NAVAL AVIATION

IN THE

FIRST WORLD WAR

Its Impact and Influence

R D LAYMAN

NAVAL INSTITUTE PRESS
Annapolis, Maryland

For Marget Murray Layman,
who is dissolved into the ocean she loved

Copyright © R D Layman 1996

First published in Great Britain in 1996 by
Chatham Publishing
1 & 2 Faulkner's Alley, Cowcross St, London EC1M 6DD

Published and distributed in the United States of America
and Canada by the Naval Institute Press, 118 Maryland Avenue,
Annapolis, Maryland 21402-5035

Library of Congress Catalog Card No. 96-69149

ISBN 1-55750-617-5

Manufactured in Great Britain

This edition authorized for sale only in the United States of America, its territories
and posssessions and Canada.

Contents

List of Plates

Author's Preface

———— · ————

Naval aviation is a very recent phenomenon in the long annals of warfare. How recent is illustrated by the fact that before I reached the age of 40 I met two persons who had known its very earliest pioneers.

The first was Mabel Hall Ely Brown Pierce, widow of Eugene Ely — the aviator who less than two decades before my birth had been the first to fly an aeroplane from a ship and the first to alight one aboard a ship. The meeting occurred because the newspaper for which I then worked assigned me to interview her in connection with her campaign for the issue of a US postage stamp honouring her first husband. The interview ignited an interest in early naval aviation — partially because of the fact that both Ely and I had spent some of our early years in Davenport, Iowa.

Ten years later, after my interest had grown into a continuing study, I interviewed (for an article in the *Cross & Cockade Journal*) Robert W Peel, who as a young Royal Naval Air Service flight sublieutenant had tried to bomb the German battlecruiser *Goeben* after her sortie against Imbros in early 1918. Hard-pressed by enemy aircraft, he was saved by a Greek naval fighter pilot, Aristides C Moraitinis, whose aerobatics drove the Briton's assailants away. They met later when Moraitinis presented Peel with a decoration. Five years earlier, during the First Balkan War, Moraitinis had become the first serving naval officer of any nationality to take part in an operational maritime combat flight when he and his observer reconnoitred Turkish warships in the Dardanelles and unsuccessfully attacked them with crude bombs. This episode, although minor and now almost completely forgotten, was history's first aeronaval engagement.

During the interval between these two interviews I became increasingly convinced that the development of naval aviation during the First World War had never been adequately explored and that its influence on that conflict had been underestimated, ignored or unrealised, submerged under misconception or myth.

During the next twenty years or so I made an attempt at a book exploring the subject by detailing both technical and operational aspects. After piling up several hundred pages of manuscript I realised that this approach would exceed my life expectancy. Moreover, as time advanced much technical data on Great War naval aircraft and aviation vessels was being investigated and published by researchers more competent than I.

Such compilations have produced many of what might be called 'nuts and bolts' books. This is *not* a pejorative term (I have written such a book myself) for it is obvious that the nuts and bolts have to be collected before they can be used to assemble anything. But because so much of this sort of material has become so readily available I concluded that a more general — even philosophical, if I may be permitted the dignity of that adjective — approach was required.

This book is the result.

Introduction

———— · ————

Aviation, in the sense of the powered heavier-than-air flying machine, is a very new factor in the history of mankind, yet so thoroughly has it been woven into the fabric of contemporary life that one can readily forget how truly new it is — that the chronological span between the Wright Flyer and the Boeing 707 is less than many a human lifetime. It can also be easily forgotten that aviation's impact on peacetime civilian society is barely more than four decades old. Had all civil aviation ceased to exist in, say, 1936, or even 1950, there would have been mild to considerable discomfort in a number of quarters but commerce and society would have continued with no severe disruptions. Today such a cessation would create global economic and social chaos.

The harsh fact is that for nearly half of its lifetime aviation was devoted primarily to the purposes of war. Emerging from adolescence during one world conflict and coming to maturity in another, it was as a child of Mars that it flourished. It can hardly be doubted that more aircraft were created for military use during the period 1914–1945 than for all other uses combined.

What path the peaceful evolution of aviation would have taken save for the First World War is one of the great imponderables of history. But even before that conflict, achievements of nineteenth-century science and technology — among them, wireless telegraphy, photography and the automatic firearm — had begun to converge to show how the aeroplane could become an instrument of war.

Once the aeroplane had become, even primitively, the warplane, it was inconceivable that it would not have aroused interest in taking it to sea — indeed, there seemed a number of reasons why it should be.

Taking the warplane to sea and employing it at sea would create naval aviation. That creation took place during 1914–18. Before the Great War many navies had experimented with aerial devices, all major navies and many minor ones had established embryonic air arms, and some had even drawn up theoretical operational doctrines for aircraft. But the experiments had been isolated episodes, aircraft had not been integrated into naval tactical or strategic thinking, and no one knew if they could perform effectively, or at all, the tasks that had been proposed or predicted for them. As the Great War began, aviation at sea, as on land, remained an incompletely tested instrument of uncertain value and unknown potential.

The historiography of First World War naval aviation stands in the way of an approach to its history. For decades the conflict's aeronaval aspects have been segregated into compartments labelled 'aero' and 'naval'. Countless books and articles on naval aviation of the period concentrate on technology or tactics, ignoring its purpose or pushing that purpose into the far background. Countless naval histories ignore even the existence of aviation, or, if acknowledging it, shove it off into a corner.

Arthur J Marder's history of the British navy in the Great War era[1] offers an example. Marder certainly does not ignore aviation — by virtue of his subject-matter he can hardly avoid it — but his only extended discussion of Royal Navy aviation occupies merely twenty-two of the 1,866 pages in his five volumes.

This dichotomy began early in English-language Great War historiography. Aviation is treated only meagerly and vaguely in the British official naval history.[2] There are eighty-three references to aircraft in the indices of its five text volumes, but the reader who tracks them down will find that not once is an aircraft identified by specific type or designation. This stands in contrast to the German official naval history,[3] which discusses aerial matters in considerable detail, down to the serial numbers of individual aircraft.

The British naval history's treatment was the result of a decision to restrict all aerial matters to the official air history, *The War in the Air*.[4] That decision was certainly political, intended to help justify the creation of the Royal Air Force as a separate service co-equal to the army and navy. It is probably not irrelevant that the subtitle of *The War in the Air* is *Being the Story of the Part Played in the Great War by the Royal Air Force* — retroactively applying to the air services the name of an organisation that had existed for barely seven months before the Armistice.

The air history, however, is far superior to the naval in aeronaval matters. The contrast is typified by the treatment accorded to the most significant shipboard aviation action of the war, the successful attack by aeroplanes from HMS *Furious* on a German airship base. The naval history dismisses it in a paragraph; the air history devotes nearly four pages to it.

The better balance of the air history provides a better perspective on several maritime aspects of the war, yet one noted aero historian has declared *The War in the Air* 'suffers' from inclusion of naval material.[5] That remarkable verb encapsulates an attitude that persists in separating naval and aero matters of 1914–18. It is an attitude blatantly at odds with reality, in which the two were inexorably intertwined.

Of course, not all historians have adopted that attitude. There are countless works dealing even-handedly with the relation of air and sea. Most of these, however, are devoted to particulars — specific operations, nationalities, geographical areas or technology. This book will attempt to take a broader view, with a three-fold aim: to describe the factors leading to and promoting development of naval aviation, how during its evolution it exerted more influence than it has been credited with, and what effect that influence had on strategy.

Before beginning, however, it is necessary to examine the role of Great War aviation on a more general basis.

Notes

1. Arthur J Marder, *From the Dreadnought to Scapa Flow: The Royal Navy in the Fisher Era, 1904–1919*, 5 vols (London: Oxford University Press, 1961–1970).
2. Sir Julian S Corbett and Henry Newbolt, *Naval Operations*, 5 vols text, 4 vols maps (London: Longmans, Green, 1920–1931).
3. *Der Krieg zur See 1914–1918*, 23 vols by various authors published between 1920 and 1966.
4. Sir Walter Raleigh and H A Jones, *The War in the Air*, 6 vols text, 2 vols maps (London: Oxford University Press, 1922–1937).
5. Robin Higham, *The Military Intellectuals in Britain: 1918–1939* (Rutgers University Press, 1966), p121, fn.

CHAPTER 1

The Reconnaissance Revolution

———————— · ————————

Aviation's principal functions on land during the Great War can be described under four headings: aerial combat, tactical offence, strategic offence, and reconnaissance (which must be extended to include direction of artillery fire). Interesting but lesser functions included aerial supply of ground forces,[1] courier and communications service, slipping spies into enemy territory and dispersing propaganda material.[2]

Of the four main functions, the last was by far the most influential. But, as Lee Kennett has noted, 'If the reconnaissance function was first in importance, it has been the last in the amount of [aviation] literature dedicated to it since 1918.'[3] It has been submerged under the tidal wave of works in every conceivable medium glorifying aerial combat and its aces.

Aerial combat was and remains a mesmerizing subject, appealing to what Robert L O'Connell has characterised as the 'Homeric conception' of individual, personalised battle[4] and standing in contrast to the anonymous mass slaughter of the ground war. It also had a strong touch of the chivalric; fighter pilots were often given the sobriquet 'knight' (*eg*, the Red Knight, the Iron Knight) or described in other terms from the vocabulary of chivalry (*eg*, the Sword of France, the Eagle of Lille), and insignia adorning aircraft often replicated the heraldry of the joust.

There truly was much chivalry and knight-errant gallantry in the air war,[5] but the romantic picture has been overemphasised — 'taken as a whole, air combat in World War I was ruthless and merciless'.[6]

The romanticisation of aerial combat has created the impression — even among scholars who should know better — that the 'gallant knights of the air' were fighting each other just for the sport of it. In fact, they were battling to win aerial superiority, or 'control of the air', as it has come to be termed. Aerial superiority is sought as a means to an end, to permit one's own aircraft to see what the enemy is doing on the ground or water below and/or to drop or fire unpleasant things at him and, equally importantly, to prevent him from doing the same.

The influence that the achievement or lack of achievement of aerial superiority had on the Great War has gone unnoticed by most generalist historians of that conflict, many of whom have dismissed aviation as trivial. 'The plane was still a minor factor in 1914–18' wrote Hanson W Baldwin. 'Throughout the war,' asserted J F C Fuller, 'air power was not sufficiently developed to warrant decisive results.' Bernard Brodie and Fawn Brodie declared flatly 'One cannot in any sense accord the airplane in the First World War the importance that it proved to have in the Second.'

Such hindsight judgments are based on an unfair comparison of the 'air power' of the two conflicts and show an inadequate investigation of aviation's role in the first. They dismiss aviation because during 1914–18 it lacked the offensive power it displayed during 1939–45. Certainly that power was greater during the second war, but it was far from insignificant during the first. Tactical attack by aircraft, *ie* offensive action in support of battlefield or near-battlefield activity, was often highly influential. Ground-attack aviation was well-developed by mid–1917 and that year and the next saw numerous actions in which aerial assault affected the fates of ground units ranging in size from squad to division. By the end of the war entire armies were being affected. Remarkable results were obtained in Macedonia and Palestine when aircraft taking over the role of cavalry in pursuing and demoralising a retreating enemy turned orderly retirements into chaotic routs. The utter disintegration of the Turkish 7th Army in September 1918 caused by unopposed bombing and strafing — in which nearly 100 artillery pieces and more than 1,000 vehicles were destroyed or abandoned — comes close to rivaling any similar aerial success in the Second World War.[7]

Strategic aerial offence — strategic bombing — has received a greater amount of attention from generalist historians, probably because it became the fundamental tenet of 'air power' philosophy: the thesis that an enemy can be more quickly and effectively defeated not by battling his armed forces but by striking directly at his economic and social infrastructures. At the same time, however, strategic attack's inability to inflict the mass destruction it inflicted during 1939–45 seems a major reason why these historians have so denigrated the 'air power' of the earlier war.

The influence of strategic bombing in the First World War can be debated endlessly to no avail, for it is difficult to quantify. It may be noted, however, that it was pioneered by the German and British *navies* — a seldom-remembered fact that will be discussed later.

The effects of both tactical and strategic offence were episodic and temporary, for aircraft were incapable of sustaining such operations for any truly extended period. The aerial function that *was* constant and consistently influential, from the opening weeks of the war until its last day, was reconnaissance.

*   *   *

That reconnaissance would be a prime duty, perhaps the only duty, of aircraft had been a foregone conclusion for many years, but it was the peculiar character of the First World War that elevated aerial observation to an importance undreamt of before 1914. Reconnaissance itself, however, had gone into an eclipse in the immediate prewar years when European armies had fallen under the spell of what has been called 'the cult of the offensive' — the doctrine that wars could be decided quickly by mass attack pressed with utmost vigour. In this scheme of things, reconnaissance was deemed to have slight value — its findings would always be incomplete and arrive too late; battle itself would clarify matters, and low-level tactical information could be obtained by the traditional cavalry screen.

This doctrine withered away bloodily during the first months of the conflict when it confronted the massive firepower that late nineteenth-century technology had placed in the hands of early twentieth-century soldiers. The result was stalemate creating that characteristic feature of the war, the continuous front. This feature spelled the end of cavalry as the traditional means of reconnaissance. It could not function frontally against the new firepower and there were no flanks around which it might manoeuvre. Even before the trench deadlock set in, aviation had shown its value in the reconnaissance role. Aerial observation was a crucial, perhaps even decisive, factor in the 1914 battles of Tannenberg and the Marne.[8]

Early aerial reconnaissance had its limitations. The aviator, like the cavalryman, had to return somewhere to impart his information, relying on memory or hastily-drawn sketches. This handicap was overcome by aerial wireless telegraphy, which eliminated the time-lag between observation and report, and aerial photography, which provided a permanent record of what had been observed and sometimes could detect things invisible to the human eye. By the end of the war photography had almost superseded visual observation. On the Western Front, where millions of aerial photos were taken by both sides, photographic observation became the *sine qua non* for operational planning.

Wireless permitted aircraft to take over direction of artillery fire, with enormous consequences. Aerial fire control remained an important factor in counter-battery work even after sound-ranging, flash-ranging and preregistration techniques were developed.

A form of aerial reconnaissance called into being by the pecularities of the war was use of low-flying craft to observe battle-field activities and report them to the engaged troops and to rear-area headquarters. Called 'infantry contact patrols' (in German, *Feldfliegerabtielungen-Infanterie*), they were often the principal way, sometimes the only way, that commanding officers could obtain information during a war in which, as John Terraine has pointed out, ground communications had grown so precariously vulnerable, battlefields so extended and the number of troops engaged so large that a general could no longer personally observe or control events.[9]

Useful as aerial reconnaissance had proved while manoeuvre was still possible during 1914, it was the long trench stasis that caused it to become invaluable. Once the trench lines were drawn and the continuous front established, knowledge of enemy strength and intentions became increasingly difficult to obtain. There were, of course, many conventional means of obtaining information, from espionage to gaining high ground (on the Western Front, the slightest of elevations became a prize to be fought for). But in general, the area behind the lines was *terra incognita*, accessible only from the air.

For this reason, there are compelling grounds to believe that aerial reconnaissance exercised a strong influence on the war's nature and duration. Charles D Bright, in an incisive study, advances with highly convincing logic and examples the argument that 'air power' (by which he actually means aerial reconnaissance) was the conflict's *decisive* factor because it could eliminate the possibility of strategic surprise.[10]

Why this should be so was again dictated by the nature of the war. The massive and lengthy buildup required for a large-scale offensive could seldom be hidden entirely from aerial discovery regardless of the many ingenious techniques devised for disguise or deception. The result was that the side able to maintain adequate aerial surveillance of the enemy could almost without exception predict where, and sometimes even when, an attack could be expected and so take defensive measures. If strategic surprise could not be achieved, the result was the stalemate that persisted for so long during the Great War.

That aviation might lead to military impasse had been predicted by H G Wells in his 1908 novel *The War in the Air*: 'With the flying machine war alters its character . . . and while there is an increase in the destructiveness of war, there is also an increased indecisiveness.' The indecisiveness that prevailed so long during the First World War, however, was not *caused* by aviation; it was caused by a period of technological history in which defensive weapons dominated the battlefield. But once the stasis was established — or so Bright argues — aviation became a major factor in *prolonging* it: '. . . if one side had achieved lengthy control of the air . . . it seems probable that more victorious attacks would have been made [and] a decision could have been reached earlier.'[11]

The problem was that truly 'lengthy' control of the air was difficult to obtain. Total air superiority (air supremacy) was never achieved save by default — when one side possessed no aircraft or too few to affect matters (the early stages of the Dardanelles/ Gallipoli and Mesopotamian campaigns are examples).

The advantages that even air supremacy might confer could, however, be nullified by such external factors as geography, climate and weather (in East Africa, for instance). Such factors aside, the main impediment to achieving lengthy control of the air was that from mid-1915 on it had to be fought for — at first on the Western Front, and eventually in nearly every theatre of conflict.

That fact returns us to the function of aerial combat. Its evolution and techniques have been so often and thoroughly described and analysed that no discussion is required here.[12] What is germane is that it created a cycle in which air superiority passed from one side to the other and back again, neither being able to hold it long enough to permit the successes on the ground it might have made possible. This state of affairs came into being by virtue of what Edward N Luttwak calls the 'reciprocal force-development effect'[13] and O'Connell describes as 'symmetrical response'.[14]

What both terms refer to is the natural tendency by the victim of a new type of weapon to adopt it himself, but if possible with improved features. This is what happened after the fighter aeroplane appeared in 1915. There ensued a technological competition in which each new type of fighter that came close to dominating the sky was eventually countered by an equal or superior type. A paradox resulted in which every effort to attain aerial superiority automatically resulted in a counter-response that prevented its attainment.

The 'symmetrical response' type could appear so quickly because of the rapid pace at which aircraft could be designed, developed and produced — sometimes within a few months. But the period required for this process was short only in comparison with the duration of the war.

If, as Bright postulates, aviation helped lengthen the war, it is unquestionably true that the duration of the war provided the time-span required for progress in aviation. Had the conflict been the short, sharply decisive clash that many of the best military minds expected in 1914, it is doubtful that the aircraft of 1918 would have been so much advanced over those of four years earlier. It was the length of the war that led governments to loosen pursestrings in lavish outpourings to finance all phases of aeronautical development and fields related to aviation. The result was progress in less than five years that surely otherwise would not have been made in a decade or more. By fostering improvement in aircraft and providing the first mass market for them — one which would not be matched by civilian demand for decades — the war exerted an influence on aviation that may have been greater than the influence of aviation on the war.

Debating which of these influences was greater is pointless. The fact is that they intertwined in a reciprocal process whereby the longer the war lasted, the more efficient aircraft could become, while the more efficient aircraft became the more possible they made the prolongation of the war.

Because of aviation's role in maintaining stalemate, Bright contends that 'the essence of air power in World War I . . . was not as an offensive but rather a *defensive* [his emphasis] weapon'. However, this judgment flies in the face of the fact that aerial reconnaissance was essential for planning offensive operations. After early 1915 no Western Front offensive by any nationality was undertaken without extensive preliminary aerial observation. For both defensive and offensive purposes, 'the action of aircraft', as

Basil Liddell Hart put it, 'formed a thread running through and vitally influencing the whole course of operations, rather than as a separate strategic feature'.[15]

That final qualifying phrase, however, should not be interpreted as implying that aviation was divorced from the strategic level, for it was on that level that aerial reconnaissance was most influential.

To demonstrate this, a line must be drawn between strategic and tactical reconnaissance — not an easy task, for their overlappings are many. The distinction has been muddied in recent years by semantic misuse equating 'strategic' with long range and 'tactical' with short range. The distinction is not of distance but of function. For First World War aviation, the distinction becomes clearer if one applies the rough-and-ready definitions of strategy as that which governs the plans, movements and dispositions of armed forces before battle is joined, and tactics as that which applies after the shooting starts. During the Great War an aircraft photographing an enemy front line in preparation for an attack was performing strategic reconnaissance, one signalling the position of a machine-gun nest to infantry was performing tactical reconnaissance.

Aerial reconnaissance could assist in achieving tactical surprise but it could seldom, if ever, prevent it. Aerial observation helped forewarn the British army of the impending German offensive of March 1918 but it could do nothing to offset the surprising novelty of German infantry and artillery tactics. Nor could it prevent the tactical surprise effected by gas at Second Ypres, mines at Messines or tanks at Cambrai.

But tactical surprise, although it might achieve great initial success, was never decisive. The war's outcome was decided by overall strategy implemented by masses of matériel and manpower. And it was during the strategic planning period that aerial reconnaissance, with the information it gathered by photographic and visual observation, made its greatest contribution.

While tactical aerial reconnaissance could influence the battlefield immediately and directly, its strategic counterpart functioned indirectly and at a greater remove in time. It was not *in* the skies but when information obtained *from* the skies was analysed at behind-the-scenes conferences that aviation most signally helped shape the course of the First World War.

* * *

By providing a means of seeing what was on that proverbial 'other side of the hill', aviation revolutionised reconnaissance. From that stemmed a larger revolution in the entire art and science of warfare comparable to that brought about by the introduction of gunpowder. This revolution would have occurred had no aircraft ever dropped a bomb or fired a shot during 1914–18.

Notes

1. The most sustained (although ultimately unsuccessful) example of this was the attempt to supply by air the besieged British force at Kut al Amara in Mesopotamia in 1916. For a concise but good account, see A P Sights Jr, 'Airlift to Kut', *United States Naval Institute Proceedings*, Vol 98 No 2, February 1972.
2. Use of aviation to augment espionage and propaganda was more extensive than generally realised. Many examples are cited in Michael Occleshaw, *Armour Against Fate: British Military Intelligence in the First World War* (London: Columbus Books, 1989).
3. Lee Kennett, *The First Air War 1914–1918* (New York: The Free Press, 1991), p258.
4. Robert L O'Connell, *Of Arms and Men: A History of War, Weapons, and Aggression* (New York: Oxford University Press, 1989), pp46 *et seq.*
5. See Piet Hein Meijering, *Signed With Their Honor: Air Chivalry in the Two World Wars* (New York: Paragon, 1988).
6. George Shiras, 'The Two Faces of Chivalry in the Air War', *Cross & Cockade Journal*, Vol 5 No 2, Winter 1964. For another corrective view, see Thomas Cripps, 'The Romance of the Dogfight: A Cautionary Tale for Historians', *Prospects*, Vol 17, 1992.
7. The Macedonia and Palestine episodes are described in Jones, *The War in the Air*, Vol 6. More recent discussion of the Palestine operation can be found in David L Bullock, 'The Application of Airpower in Allenby's Megiddo Campaign', *Over the Front*, Vol 8 No 1, Spring 1993, and Richard P Hallion, *Strike From the Sky: The History of Battlefield Air Attack, 1911–1945* (Washington: Smithsonian Institution Press, 1989).
8. The most detailed accounts of the role and influence of aerial reconnaissance in these battles are given in John R Cuneo, *The Air Weapon 1914–1916*, Vol 2 of *Winged Mars* (Harrisburg, Pa.: Military Service Publishing Company, 1947). For aviation at Tannenberg, see also Dennis E Showalter, *Tannenberg: Clash of Empires* (Hamden, Conn.: Archon Books, 1991). An appreciation of the work of British aerial observers at the Marne was given by General Joffre — see Sir Edward Spears, *Liaison 1914: A Narrative of the Great Retreat* (New York: Stein and Day, 2nd ed 1968), p414.
9. John Terraine, *The Smoke and the Fire: Myths and Anti-Myths of War 1861–1945* (London: Sidgwick & Jackson, 1980).
10. Charles D Bright, 'Air Power in World War I: Sideshow or Decisive Factor?', *Aerospace Historian*, Vol 18 No 2, summer 1971. Bright does not specifically distinguish between tactical and strategic surprise, but it is clear from his context that he refers to the latter.
11. Ibid.
12. The most recent and one of the best works on this subject is Richard P Hallion, *Rise of the Fighter Aircraft 1914–1918* (Baltimore: Nautical & Aviation Publishing Company, 1984).
13. Edward N Luttwak, *Strategy: The Logic of War and Peace* (Cambridge, Mass: Harvard University Press, 1987).
14. O'Connell, *Arms and Men*, op cit.
15. Basil Liddell Hart, *The Real War 1914–1918* (Boston: Little, Brown and Company, reprint ed. 1964), pp313–14.

CHAPTER 2

Contrast of Land and Sea

The four main functions of aviation over land during 1914–18 were also performed over the sea, although often differing in degree. Before describing them, it is necessary to define naval aviation and to examine in what respects it differed from aviation functioning on the land fronts.

Probably the simplest definition of naval aviation is: any and all aerial elements operated by a navy and/or on behalf of a navy. As such, it becomes an element of sea power to be employed in pursuit of traditional maritime objectives, of which the most primary is command of the sea — or, as it has recently come to be called, sea control. However, its flexibility permits it to take a broader role in what has been termed power projection, *ie* extension of sea power over land by means of the air.

Functioning in either role, a basic — although not a sole — characteristic of naval aviation is *flight over water*. This fact creates circumstances that differ from minor to extreme degree from those governing operational and technical aspects of aviation employed solely in support of land forces.

From the first introduction of aircraft into warfare, the fact that these differing circumstances require different approaches to aviation, different disciplines and doctrines, and, often, different types of aircraft, has been difficult to appreciate or accept — indeed, it has often been denied or outright rejected. The ability of aircraft to operate flexibly over both land and sea, especially in an element and dimension so distinct from that in which ships operate, has seemed to many to make aviation a separate entity, far removed from traditional aspects of naval warfare. The fact that the sky has no boundaries is responsible for the creation and development of air power philosophy, one main object of which during the 1920s and 1930s was the dethronement of sea power.

The history of two great wars and a number of lesser ones, however, has shown that aviation, in serving either sea control or power projection, functions more effectively and influentially as a component of sea power than as a separate entity — that it has endowed sea power with greater strength, versatility and influence than it ever possessed before the air age.

The possibility of this endowment was predicted, or at least suspected, well before 1914, but only a few visionaries could conceive of how central aviation would become to naval warfare. The process leading to that had to be undertaken pragmatically; navies had to learn under the stress and practicalities of wartime what aviation could and could not accomplish.

* * *

The revolution that aerial reconnaissance wrought on land was paralleled at sea during the Great War, but its influence was not as pervasive or consistant. A basic reason was the nature of the naval war, in which the equivalent of the continuous front could not arise. Beyond that, factors of geography and technology, separately or in combination, often limited or inhibited aerial activity at sea.

Technologically, although aircraft improved tremendously in all areas of performance between 1914 and 1918, there was still in the latter year no such thing as a totally reliable aeroplane or an assuredly safe flight. The hazards of flying were myriad; engine or other mechanical failure could occur for innumerable reasons, and weather was always a threat.

These hazards were shared by all aviators everywhere, but their potential for misfortune was greater for naval fliers because flight over water was inherently more dangerous and difficult than over land. Oceanic weather is often more rapidly changeable, storms more frequent and more violent, fog more abundant, wind, temperature and atmospheric pressure more capricious. Moreover, the naval aviator faced not only the problems of weather aloft but also often had to contend with the state of the sea.

Mechanical failure was usually more life-threatening over water than over land. An aviator coming to grief over land usually had at least a sporting chance of finding a safe spot to alight, of coming down in friendly territory, of being rescued, even if by the enemy, and if injured, of receiving medical assistance. Not so at sea, where nothing was 'safe' or 'friendly'.

This situation resulted in far more naval air casualties from accidents than from combat. Operational or training accidents accounted for more casualties on land as well, but because of the factors mentioned above it is probable that the percentage of *fatalities* resulting from accidents was higher among naval fliers.

Adding to the perils of the naval aviator was the greater difficulty of navigating over sea. Above land, natural features and such man-made guides as roads and railway lines could serve to establish position. This was true also for an aircraft operating along a coastline, where it could be piloted in the exact definition of the verb, but once out of sight of land only artificial aids were available. Celestial navigation could be helpful, but in general dead reckoning was the only feasible way an aviator could determine where he might be over the waves.

Instruments and techniques for aerial navigation were crude in 1914 and far from reliable by 1918, although much progress had been made.[1] The danger of becoming lost at sea persisted even after the advent of elaborate electronic navigational devices — as witness the two seaplanes catapulted from the US cruiser *Boise* in the Pacific one August day in 1942, never to be seen again.[2]

'Never to be seen again' was the epitaph for many a Great War naval aviator. It was the fate, for instance, of an experienced British pilot, Flight Commander B D Kilner, who took off from HMS *Vindex* on 25 September 1917 in pursuit of a German airship and vanished forever.[3]

The longer the distance requiring flight over water, the greater the chances for navigational error became. In some areas, for example the upper Adriatic, the northern English Channel, off the mouth of the Dardanelles, distances between hostile coasts were relatively short. But in the fulcrum of the naval war, the North Sea (as well as other regions), the contending fleets were separated by hundreds of miles that no aeroplane could span and still return.

The operational reach of coastal-based aircraft in such areas was therefore limited by the interrelated factors of endurance (how long an aircraft could stay aloft) and radius (how far it could fly and do something useful while retaining enough fuel to get back again). Obviously, the farther an aircraft could fly and the longer it could stay in the air, the greater was its usefulness — a fact that stimulated development of large, long-range aircraft. Thus by the end of the war Britain and Germany had produced big seaplanes with endurance of up to nine to twelve hours.[4]

This fact also accounts for the extensive naval use of the airship, which had inherently longer radius and greater endurance than the aeroplane, because the power that propelled it was not required to keep it aloft.

Finally, the need to conquer distance at sea was a major stim-
ulus (although not the only one) to the creation of shipboard
aviation, leading ultimately to the flight-deck carrier.

In addition to the technical problems that had to be overcome
before aviation could be useful at sea, operational needs posed
other difficulties. It is elementary that information gained by reconnaissance, if it is to be of any value, must be timely and accurate. Timeliness was even more important at sea, simply because
warships move far more rapidly than land forces and can change
location, direction and formation far faster. A First World War
army corps took many hours, even days, to pass a given point and
could not readily be rerouted, dispersed or redeployed, but a
squadron of warships could be many miles away in any direction
of the compass within an hour of being sighted.

Timely transmission of information from air to sea thus demanded a system of speedy, reliable communications. Several
methods had been tried before the war — signalling by light or
smoke flares, dropping messages in canisters — and some of
these would be used early in the conflict. Their mutual drawback
was that all required the aerial observer to return to within visual
distance of the ship or fleet for which he was scouting. This
created a dilemma: if he returned, he would lose sight of his
quarry and might very well be unable to regain it; if he remained, he would be unable to communicate the results of his
observation.

The dilemma was eliminated by wireless, which became the *sine
qua non* for naval aerial reconnaissance. Wireless-equipped aircraft could not only impart 'real time' information, they could
spot for gunfire. Spotting against ships, although practiced during the war, saw almost no operational use, but it was employed
extensively for shore bombardment, enabling warships to strike at
land targets at greater range and with greater accuracy than ever
before. It debuted in the shore bombardment role during the
Dardanelles/Gallipoli campaign in early 1915. Initial results were
unsatisfactory, owing to crude wireless equipment and lack of
experience, but improvements came rapidly and by the end of the
campaign warship guns guided by air were hitting with remarkable accuracy at extreme range.[5]

Although wireless could assure timeliness, it could not guarantee accuracy of the information it transmitted, for aerial observation at sea teemed with chances and reasons for error or
misjudgment.

Navigational inaccuracy was one major reason; an aerial observer misjudging his own position naturally incorrectly reported the position of his object of observation. Equally serious was misidentification of ship type or nationality, which persisted even after special training in identification. Such errors could be dangerous. British submarines were frequently bombed by friendly aircraft, and one was sunk in 1918 in a mistaken-identity attack by a French airship.

The flip-side of that coin was misidentification of aircraft by warships, although this was less of a danger during the First World War than the Second World War, when 'friendly' fire caused countless casualties. In what was probably the first incident of this kind — and one of the most inexplicable — German destroyers fired at a German airship during the Battle of Heligoland Bight in 1914.[6]

* * *

In August 1914 nascent naval aviation was composed of three basic functional types of aircraft: landplanes[7] and airships operating from land bases, seaplanes operating from coastal waters or lakes[8] and, by the end of that month, seaplanes carried aboard ships. These would be joined during the war by landplanes and seaplanes flying from shipboard platforms or decks and by observation balloons towed by surface vessels.

Aircraft operating from land or coastal waters could co-operate with and assist surface forces to the limits of their radii and endurance if co-ordination could be arranged — something rarely achieved during the First World War. Beyond these limits, a surface force would have to take its aerial component with it. For that reason, the seaplane had been deemed in prewar years to be the aircraft best suited — indeed, ideally suited — for naval use. Operating from the same medium in which ships floated, it seemed to have the ability to function anywhere in the world. It proved not to be that simple, for reasons to be examined later, but in 1914 there was the apparently irrefutable fact that if aircraft were to assist warships beyond range of flight from coasts they *had* to be able to function from water.

The seaplane had developed into two types — the floatplane, in which the appendages it required to operate from water were attached externally to the fuselage, and the flying boat, in which the fuselage provided flotation in the form of a water-navigable hull. Addition of a wheeled undercarriage to either type turned it into an amphibian, able to function from either land or water.

The flying boat is inherently stronger in water and can be made extremely seaworthy, although at the cost of increase in size and weight. The floatplane, usually much lighter and so more nimble in the air, is more subject to wave stress and so less seaworthy. The latter may have either twin or single floats. Twin floats provide greater stability in water but also are more affected by wave stress than the single float, which because of its lesser stability requires auxiliary under-wing floats. Many 1914–18 twin-float types also had auxiliary tail floats. Both types often required an increase in wing and/or rudder surface to assist in manoeuvring in the water.

Seaplanes are burdened by handicaps not afflicting landplanes, the chief of which is that the extra weight and added drag imposed by their configuration for operation from water impairs their performance in the air, including their speed.[9] Even more handicapping is their total dependence on the state of the sea; even if launched directly from a ship, they must end their flight in water. Relatively calm water is imperative, but, paradoxically, a total calm can frustrate take-off because ever-present surface suction straining against aerodynamic lift makes it intrinsically more difficult to raise weight from water than from land.

The solution to these problems lay in the combination of more powerful engines (in fact, the seaplane was a spur to their development) and efficient floats and hulls patterned on the configuration of hydroplaning boats. Such designs appeared during the war, but many floatplanes still had to rely on clumsy, box-like pontoons that were hydrodynamically inefficient and structurally weak. The floats of the British Sopwith Schneider and Baby seaplanes, for example, were notorious for their tendency to break up under wave stress.

Water density, as determined by its salinity, could affect flotation. A French attempt to operate seaplanes from Montenegro's Lake Scutari in 1914 failed because their floats could not function efficiently in fresh water. Tropical heat and humidity could do unpleasant things to aeroplanes, as British aviators discovered in East Africa and the Red Sea, where radiators boiled dry, rubber and glue melted, wood warped, propellers cracked, fabric rotted and altitude and rate of climb were adversely affected.

Among potential perils lurking to bedevil seaplanes was one unique to those powered by rotary engines. In this power plant, which was much favoured during the Great War era, the entire machinery together with the propeller revolved at high speed around a fixed crankshaft. Being air-cooled and so requiring no radiator system, the rotary was lighter than a liquid-cooled engine and thus produced a higher ratio of horsepower to weight. Its disadvantages were a high rate of fuel consumption and mechanical complexity requiring careful maintenance. It had only two power settings, on and off, and was regulated by alternating them. Prolonged taxiing on the water at low speed, sometimes necessary to reach a take-off position or clear a harbour, could cause a rotary to overheat and seize up. Also, its delicate mechanism was easily clogged or abraded by foreign matter. Rotary-powered French seaplanes operating in the sand-laden air of the Near East in early 1915 often could fly no more than twenty hours before their engines demanded overhaul.[10] This problem was also one reason why the Royal Naval Air Service No 2 Wing in the Aegean abandoned use of its rotary-powered French aeroplanes later in 1915.

* * *

The seaplane has been discussed at length because as a type it dominated the inventories of all naval air arms during the Great War and saw the most operational use at sea. From the technological standpoint, its limitations were caused by problems common to all aeroplanes of the period. Its additional handicap, it must be stressed again, was imposed by the features it required for operation from water. Its purely military functions were inhibited by that handicap plus the general hazards of maritime flight.

Succeeding decades would see the increasing erosion of its utility for naval use and its final demise in that role, for reasons beyond the scope of this study. That fate, of course, could not have been foreseen in 1914; the seaplane was then quite a new type, the first successful one having flown only four years earlier,[11] and seemed to hold great promise as a tool for navies. Indeed, it did fulfill that promise to a considerable extent. But its limitations constitute one important reason why, as noted at the start of this chapter, aerial reconnaissance did not exert as *consistant* an influence on the naval side of the war as it did on the land fronts.

Notes

1. See Monte Duane Wright, *Most Probable Position: A History of Aerial Navigation to 1941* (University Press of Kansas, 1972).
2. This incident is described in Mike Stankovich, 'The Hardest Choice', *Naval History*, Vol 2/1/2, Winter 1988.
3. C F Snowden Gamble, *The Story of a North Sea Air Station* (Oxford University Press, 1928), p299, fn.
4. These were the British Felixstowe F-series flying boats and the German Dornier Rs.-series flying boats and Staaken 8301 floatplane. For details, see J M Bruce, *British Aeroplanes 1914–1918* (London: Putnam, 1957) and G W Haddow and Peter M Grosz, *The German Giants: The Story of the R-planes 1914–1919* (London: Putnam, 1962).
5. See R D Layman, 'Over the Wine-Dark Sea: Aerial Aspects of the Dardanelles/Gallipoli Campaign', Pts 1 and 2, *Over the Front*, Vol 9 No 1, Spring 1994.
6. Douglas H Robinson, *The Zeppelin in Combat: A History of the German Naval Airship Division, 1912–1918* (London: G T Foulis, 1962), p41.
7. 'Landplane' as used in this study refers to aircraft with wheeled undercarriages as distinguished from seaplanes. 'Aeroplane' is used as a generic term for the heavier-than-air flying machine.
8. Lake bases for seaplanes did not figure importantly until later in the war and then primarily in the Baltic and Black Sea regions.
9. This handicap was not significant during most of the Great War. Italy and Austria-Hungary produced flying boat fighters, and Germany floatplane fighters, capable of holding their own against landplanes. The seaplanes created for the Schneider Trophy races of the 1920s and 1930s were the fastest aircraft of their time, setting many speed records. But although they contributed greatly to the advancement of aeronautical design they were militarily useless; their only payloads were their pilots and fuel.
10. *Capitaine de Vaisseau de Réserve* De'Escaille (no further identification), 'Une escadrille d'avions de la Marine française au Canal de Suez (1914–16)' in *Revue des Forces Aériennes*, No 12.
11. The first powered flight from water, as distinguished from gliding flight, was made by Henri Fabre on 28 March 1910 in a floatplane of his own design. The first take-off from water of a flying boat was made by Glenn Curtiss on 10 January 1912. For a description of Fabre's craft and succeeding developments in the evolution of the seaplane, see H F King, *Aeromarine Origins: The Beginnings of Marine Aircraft, Winged Hulls, Air-Cushion and Air-Lubricated Craft, Planing Boats and Hydrofoils* (London: Putnam, 1966) and Henry R Palmer Jr, *Famous Aircraft: The Seaplanes* (Dallas, Texas: Morgan Aviation Books, 1965).

CHAPTER 3

The 'Battleship Admiral' and Other Myths

———— · ————

Many of naval aviation's achievements during the Great War continue to be obscured by a smoke screen laid down in the 1920s and 1930s by air power proponents agitating for creation of independent air forces. Their arguments focused almost entirely on use of aircraft as offensive weapons, to the neglect of other functions.

Their main thesis was that aircraft had made the battleship, the symbolic keystone of sea power, obsolete, or soon would do so. The reputed ability of aviation to drive it from the seas was shouted to the skies, and the clamour became even more strident after 'Billy' Mitchell,[1] later to be canonised as the infallible pope of air power, actually sank one (the obsolescent German dreadnought *Ostfriesland*) in 1921.

Credibility was lent to the air power credo by some ranking naval figures of the time, including the American Rear Admiral William S Sims and the British Admiral Sir Percy Scott.[2] The latter became practically rabid in preaching that aircraft had rendered the battleship extinct. Even Lord Fisher (Admiral John Fisher), the creator of the dreadnought, predicted its demise.

The credo, however, collided with the incontrovertible fact that battleships, and all other armoured warships, had proved invulnerable to aerial attack during 1914–18. Instead of accepting this reality, however, the air enthusiasts sought to attribute it to lack of use, or misuse, of the aerial weapon. They created a scapegoat to blame for this supposed state of affairs — a straw man who has gone into legend as the 'Battleship Admiral'. This creature was a purblind reactionary who resisted innovation in any form but especially scoffed at aviation and was determined to block it at every turn. He was at the helm of every navy and, of course, belonged to the 'Gun Club', the nebulous but powerful fraternity composed of believers in the big gun behind heavy armour as the be-all and end-all of naval warfare and which was responsible for any failure of aviation to live up to its potential. He was, as described in an oft-quoted remark by an anonymous RNAS officer, 'solid ivory from the jaws up, except for a little hole from ear to ear to let useful knowledge go in and out'. If aircraft had not performed wonders during the war, it was the fault of such dunderheads who ignored, neglected or thwarted aviation through sheer stupidity or prejudice.

There is some truth to this view, although it has been much exaggerated. An example of how it could be twisted to transfer blame from technical reality is seen in Rear Admiral Murray F Sueter's discussion of Royal Navy development and use of torpedo aeroplanes in his semi-autobiographical philippic *Airmen or Noahs*.[3] The disgruntled former director of the Admiralty's Air Department notes their successes at the Dardanelles ('Three shots, three hits — 100 per cent of hits!') and from these extrapolates that 'the morning after [the Battle of] Jutland . . . would have been ideal for making [an aerial] torpedo attack on the retreating German Fleet'.[4] He then laments the delay in development of torpedo aeroplanes, which he claims (with some justice) to have inaugurated, attributing it to his transfer to a command in the Adriatic, whereupon everyone else in the navy supposedly lost interest in the idea.

Sueter also claims, seven months before Jutland, to have proposed to the Admiralty the construction of 200 'invisible-winged [whatever that may have meant] torpedo machines' but the request had been refused. He advances no documentation for this assertion, and I have been unable to find any. He did indeed, in October 1916, instigate development of what resulted in the Sopwith T 1 Cuckoo torpedo landplane, of which many were eventually ordered — an order he castigates as coming 'too late to be of the slightest use in the War'.[5]

Sueter's attack on the Admiralty — against which he had a personal axe to grind[6] — contains a number of half-truths and willful or inadvertent distortions of fact. Torpedo machines *had* been developed, otherwise there would have been none at the Dardanelles, but these floatplanes were far from satisfactory and their successes, which have been much overrated, were achieved only with a great deal of difficulty. In citing the three successes, Sueter ignored the many other times that such craft could not even take off under the weight of their missiles and how poorly they performed under that weight.

Even if Cuckoos had been available by the time of Jutland, they would have to have been carried to the battle site by ships, and there was only one RN vessel in 1916 with a deck from which they could have flown. Seaplanes, of course, would have been at the mercy of the elements, which could never be counted upon to be charitable — as Sueter discovered when his one and only attempt to mount a torpedo attack by seaplanes in the Adriatic was thwarted by a gale.

Sueter's criticism of the Admiralty's failure to act earlier on torpedo planes is justified, but the fact remains that it finally *did* act, and only clairvoyance would have foreseen that the War would have ended before the craft entered service. Actually, a squadron of Cuckoos was embarked on HMS *Argus*, the RN's first flight-deck carrier, at the time of the armistice.

* * *

Unquestionably, naval hierarchies did sometimes find aviation a difficult proposition, navies not being immune to the streak of conservatism found in most military (and other societal) organisations. Conservatism *did* at times result in suspicion, distrust or even rejection of aviation. There really were, if not the archetypal 'Battleship Admirals', naval officers and civilian administrators who regarded it with attitudes ranging from mild skepticism to outright loathing. But the degree to which these attitudes affected or retarded aviation has often been exaggerated, and it has often been forgotten or gone unrecognised that objections to aircraft were far more frequently based on valid technical, maritime or operational considerations than on ignorance or personal bias.

These considerations stemmed from the elementary fact that throughout the war, but especially in its early years, the aeroplane was greatly inferior to the surface vessel in radius, endurance, navigational accuracy, weather-worthiness and mechanical reliability. It rarely could match the surface craft in offensive punch, and always lacked the ability to project it accurately.

An example of a valid reason for rejecting use of aircraft can be found in the negative response by Vice Admiral Sir Lewis Bayly to an Admiralty proposal in late 1916 to establish seaplane bases in southern Ireland for anti-submarine patrolling in his Western Approaches Command. He was, as the British air history notes, 'lukewarm about aircraft cooperation, chiefly because no sloops could be spared to leave their patrol to attack a submarine if and when one was reported by aircraft, or to rescue a seaplane down on the water from engine trouble or other cause'.[7] The unreliability of aircraft caused Bayly to declare: 'If sloops have to look after them, to rescue or mother them, then the seaplanes will be a hindrance and a serious nuisance. If seaplanes . . . can look after themselves, they will be useful. If not, they will be an offence.'[8]

The air historian has to admit that this objection — which was similar to others voiced elsewhere for much the same reasons — 'must in fairness be stated [to have been] founded on experience with some of the earlier and less reliable types of aircraft'.[9] When more reliable types appeared, Bayly changed his view and seaplane bases were established.

It is delusory to transfer blame for such shortcomings of aircraft from the realm of technological fact to the mentality of naval officialdom. The admirals of 1914–18 are indeed open to criticism in regard to aerial matters, but the view that aviation was blindly and unreasonably rejected by naval authorities belongs, as John R Cuneo has written of another misconception, 'to the folklore of aviation rather than its history'.[10]

*   *   *

Strangely, in view of its world leadership in the development and employment of all phases of maritime aviation before and during the Great War, the British navy has become the target of inordinate criticism of its air policies. Not only aeroplane buffs, whose ignorance may be excusable, and air power theorists, whose prejudices are predictable, but naval scholars of the highest order have joined in the mud-slinging.

Here is a typical popular assessment, written as late as 1964: 'Of all the fighting arms of World War I, none was more obscure or more slighted than England's [sic] Royal Naval Air Service. Considered a practically useless appendage by many senior Admiralty officers, fleet air was consistently treated as an orphan, an annoying offspring that got in the way of His Most Britannic Majesty's rule of the sea. When not continually sent out on endless, fruitless patrol, pilots were treated little better than naval ratings, as if to make them rue the day they had ever chosen a career in the air over the more orthodox calling of the sea. The monotonous slate gray expanse of the North Sea . . . became a common sight to aviators who were fobbed off on time consuming assignments just to keep them off ship and out of the captain's hair.'[11]

This tissue of sarcastic nonsense can be dismissed as just that, but serious attention must be paid to criticism from the higher end of the spectrum. Marder, concluding his discussion of British naval aviation, writes of 'the Admiralty contempt of the air' and quotes Stephen Roskill anent 'the dislike of blue water sailors for the noisy and smelly machines which desecrated the decks and paintwork of the ship — and of the unconventional and out-spoken young men who flew them'.[12] This judgment deserves analysis as encapsulating some of the attitudes British naval officers supposedly felt toward aircraft aboard ships.

First, one wonders if 'blue water sailors' really found a 100-horsepower aero engine any noisier than sustained salvos from 15in guns, or the aroma of petrol or oil more noxious than the powder fumes from those guns. Sailors must put up with a number of discomforts, especially in wartime, and it is difficult to believe that two more petty affronts to ear and nose were not taken in their stride.

Then there is the matter of the desecrated paintwork. The objection to aircraft because they leaked fuel or lubricants has been cited so often as to seem apocryphal, although it can be authenticated in some cases. But the brightly holystoned decks and gleaming paintwork so prized in the Victorian and Edwardian navies had gone by the board even before the war. Until the so-called dazzle camouflage was introduced later in the war, British ships were painted in various shades of gray and/or black. A few blotches of oil would hardly have marred their appearance, and it seems highly doubtful that the captain of a cruiser on North Sea patrol would have considered his ship's appearance a matter of great priority.

The objection, however, may not have been as absurd as it might seem and as it has been made out to be. Of the 11,843 officers and ratings officially listed as having died from non-combat causes,[13] a percentage — the exact number appears unknown but likely was in the hundreds — lost their lives from being washed or simply slipping overboard. This hazard was especially prevalent in the blusterly North Sea, where the Grand Fleet lost many a man in rough weather. Surely any prudent captain would have been concerned about the addition of a slick, slippery substance to the rolling decks his crew had to tread.

Another, and reasonable, objection to aircraft aboard ship was the necessity for a launching platform if aeroplanes (whether landplanes or seaplanes on trollies) were to take off directly from the vessel. These structures took up considerable space and almost always restricted, or even totally masked, the training arcs of guns. The fixed three-track ramps fitted on the light cruisers *Aurora, Arethusa, Penelope* and *Undaunted* in 1915 made fire from the forward guns impossible and seriously interfered with working of capstans and cables. The weight of fixed platforms placed on some cruisers later on in the war affected the ships' stability.

These problems were solved with the development beginning in 1917 of rotating platforms — mounted either as separate structures or, on capital ships, atop main-battery turrets, which served to train them — and experiments proving, that with empennage elevated, the light aircraft of the period required only very short runs to take off against felt wind.

The combination of the rotating platform and short take-off conferred two benefits: it eliminated the need for a ship to steer directly into the wind in order to launch aircraft (an important consideration for capital ships, which dared not leave the line of battle) and it allowed the platforms to be shortened drastically. The ramps on the cruisers mentioned above were 120ft long; some rotating platforms were as short as 37ft. The shorter length, of course, lessened weight.

This development, coupled with the continuing demonstration of the value of aviation at sea, resulted in a large-scale equipping of Royal Navy vessels with aircraft during late 1917 and throughout 1918. If Admiralty 'contempt for the air' had been as rife as Marder would have us believe, the Sea Lords would hardly have authorised such a large investment in matériel, money and manpower in this programme.

Undoubtedly by the end of the war there lingered in the Royal Navy individual cases of distrust or dislike of aviation, but the belief that anti-air attitudes were widespread or affected naval air policy is refuted by statistics. Had the Grand Fleet sortied *en masse* on 11 November 1918 with all vessels carrying their full aerial complements, its capital ships and cruisers would have been carrying a total of 103 aeroplanes.[14] It would also have been supported by five specialised aviation vessels: a full flight-deck carrier, *Argus*; two quasi-flight-deck carriers, *Furious* and *Vindictive* (a similar vessel, *Campania*, was lost by collision on 5 November 1918), and two seaplane carriers with launching platforms.

Leaving the 'Battleship Admiral' becalmed in his supposed Sargasso Sea of reactionary ignorance, let us examine the attitudes toward aviation evinced by real personages occupying seats of naval authority before and during the Great War.

Notes

1. It is *de rigueur* for US aviation writers never to refer to Mitchell as William but always as 'Billy', apparently in the peculiar American belief that a nickname confers some sort of democratic credibility. It is also mandatory to title him 'General', although his temporary rank as Brigadier General lapsed when he was not reappointed Assistant Chief of the Air Service in 1925 and he reverted to his permanent rank of Colonel. This is usually and inaccurately called a demotion. All biographies of Mitchell to date are hagiographic, but for the main facts of his life and career, see Roger Burlingame, *General Billy Mitchell: Champion of Air Defense* (New York: McGraw-Hill, 1952).

2. For Scott's views on aviation, see Peter Padfield, *Aim Straight: A Biography of Admiral Sir Percy Scott* (London: Hodder and Stoughton, 1966), pp273 *et seq.*

3. Murray F Sueter, *Airmen or Noahs: Fair Play for Our Airmen — The Great 'Neon' Air Myth Exposed* (London: Sir Isaac Pitman and Sons, 1928).

4. Ibid, p54.

5. Ibid.

6. Sueter became *persona non grata* with the Admiralty when, in seeking recognition for his work in development of the tank (described in *Airmen or Noahs*), he wrote directly to King George V. For this breach of professional protocol, he was recalled from his Adriatic command, placed on half-pay, denied further responsibilities and was refused permission to transfer to the Royal Air Force when it was created in 1918. Elected to Parliament in 1921, he spent the next several years there fulminating against the Admiralty.

7. Jones, *The War in the Air*, Vol 4, p46.

8. Ibid.

9. Ibid, p47.

10. John R Cuneo, *The Air Weapon 1914–1916*, Vol 2 of *Winged Mars* (Harrisburg, Pa.: Military Service Publishing Co, 1947), p1.

11. Anson McCullough, 'Black Flight', *Air Classics* No 2, 1964.

12. Marder, *Dreadnought to Scapa Flow*, Vol 4, 1917: *Year of Crisis*, p24.

13. Newbolt, *Naval Operations*, Vol 5, Appendix K, p434.

CHAPTER 4

Admirals and Aviation — The Reality

As the war began, the largest, best-organised and most experienced naval air arm was that of Great Britain. It had started life as the Naval Wing of the Royal Flying Corps, created in 1912 (the other components being a Military Wing and a Central Flying School), but quickly began divorcing itself from the parent organisation and styling itself the Royal Naval Air Service — a title officially accepted in 1914 — although it remained *de jure* an arm of the RFC until 1915.[1]

Its prewar development owed much to an individual who while not an admiral was probably the closest a civilian ever came to being one: Winston S Churchill, First Lord of the Admiralty from October 1911 to May 1915. The RNAS became his special pet, and although he declared himself in favour of a unified air service[2] he acquiesced in, or even instigated, the moves that separated it from the RFC. With his love of gadgetry, he immersed himself in technical matters, encouraging such innovations as the torpedo plane, the flotation bag and the folding wing. He claimed — and no-one has successfully disputed it — to have coined the word 'seaplane' to replace the cumbersome 'hydroaeroplane'.

Churchill enjoyed the company of aviators; one early RNAS flier recalled being entertained by the First Lord aboard the Admiralty yacht *Enchantress* 'as though the only thing [Churchill] was interested in was naval aviation'.[3] In fact, after going aloft a few times as a passenger, Churchill took flying lessons. He gave it up only upon the urgent appeals of his friends, political colleagues and, most importantly, his wife. 'It was a wrench' to abandon flying, he wrote in June 1914, 'because I was on the verge of taking my pilot's certificate.'[4]

While Churchill was wielding benign high-level influence over the RNAS, its day-to-day administration was under the direction of

Murray Sueter, then with the rank of captain and far from the embittered critic of the Admiralty we encountered in the previous chapter. Sueter, named director of the Admiralty's Air Department when it was created in November 1912, came to aviation with an impressive technical background in torpedoes, submarines and wireless. He had been a member of the Advisory Committee for Aeronautics in 1909, was a delegate to the first International Conference on Aerial Navigation in 1910 in Paris, and in the same year was named to head an inspectorate formed to oversee construction of the Royal Navy's first, ill-fated rigid airship.[5]

A technical innovator of the first order, Sueter has been called (perhaps with some exaggeration) 'the clever, iron-willed creator of British naval flying in all its aspects'.[6] One early RNAS aviator was to state that Churchill and Sueter together were 'the two people most responsible for anything the Navy did to help Naval Aviation'[7] before the war.

During the prewar years much attention was paid to the airship, especially after the rigid type, capable of long radius and great endurance, was perfected by Germany's Ferdinand *Graf* von Zeppelin. It was in an effort to emulate Zeppelin's craft that the construction of the airship mentioned above was undertaken. But HMS *Airship No 1*, nicknamed *Mayfly*, was a failure, breaking up before even getting aloft.[8] This soured the Admiralty against the type for a time, but interest revived as German success with it continued.

The revival was due at least in part to the representations of Vice Admiral Sir John Jellicoe, destined to command the Grand Fleet at the outbreak of war. He became a convert to aeronautics after flying in the commercial Zeppelin *Schwaben* at Potsdam on 15 November 1911.[9] Realising the potential of such craft for naval reconnaissance, he called for British construction of them. The resulting muddled British rigid airship programme, however, came to fruition too late in the war. Meanwhile, Jellicoe found himself confronted during 1915–16 by an enemy becoming liberally supplied with airships and was in an almost perpetual dither about that fact. The consequences will be discussed later.

Jellicoe's successor as Grand Fleet commander, Vice Admiral Sir David Beatty, was equally concerned about enemy aviation but projected more positive uses for the RN's own air arm than had his predecessor. He convened an aircraft committee that made important and far-reaching decisions, persistently pressed for improved techniques of aerial reconnaissance and fire-control, pushed through over staff opposition the use of captive balloons for fleet observation as well as anti-submarine work, created the fleet's first formal squadron of aviation vessels and with it the first flag-rank aviation staff position and pestered the Admiralty for torpedo planes, and the ships to carry them, to attack the German fleet in its harbours. Beatty had high praise for the work of the only British aircraft to fly at Jutland[10] and in a postwar speech sagely predicted 'that in the future the Commander-in-Chief of a fleet may be quartered on board an aircraft carrier'.[11]

Below the high pinnacles of authority occupied by Jellicoe and Beatty were several other RN officers who became exponents and practitioners of aviation at sea. One such leading figure was Commodore Sir Reginald Tyrwhitt, commander of the Harwich Force (of cruisers and destroyers), who 'at once grasped the possibilities' of the offensive uses of ship-borne aircraft 'and persisted, in spite of repeated setbacks, with their development'.[12]

Tyrwhitt's partner at Harwich during the early months of the war was Commodore Sir Roger Keyes, an aviation enthusiast who later made extensive use of aircraft as commander of the Dover Patrol, as had his predecessor, Admiral Sir Reginald Bacon.

Two others who had innovative ideas about aviation are worthy of mention: Vice Admiral Sir Robert Arbuthnot, remembered today only for his death at Jutland, and Vice Admiral Sir Ernest Troubridge, well known for his ill-fated chase of the German battlecruiser *Goeben* early in the war and far less so for his tenure as head of the British Naval Mission to Serbia.[13] In 1915 Arbuthnot proposed equipping submarines with aircraft to be stowed in watertight containers, an idea considered by an Admiralty subcommittee[14] and the forerunner of many similar schemes studied or implemented by several navies between the World Wars. Three years earlier, Troubridge had drawn up a detailed and well-conceived programme for organisation and equipment of a naval air service.[15] These facts tend to refute strongly Marder's assessment of Arbuthnot as 'without much imagination'[16] and Troubridge as lacking 'a creative brain or much interest in weapon development'.[17]

That Troubridge could put his idea on paper in 1912 attests to the degree that interest in aviation had permeated British naval thought in the prewar years. Surely it cannot be imagined this would have been the case had the Royal Navy's officer corps been, as charged by one critic, characterised by 'punctilious ritual, ignorance of technical progress, and remoteness from the reality of a modern fleet'.[18]

* * *

'German naval use of aviation in both World Wars was extremely limited in terms of success and experimentation', states the editor of a bibliography of German military aviation, who then asks 'Why was this?'[19] As far as the Second World War is concerned, the answer can be given in three words: Hermann Wilhelm Göring.[20] For the First World War, the premise leading to the question is false. The German navy of 1914–18 not only achieved a number of aeronautical successes but experimented with many innovative techniques of future significance. It was the first to employ aircraft (airships) for long-range oceanic reconnaissance; it realised the importance of achieving aerial superiority over disputed waters, fostered the development of the torpedo plane and employed it more extensively than the Royal Navy, pioneered aerial mine-laying and use of aircraft in anti-commerce warfare, and developed wireless-guided aerial navigation. It instigated construction of aircraft for use aboard submarines, experimented with aerial control of explosive missiles and surface attack boats and even earmarked vessels for conversion to seaplane carriers marginally earlier than the Royal Navy.

Many of the experiments were inconclusive or achieved only limited success, but taken as a whole the German naval air arm was by late 1917 quantitatively and probably qualitatively the strongest and most effective of all those of the continental powers. Its growth and achievement by that data contrasts remarkably with its status at the start of the war. In August 1914 the *Kaiserliche Marine* possessed only a couple of dozen heterogeneous seaplanes — several of foreign manufacture, several unfit for operational use — and a single airship unequipped for combat (two earlier Zeppelins had been lost in prewar accidents that had wiped out almost the entire cadre of naval airshipmen).

The paucity of seaplanes cannot be blamed on the Kaiser's admirals. As early as October 1910, only seven months after the first powered flight from water had been made, *Grossadmiral* Alfred von Tirpitz, Secretary of State of the Imperial Naval Office (*Reichsmarineamt*), ordered investigation of heavier-than-air machines for naval use. Early the next year funds eventually totalling 200,000 marks were allocated for seaplane research and development. This was undertaken by the *Kaiserliche Werft* at Danzig, where the first German seaplane was eventually produced.[21]

Technical criteria for seaplanes were drawn up in expectation that the private aircraft industry would build craft to these specifications for sale to the navy. The expectation proved wrong: 'Because of their inland location and the fact that landplanes were easier and more profitable to construct, the aircraft firms were reluctant to accept the challenge and expense of seaplane development.'[22] Repeated invitations to bid for seaplane contracts were snubbed, accounting in large part for the navy's purchase of foreign machines. One reported reason for the German firms' reluctance was the navy's insistance that all its seaplanes be amphibious. Industry interest finally began to be expressed when the amphibious requirement was dropped in January 1913, and a number of companies developed seaplanes to compete for naval purchase.

But the time lost could not be regained, and February 1915 found the navy with only half the 120 seaplanes it had projected to be in service at that time. By then the dominance of the army in competition for allocation of airframes and aero engines had become another factor retarding naval air expansion.

The German navy's difficulty in obtaining aircraft refutes another myth — the myth would have it that aviation was beating vainly at the closed door of naval officialdom, but here was a case of aviation refusing to enter a wide-open portal.

An influential figure in early German naval aviation was *Grossadmiral Prinz* Heinrich of Prussia, younger brother of Kaiser Wilhelm II. Prince Henry, as he was known to the English-speaking world, became an air enthusiast in his middle years and, like Churchill, took up flying personally. Unlike Churchill, he stayed the course and became a certified aviator in 1910 at the age of 48. He quickly established himself as a prime patron and promoter of all phases of German aviation, lending the prestige and wielding the influence that his standing in both the royal family and the navy conferred on him.

It was pressure from Heinrich that helped persuade Tirpitz to accept the Zeppelin for naval service, something he had resisted for reasons that will be examined later. Heinrich had become impressed with the potential of the airship after a flight in Zeppelin *LZ 3* on 17 October 1908 that lasted only five minutes short of six hours.[23]

On 30 July 1914, Kaiser Wilhelm, in what apparently was a fit of nepotism, appointed Heinrich commander of naval forces in the

Baltic (*Oberbefehlshaber der Ostseestreitkräfte*), against the wishes of his naval advisers, including Admiral Georg Alexander von Müller, Chief of the Naval Cabinet. To the surprise of Müller and others, Heinrich's leadership, if not brilliant, proved 'satisfactory in the extreme'.[24] He certainly employed aviation extensively and effectively; he successfully insisted that a proportion of airships be allotted to the Baltic, and persuaded *Konteradmiral* Ehler Behring to embark seaplanes on the armoured cruiser *Friedrich Carl* for reconnaissance over the Russian coast, 'the first example in the war of airplanes accompanying a task force'.[25] The Baltic was the site of the first German torpedo plane operations, the only area in which aerial mine-laying was undertaken by any navy, and the only theatre where German seaplane carriers were employed as aggressively as their British counterparts elsewhere.

In the main arena of the naval war, the North Sea, all the successive commanders of the High Seas Fleet — Admirals Friedrich von Ingenohl, Hugo von Pohl, Reinhard Scheer and Franz Hipper — were acutely aware of the value of aviation. As early as February 1914, von Pohl, then chief of the Admiralty Staff (*Admiralstab*), 'was . . . asking for seaplanes, not just as defensive weapons . . . but also, more significantly, as offensive weapons and reconnaissance to compensate for the German fleet's lack of cruisers'.[26]

Scheer, who in his postwar book lamented the shortage of scouting seaplanes during the early months of the conflict, attached great importance to aerial reconnaissance, as will be discussed later.

Hipper (von Hipper after his elevation to the Baverian nobility in 1916) was equally aware of aviation's value in his capacity as Flag Officer, Reconnaissance Forces (*Befehlshaber die Aufklärungsschiffe*) during 1913–18 before taking command of the fleet. In 1915, advocating aircraft for anti-submarine work and the equipping of cruisers with wireless-carrying seaplanes, he asserted in a memo: 'Should we make as great an effort in air weapons as we have in the undersea it would give us absolute superiority over all other nations in the world.'[27]

It is apparent from the sentiments expressed above that the German navy, both before and during the war, possessed a thoroughly air-minded group of high-ranking officers. It was a misfortune not of their making that they were forced to enter the conflict with a weak aerial weapon.

* * *

The air arm of Austria-Hungary's *Kaiserlich und Königlich Kriegsmarine* (Imperial and Royal Navy) was fostered by its prewar commander, Admiral Rudolph *Graf* Montecuccoli, who himself went aloft a number of times — probably the first chief of a major navy to do so.[28] The *KuK* air arm at the start of the war was about on a par in terms of numbers and equipment with that of its much larger German ally. It had gained some slight operational experience, having taken part in peace-keeping efforts in Albania in 1913, and flew the Great War's first combat missions in late July 1914.

The navy's first wartime commander, Admiral Anton Haus, was equally, if not even more, appreciative of aviation as Monte-cuccoli. Haus 'praised [aviators] and termed them the first elite corps of the navy. [He] marvelled at the spirit shown by everyone once they [*sic*] could fly, and noted with approval that a call for aerial observers for reconnaissance flights had resulted in all Fre-gattenleutnants in the fleet at Pola, without exception, volun-teering'.[29] Integration of air and surface elements was remarkably smooth; as one historian put it, 'There does not appear to have been any friction or competition between aviation and other branches of the navy.'[30]

When Italy entered the war in May 1917, Austro-Hungarian superiority in aerial matériel, plus personnel who had had ten months of operational experience, enabled the *KuK* navy to take control of the Adriatic skies and hold it for all practical purposes until overwhelmed numerically in 1917.

Austria-Hungary's aerial Achilles' heel was the fact that the empire lacked the resources to support an extensive aeronautical industry, excellent as some of that industry's products were.[31] As a result, the army came to rely increasingly on German aircraft. The navy, however, was equipped largely with aircraft of indigenous design and manufacture throughout the war.

*   *   *

The French navy had a long association with aeronautics, predat-ing even the siege of Paris during the Franco-Prussian War, when sailors were active in constructing and manning the balloons that flew from the city.[32] A naval heavier-than-air branch was established informally in 1910 and given official status in 1912. That year the Ministry of Marine authorised the conversion to a seaplane carrier of the first warship anywhere to be permanently configured as an aviation vessel — the former torpedo-boat carrier *Foudre*, which had lofted balloons in turn-of-the-century naval exercises and from which in 1914 the first French shipboard take-off of an aeroplane would be made.

Nursed through its formative years under the successive commands of two captains who would achieve flag rank, René Daveluy and Louis-Ernest Fatou, the air arm remained small in 1914 but was on the verge of considerable expansion. Specifications had been issued for shipboard aeroplanes, launching and retrieval devices for them were being investigated, negotiations were under way for purchase of a merchant vessel for conversion to a seaplane carrier, plans for a specialised aviation ship were being drawn up and a large fleet of airships was projected.[33] All of this came to an abrupt halt with the outbreak of war, at first under the soon-to-be shattered illusion that the conflict would be too short for the programme to be completed. Consequently, as hostilities began the naval air service numbered no more than twenty or so aeroplanes, including only eight seaplanes, and possessed no airships.

By the time the Western Front was established, unforeseen economic strains further stalled naval air expansion. A considerable portion of France's northeastern industrial area, with its mines, smelters and factories, had fallen under German occupation and nearly a quarter of France's industrial labour force had been lost. This problem was exacerbated by the sudden need for armaments of all kinds, including demands for aircraft and aero engines not only by the French services but by those of the other allied powers — demands that became more pressing as the war continued. Heroic achievements of industrial mobilisation and organisation finally surmounted these problems, but naval aviation was perforce given low priority. It did not begin to be revived on a large scale until 1916, in response to the mounting submarine menace, with consequent emphasis on flying boats and airships.

The ambitious prewar programme proves the French naval hierarchy was cognizant of the value of aviation, but it was not implemented first because of the belief in a short war and then because of unexpected wartime exigencies.

* * *

Italy was the first nation to employ a truly organised national air force, in North Africa during its 1911–12 war with Turkey.[34] Naval aspects of this employment were the use of a ship-lofted balloon to spot ship gunfire against shore targets (the first use of this technique since the American Civil War) and refuelling of airships from a surface craft.

Italian naval aviation, however, advanced only slightly in the years before the Great War, despite a number of innovative experiments and suggestions. Some of the earliest attempts to develop the torpedo plane were made by *Capitano de Genio Navale* Allessandro Guidoni and the Argentine/Spanish Marquis Raul Pateras Pescara (later a pioneer of the helicopter). Guidoni also drew up plans for conversion of the old cruiser *Piemonte* into a seaplane carrier, and experiments with shipboard operation of seaplanes were made on the battleship *Dante Alighieri* and the armoured cruisers *Amalfi* and *San Marco*.[35]

When Italy entered the war, a chain of naval air bases was under development and the cruiser *Elba*, which had earlier operated balloons during naval manoeuvres, had been outfitted as a seaplane mothership. Naval aircraft, however, numbered no more than thirty, all of foreign manufacture, half of them American Curtiss seaplanes suitable only for training.

Italian aviation made striking progress during the war, thanks to such figures as the aeronautical genius Gianni Caproni and pioneer air power philosopher Guilio Douhet. Its maritime component, however, although it fought hard and valiantly, never achieved a status comparable to those of other navies. With the establishment in 1923 of the independent air force, the *Regia Aeronautica*, the naval air arm underwent an eclipse from which it never recovered.

* * *

The Imperial Japanese Navy had used balloon observation to spot fire for a shore-based battery at Port Arthur, but lacked a formal air organisation until June 1912, when a Naval Aeronautic Research Committee was formed. One of its first acts was to dispatch five junior officers to flying schools in the United States and France. They returned as trained aviators, bringing with them the navy's first aircraft, a US Curtiss and two French Maurice Farmans, all floatplanes.

One of the Farmans took part in naval manoeuvres during October and November 1913, operating from a former merchant vessel crudely fitted out as a seaplane carrier, the *Wakamiya Maru*. That vessel had the distinction of being the first aviation vessel to see combat when attached to Admiral Kato Sadakichi's fleet during the August–November 1914 siege of the German protectorate of Tsingtao on the Chinese mainland. Her four seaplanes joined Japanese army aircraft in scouting and bombing missions.[36]

After Tsingtao, little is heard of Japanese naval aviation during the rest of the war, for the IJN mounted no more major operations. But the conflict had great influence on the navy, which assidiously studied British maritime air operations and developments (there was, for instance a Japanese observer aboard HMS *Furious*). 'During the late war', asserted the officer who headed a British navy air mission to Japan during 1921–23, 'it is no idle boast to say that the Japanese Navy became impressed with the work of our own Naval Air Service and convinced of the necessity of having a similar organisation.'[37]

This British mission, instigated by the Navy Minister, Admiral Kato Tomosaburo,[38] thoroughly tutored the IJN in all aspects of naval flying. During the same period the Mitsubishi industrial complex, in a move facilitated by the navy, hired talented British aeronautical engineers who designed the first Japanese carrier aircraft.[39] And in 1922 the aircraft carrier *Hosho* was commissioned — the world's first specially-designed, built-from-the-keel flight-deck vessel to reach completion.[40]

* * *

The Russian navy began its association with aeronautics almost as early as the French. Use of the air to extend vision at sea was suggested before the turn of the century by Vice Admiral Stepan O Makarov, one of the ablest and most outstanding Tsarist officers of the steam era. In a discussion of the importance of scouting, after urging 'we should do all in our power to increase the limits of our own horizon', he recommended that for this purpose 'it would be well to experiment with aerostatic devices to determine how far they may be useful in war'.[41]

By 1900 'aerostatic parks' (balloon fields) had been established on the Baltic and Black Sea coasts and a number of warships had experimentally lofted balloons.[42] Later experiments involved man-lifting kites. There was a flurry of lighter-than-air activity at Vladivostok during the Russo-Japanese War, while at the same time in the Baltic the Imperial Navy converted a merchant ship into the world's first sea-going balloon vessel, although it saw no operational service.[43]

The navy began to enter the heavier-than-air field in 1910, with a substantial impetus supplied by Grand Duke Alexander Mikhailovich, a cousin of Tsar Nicholas II who held naval flag rank. He was presiding over a two-million rouble fund (roughly $1.2 million or £675,000) raised by public subscription during the Russo-Japanese War to build warships. While in France, Alexander was impressed by Louis Blériot's English Channel flight and 'decided to act at once and introduce the heavier-than-air flying machines in Russia'.[44]

After receiving strong public support for this venture, he used the money to purchase aeroplanes in France and pay for flight training of selected officers, arrangements assisted by Nicolas de Basily, secretary of the Russian Embassy in Paris.[45] Later in the year Alexander used part of the fund to purchase land for a flight school near the Black Sea Fleet's base at Sevastopol in the Crimea. (The southerly location was chosen because it had a long summer season and a more clement climate for flying — it was for the same reason that the French navy concentrated its flight training on the Mediterranean coast and the US navy in Florida and southern California.)

Groundwork having been laid and naval aviators trained, an air arm began to be organised in 1912. In the spring of that year, Vice Admiral Nikolai O Essen, commander of the Baltic Fleet, ordered Captain[46] Adrian I Nepenin, chief of what was called the Combined Services, to form an aviation section within it. ('Combined Services' was a shorthand term for *Sluzhba Nabluideniia i Sviazi*, which may be translated as Service of Reconnaissance and Liaison or Service of Scouting and Communications.)

Nepenin deputed the responsibility to his lesser in grade (although long-time associate), Captain Boris P Dudorov, a veteran of the Russo-Japanese War who had been a prisoner after the fall of Port Arthur and later an outstanding student at the Naval Academy.[47]

Dudorov proceeded to organise a staff, create air bases and tour France to acquaint himself with aeronautical progress (of which he had initially no knowledge) and arrange for purchase of seaplanes, which the infant Russian aircraft industry had yet to produce. Upon the outbreak of the war he became chief of the Baltic Fleet's air arm and was responsible for, among other innovations, creation of that fleet's first and only aviation vessel.[48]

In all his efforts, both before and during the war, Dudorov records receiving strong support, encouragement and co-operation from the Naval Minister, Admiral Ivan K Grigorovich, and the successive chiefs of the Naval General Staff, Vice Admirals Aleksandr A Liven and Aleksandr I Rusin, and even from Tsar Nicholas himself.[49] It is possible to suspect that the support was politically motivated, but, for whatever reason, naval aviation received favourable backing from the highest ranks of officialdom.

An air service for the Black Sea Fleet was also established in 1912, also as a section of the Combined Services, with an initial strength of five seaplanes.[50] Some of the most innovative aero-naval operations of the war would be initiated and conducted by the two successive commanders of the Black Sea Fleet, Vice Admirals Andrei A Eberhardt[51] and Aleksandr V Kolchak.

* * *

Although both sides had lofted observation balloons from surface vessels during the American Civil War,[52] the US navy evinced no further interest in aeronautics for many years. In 1898 Assistant Secretary of the Navy Theodore Roosevelt had tried but failed to enlist naval technical and financial support for Samuel P Langley's ultimately unsuccessful 'Aerodrome' flying machine.

Six years later, aeronautics came to the favourable attention of Admiral of the Navy George Dewey, the hero of Manila Bay and for seventeen years the first president of the navy's General Board, a panel of officers established in 1900 to advise on policy and technical matters. After witnessing lighter-than-air flights at the St Louis Exposition in 1904, Dewey reportedly told aeronauts 'If you can fly higher than the crow's nest, we can use you.'[53] He was subsequently to exercise remote but beneficial influence on the creation of USN aviation.

That creation can be credited more to the force of public opinion than to any other factor. Correspondence to the Navy Department urging investigation of aviation became so insistent that in September 1910 an officer was designated to cope with it. The choice fell on Captain Washington I Chambers, selected for his general expertise rather than knowledge of aviation — of which, like Dudorov, he had none. To remedy his ignorance he immersed himself in aeronautical literature and attended the first large-scale US aerial display and competition, at Belmont Park, New York. As his knowledge deepened and his interest grew, he widened his basically secretarial role into a self-conferred mandate to establish a naval air service.[54]

Often assisted by Assistant Secretary of the Navy Beekman Winthrop and with Dewey hovering benignly in the background, Chambers arranged for the world's first shipboard take-off and landing by an aeroplane, initiated work resulting in the first successful aircraft catapult, and eventually headed a committee that drew up an ambitious and comprehensive — although never implemented — plan for a naval air organisation.[55]

On 1 October 1910, only a few days after Chamber's assignment to aviation correspondence, the General Board issued a recommendation (in which Dewey's hand can be discerned) that provision for accommodation and operation of aircraft be made in the design of scout cruisers. Nothing came of this, however, for the board could only recommend.

Hard on the heels of this, a new and junior member of the board, Captain (later Rear Admiral) Bradley A Fiske, laid before it a proposal for defence of the Philippines by a fleet or 400 or more torpedo-carrying aircraft. The state of aviation being what it was in 1910, this was obviously a visionary idea impossible to achieve, and a more senior board member, Rear Admiral Richard Wainwright, can hardly be criticised (although he has been) for condemning it as a 'wildcat' scheme.

Fiske remained smitten with the concept of the torpedo plane and in 1912 received a patent for an aerial torpedo-carrying and launching device. Even earlier than Sueter, then, Fiske was an ardent advocate of the air-borne torpedo, and lived to see his belief in it vindicated.[56]

USN aviation made its official debut in 1911 with training of a small number of junior officers as fliers and acquisition of a few aeroplanes. It progressed by fits and starts for the next few years, lacking funds and, in contrast to the British navy, a formal organisational status. The latter problem was caused by the navy's bureau system, in which each bureau chief controlled his own fiefdom, answerable to no central authority below the Secretary of the Navy. Elements of aviation were parcelled out among the bureaux of Engineering, Construction and Repair, Navigation, and Ordnance — a situation guaranteed to make co-ordination difficult. An Office of Aeronautics was established in July 1914 but lapsed for all practical purposes in October 1915 when it was subordinated to the Office of Naval Operations. Aviation did not achieve bureau status until 1921.[57]

Some slight operational experience was gained when a few aircraft flew reconnaissance missions during the American seizure of

In the beginning—the Greek destroyer *Velos* towing a Farman seaplane back to port after its flight over the Dardanelles in February 1913 that occasioned the first verified skirmish between warships and an aeroplane. (Courtesy of August G Blume)

This photograph is believed to show Flight Commander B D Kilner taking Sopwith Pup 9927 off HMS *Vindex* in pursuit of a Zeppelin—a chase from which he never returned. 'Never to be seen again was the epitaph for many a Great War naval aviator.' (Fleet Air Arm Museum)

Rear Admiral Sir Murray F Sueter, 'the clever, iron-willed creator of British naval flying'. (Fleet Air Arm Museum)

Admiral Sir John R Jellicoe, commander of the Grand Fleet, 1914–16, who was continually frustrated by what he believed was the advantage that airships gave to the German navy. (US Naval Historical Center)

A Sopwith fighter aboard a rotating platform on a British light cruiser. Such platforms permitted a ship to launch aircraft without having to change course into the wind. (Author's collection)

Admiral Reinhard Scheer, who as commander of the High Seas Fleet maintained great but ill-placed reliance on airship reconnaissance. (US Naval Historical Center)

Rear Admiral Bradley A Fiske in 1914—an early and ardent advocate of the torpedo plane, he lived to see his faith in it justified. (US Naval Historical Center)

Rear Admiral William A Moffett in his rank of commander *c* 1912–14. As first and long-time chief of the US Navy's Bureau of Aeronautics, he was responsible for integration of aviation into the fleet. (US Naval Historical Center)

Hansa-Brandenburg W 29 floatplane fighters, prime weapons in the fight for aerial control of the narrow reaches of the North Sea and which 'could out-perform nearly any type thrown against them'. (Courtesy of Peter M Grosz)

Veracruz, Mexico, in April 1914. Although this service was late and limited, it earned the commendation of Rear Admiral Frank Jack Fletcher, commander of the naval forces at Veracruz.[58]

The Great War made a convert to aviation of Rear Admiral William S Sims, commander of US naval forces in Europe. He endorsed and helped facilitate an aerial offensive against German submarine bases, nudged the General Board toward favourable consideration of aircraft carrier construction, and praised the work of naval aviators in his memoirs, declaring that 'aircraft were an important element in defeating the German campaign against merchant shipping'.[59] In the immediate postwar years, Sims joined Fiske as a vigorous champion of aviation, foreseeing the eclipse of the battleship and predicting the aircraft carrier 'as the agent that would revolutionize warfare at sea'.[60]

A somewhat more belated but even more influential convert to aviation was Captain (later Rear Admiral) William A Moffett, who became the first chief of the new Bureau of Aeronautics. He 'integrated the use of airplanes and airships with fleet operations, managed the introduction of new technology — most notably the aircraft carrier — and rationalised procurement and personnel.'[61]

All this lay in the future when the United States entered the war in April 1917 with a naval air arm greatly inferior in numbers of aircraft and personnel to those of even Austria-Hungary and Italy. The inferiority was not only in numbers — all US naval aircraft in service were obsolete by European standards.

*   *   *

In this chapter we have examined the favourable views of aviation held by a number of leading naval figures, as expressed in documented words and, in some cases, in deeds. It would be folly to claim that this opinion was shared all by *all* officers in *all* navies. There was certainly much skepticism, from the lowest ranks to the highest. But, as I have tried to emphasise earlier, much of the skepticism stemmed less from ignorance or reactionary conservatism than from realistic technical considerations. For the rest of this book we shall explore how these realistic objections were overcome as aviation proved it could be — and even in an early state *was* — an important adjunct to sea power.

Notes

1. Sources describing the genesis of British military and naval aviation are myriad. One of the earliest but still one of the best is C F Snowden Gamble, *The Air Weapon: Being Some Account of the Growth of British Military Aeronautics from the Beginnings in the Year 1773 Until the End of the Year 1929* (London: Oxford University Press, 1931). This was to be the first of a series of volumes of which no more were published.

2. This view was put forward in ADM 1/8621, 'Some Minutes by Mr Churchill on Aviation Matters September–December 1913', reproduced in Stephen W Roskill, ed., *Documents Relating to the Naval Air Service*, Vol 1, 1908–1918 (London: Navy Records Society, 1969), pp115–124. No further volumes published.

3. Richard Bell Davies, *Sailor in the Air: The Memoirs of Vice Admiral Richard Bell Davies* (London: Peter Davies, 1967), p85.

4. Quoted in Mary Soames, *Clementine Churchill: The Biography of a Marriage*, (New York: Paragon House Publishers, reprint ed 1988), p134. Churchill's aptitude for flying has been questioned. Oliver Stewart, in ' " Creative Instrument": Sir Winston Churchill and Aviation' (*Air Pictorial*, Vol 27 No 3, March 1965), states that for Churchill 'The huge scope of aviation's possibilities enthralled him rather than the acquirement of piloting skills.' I think that, had he had the chance to acquire experience, Churchill would have made an excellent aviator. He had been a skilled cavalryman and a crack polo player, and it is well attested that in the early days of aviation the qualities required for good horsemanship also made for good airmanship.

5. There is no formal, full-length biography of Sueter, but for a good summary of his career see Edward Chilton, 'Rear Admiral Sir Murray Sueter, CB' *Cross & Cockade (Great Britain) Journal*, Vol 15 No 2, 1984.

6. Harald Penrose, *British Aviation: The Pioneer Years 1903–1914* (London: Putnam, 1967), p593.

7. Charles R Samson, 'History of Naval Aeroplanes and Seaplanes,' Air 1/724/76/2, quoted in Alfred Gollin, *The Impact of Air Power on the British People and Their Government, 1909–14* (Stanford University Press, 1989), p181.

8. For details, see Robin Higham, *The British Rigid Airship, 1908–1931: A Study in Weapons Policy* (London: G T Foulis, 1961).

9. Douglas H Robinson, *Giants in the Sky: A History of the Rigid Airship* (Seattle: University of Washington Press, 1958), p151.

10. See R D Layman, 'Engadine at Jutland', *Warship 1990* (London: Conway Maritime Press, 1990).

11. The speech was delivered at the London Lord Mayor's banquet, 9 November 1923; quoted in W S Chalmers, *The Life and Letters of David, Earl Beatty* (London: Hodder and Stoughton, 1931), p466.

12. William Jameson, *The Fleet That Jack Built: Nine Men Who Made a Modern Navy* (New York: Harcourt, Brace & World, 1962), p466. 'At once' may not be exactly accurate; Tyrwhitt had initial misgivings about aircraft after their fragility was displayed in his early operations. His opinion, however, did change quickly: see A Temple Patterson, *Tyrwhitt of the Harwich Force: The Life of Admiral of the Fleet Sir Reginald Tyrwhitt* (London: Macdonald, 1973) and R D Layman, *The Cuxhaven Raid: The World's First Carrier Air Strike* (London: Conway Maritime Press, 1985).

13. Troubridge's chase of the *Goeben* is described in so many sources that a list of them would run to pages. For his lesser-known work in Serbia, see Charles E J Fryer, *The Royal Navy on the Danube* (Boulder, Colo.: East European Monographs, 1988) and Paul G Halpern, *A Naval History of World War I* (Annapolis: Naval Institute Press, 1994).

14. ADM 116/11140, Public Record Office.

15. Air 1/626, Public Record Office, reproduced in Roskill, *Documents*, pp29–32.

16. Marder, *Dreadnought to Scapa Flow*, Vol 2, p442.

17. Ibid, p22.

18. Correlli Barnett, *The Swordbearers: Supreme Command in the First World War* (New York: William Morrow, reprint ed 1965), p187.

19. Edward L Homze, ed and comp, *German Military Aviation: A Guide to the Literature* (New York and London: Garland Publishing, 1984), p52.

20. That German aerial success at sea was 'extremely limited' in the Second World War might well be disputed by the ghosts of the thousands of sailors, naval and mercantile, killed in every body of water over which the *Luftwaffe* operated. For that conflict, Homze's sentence might have been better phrased not as German *naval use* of aviation but German use of *naval aviation*.

21. This was a standard Albatros pusher fitted with a single float. See John R Cuneo, *Winged Mars*, Vol 1, *The German Air Weapon — 1870–1914* (Harrisburg, Pa.: Military Service Publishing Co, 1942), p111, and John Howard Morrow Jr, *Building German Airpower, 1909–1914* (Knoxville: University of Tennessee Press, 1976), p89.

22. Morrow, ibid.

23. Robinson, *Giants in the Sky*.

24. Walter Görlitz, ed, *The Kaiser and His Court: The Diaries, Note Books and Letters of Admiral Georg Alexander von Müller, Chief of the Naval Cabinet, 1914–1918* (New York: Harcourt, Brace & World, 1959), p15.

25. Cuneo, *Air Weapon*, p347. The aircraft were floatplanes, an Albatros WDD and a Rumpler 4B.12. The Rumpler was still aboard and lost when the cruiser was sunk by Russian mines on 17 November 1914.

26. Morrow, *Building German Airpower*, p93.
27. Quoted in Tobias R Philbin, *Admiral von Hipper: The Inconvenient Hero* (Amsterdam: B R Grüner, 1982), p122.
28. Anthony Sokol, *The Imperial and Royal Austro-Hungarian Navy* (Annapolis: US Naval Institute, 1968).
29. Paul G Halpern, *The Naval War in the Mediterranean 1914–1918* (Annapolis: Naval Institute Press, 1987), p39.
30. Sokol, *Austro-Hungarian Navy*, p75.
31. The assertion by Sokol, op cit, that the Austro-Hungarian 'aviation industry did not falter until, towards the end of the war, it ran out of some of the raw materials it needed for the manufacture of engines' (p111) is far from correct. For the many problems plaguing that industry throughout the war, see John H Morrow Jr, *German Air Power in World War I* (Lincoln, Neb.: University of Nebraska Press, 1982), pp167–185. For technical details of Austro-Hungarian naval aircraft, see Heinz J Nowarra *et al*, *Marine Aircraft of the 1914–1918 War* (Letchworth, Herts.: Harleyford Publications, 1966); Franz Selinger, 'A Checklist of Austrian Naval Aircraft', *Cross & Cockade Journal*, Vol 9 No 1, Autumn 1968, and René Greger, *Austro-Hungarian Warships of World War I* (London: Ian Allan, 1976). Sokol, op cit, gives a statistical summary of *KuK* aerial operations. Operations are described in Peter Schupita, *Die k.u.k seeflieger: chronik und dokumentation der österreichisch ungarischen marineluftwaffe 1911–1918* (Coblenz: Bernard & Graefe, 1983).
32. This story is told in John Fisher, *Airlift 1870: The Balloon and Pigeon Post in the Siege of Paris* (London: Max Parish, 1965).
33. For early development of French naval aeronautics and details of the prewar expansion programme, see R D Layman, *To Ascend From a Floating Base: Shipboard Aeronautics and Aviation, 1783–1914* (Cranbury, NJ, and London: Fairleigh Dickinson University Press and Associated University Presses, 1979). See also Francis Dousset, *Les porte-avions français des origines (1911) à nos jours* (Brest and Paris: Éditions de la Cite, 1975).
34. This is described in Giorgio Aspostolo, 'The Birth of Italian Aviation: The Libyan War', *The Airpower Historian*, Vol 9 No 3, July 1962; D J Fitzsimmons, 'The Origins of Air Warfare', *Air Pictorial*, Vol 34 No 2, December 1972, and Don Fiore, 'Airplane's Baptism by Fire', *Aviation Heritage*, Vol 1 No 1, September 1990. For the naval aspects, see Layman, *To Ascend*.
35. By far the best source on the origins and development of Italian naval aviation is Erminio Bagnasco, *La portaereri nella marina italiana: idee, progttie e realizzazioni dalle origini a oggi* (Rome: Rivista Marittima, 1989).
36. This vessel was the former British merchantman *Lethington*, a blockade runner captured during the Russo-Japanese war. For particulars and a brief history, see R D Layman, *Before the Aircraft Carrier: The Development of Aviation Vessels 1849–1922* (London: Conway Maritime Press, 1989). For early Japanese naval aviation, see Katsu Kohri, Ikuo Komori and Ichori Naita, *The Fifty Years of Japanese Aviation 1910–1960*, 3 vols (Tokyo: Kantosha Co., 1960–61); Robert C Mikesh and Shorzoe Abe, *Japanese Aircraft 1910–1941* (London: Putnam, 1990); Eiichiro Sekigawa, *Pictorial History of Japanese Military Aviation* (London: Ian Allan, 1974); James A Tindal, 'A Brief History of Early Japanese Aviation', *World War I Aeroplanes*, No 120, July 1988; Toshikazu Ohame and Roger Pineau, 'Japanese Naval Aviation', *US Naval Institute Proceedings*, Vol 98 No 12, December 1972, and Robert C Mikesh, 'The Rise of Japanese Naval Air Power', *Warship 1991* (London: Conway Maritime Press, 1991).
37. Colonel the Master of Sempill (William Francis Forbes-Sempill, later Lord Sempill), 'The British Aviation Mission to the Imperial Japanese Navy', *The Journal of the Royal Aeronautical Society*, Vol 28 No 165, September 1924. This article is a transcription of a paper read at the twelfth meeting of the society's 59th session. See also Frida H Brackely, *Brackles: Memoirs of a Pioneer of Civil Aviation* (Chatham: W & J Mackay, 1952).
38. Kato is the surname of the two admirals mentioned, but they were not related.
39. This group had been affiliated with the Sopwith Aviation Co, which went into liquidation in 1920. It was headed by Herbert Smith, who was responsible for many of Sopwith's wartime designs. For its work in Japan, see John Crampton, 'Herbert Smith — Aircraft Designer', *Air Pictorial*, Vol 37 No 6, June 1975.
40. This distinction has often been given to the British carrier *Eagle*, but although that vessel was designed and launched earlier than *Hosho* she was not completed until fourteen months later than the Japanese ship. It has been reported that a British naval architect, or perhaps more than one, had a hand in *Hosho's* design, but I have been unable to confirm this.
41. Stepan O Makarov, *Discussion of Questions in Naval Tactics*, John B Bernadou, trans, (Annapolis: Naval Institute Press, 1990), p210. This is a translation of *Voprosy morskoi taktiki i podgotovki ofitserov*, originally published by the US Office of Naval Intelligence in 1898. Makarov, who took command of the Russian Pacific Fleet in March 1904, is credited with reinvigorating it after its initial setbacks, but was killed the next month when his flagship was sunk by a mine. For a concise biography, see his listing by Patrick J Rollins in *The Modern Encyclopedia of Russian and Soviet History*, Vol 21 (Gulf Breeze, Fla: Academic International Press). A shorter summary of his career is given in Donald Miller, 'Admiral Makarov: Attack! Attack! Attack!', *US Naval Institute Proceedings*, Vol 91 No 7, July 1965, which Rollins asserts is 'inaccurate in several details'.

42. See Layman, *To Ascend*. See also R D Layman and Stephen McLaughlin, 'The Shipboard Balloon–The Beginnings of Naval Aeronautics,' *Warship 1992* (London: Conway Maritime Press, 1992).

43. For details of this vessel, the *Russ* (also sometimes spelled *Rus*), see Layman, *Before the Aircraft Carrier*.

44. Alexander [Mikhailovich], Grand Duke of Russia, *Once a Grand Duke* (New York: Farrar & Rinehart, 1932), p237.

45. Nicolas de Basily, *The Abdication of Emperor Nicholas II of Russia* (Princeton, NJ: Kingston Press, 1984); reprint ed of *Nicolas de Basily, Diplomat of Imperial Russia 1903–1917* (Palo Alto, Calif: Board of Trustees of Leland Stanford Junior University, nd). De Basily took a great technical interest in aviation, flew as a passenger many times and was responsible for procuring a number of foreign aeroplanes for Russia. See *The Abdication*, pp40–45.

46. In the Russian navy of this period there were two grades below that of rear admiral — *Kapitan 1 Ranga* (captain 1st rank) and *Kapitan 2 Ranga* (captain 2nd rank), the latter corresponding roughly to commander in the British and American navies. Many contemporary and even more later sources fail to make a distinction between the two, so I have chosen to use simply 'captain' for either.

47. After the popular revolution of early 1917, Dudorov became First Deputy Minister for Strategic and Political Questions under the acting Naval Minister of the Provisional Government. In May 1917 he accepted the post of naval attaché at the Russian Embassy in Tokyo. By 1919 he had attained the rank of Rear Admiral, although the date of this promotion and under what authority it was made are unclear. In 1923, disillusioned with politics, he emigrated to the United States and died in 1965 in Palo Alto, California.

48. For details of this vessel, the *Orlitza*, see Layman, *Before the Aircraft Carrier*.

49. Boris P Dudorov, 'Russian Aviation in the Baltic Sea 1912–1917', Nicholas Cook, trans. In this unpublished and undated manuscript, Dudorov describes in detail his aviation work before and during the Great War. I am indebted to Andrei Alexandrov, Harry Woodman and August G Blume for a copy of it. Dudrov apparently drew upon it for an article in *Morskiia zapiski* (Naval Records), the Journal of the Society of Officers of the Russian Imperial Navy (published in the United States), Vol 6 No 1, April 1943.

50. *Kapitan 2 Ranga* S I Berdnikov and Lieutenant Colonel Ye A Golosuyev, T G Martin, trans, 'How Naval Aviation Was Born', excerpted from *Morskoy Sbornik*, No 10, 1970, in *FPDS Newsletter*, Vol 6 No 4, 1978. See also R D Layman, 'Euxine Wings — Russian Shipboard Aviation in the Black Sea: 1913–1917', *Cross & Cockade Journal*, Vol 15 No 2, summer 1974, although there are a number of inaccuracies in this article.

51. This officer was of Swedish ancestry, and in Swedish his surname is transliterated from the Russian as Ebergardt. I have chosen to use the spelling most commonly given in English-language sources.

52. For information on this, see Layman, *To Ascend*, which gives a considerable bibliography.

53. George van Deurs, *Wings for the Fleet: A Narrative of Naval Aviation's Early Development, 1910–1916* (Annapolis: US Naval Institute, 1966), p3.

54. Chambers still lacks a formal, full-length biography. Discussions of his career and achievements can be found in van Duers, op cit, and Archibald D Turnbull and Clifford L Lord, *History of United States Naval Aviation* (New Haven: Yale University Press, 1949).

55. For details, see Turnbull and Lord, op cit.

56. Fiske's own description of his fight for the torpedo plane is given in his memoirs, *From Midshipman to Rear Admiral* (New York: The Century Co, 1919), pp642–688. See also Paolo E Coletta, *Admiral Bradley A Fiske and the American Navy* (Lawrence, Kan: Regents Press of Kansas, 1979), pp187–197. Believing that the navy had infringed his 1912 patent, Fiske in 1922 instigated litigation that was finally decided against him in 1931. For the story, see Coletta.

57. This tangled tale of bureaucratic in-fighting is described in Turnbull and Lord, *United States Naval Aviation*.

58. Jack Sweetman, *The Landing at Veracruz: 1914* (Annapolis: Naval Institute Press, 1968), p149.

59. William Sowden Sims with Burton J Hendrick, *The Victory at Sea* (New York: Doubleday, Page & Co, 1920), p320.

60. Charles M Melhorn, *Two-Block Fox: The Rise of the Aircraft Carrier, 1911–1929* (Annapolis: Naval Institute Press, 1974). For Sims' views on aviation, see this volume and Elting E Morison, *Admiral Sims and the Modern American Navy* (Boston: Houghton Mifflin, 1942).

61. From the dust jacket of William F Trimble, *Admiral William A Moffett: Architect of Naval Aviation* (Annapolis: Naval Institute Press, 1994). This biography supersedes Edward Arpee, *From Frigates to Flat-Tops* (Chicago: The Lakeside Press, 1953) but the earlier volume is still useful.

CHAPTER 5

Aerial Combat

——————— · ———————

The stereotypical image of the First World War in the air is the goggled fighter pilot hunched over blazing machine-guns. It is not an image of much application to 1914–18 naval aviation. Aerial combat, which evolved for the reasons discussed in Chapter 1, was far less frequent over the sea than over land.

The reasons were various. One was the lesser likelihood of hostile aircraft encountering each other over wide stretches of trackless water. On the land fronts, with their fixed trench lines and associated geographical features, it would become obvious where and why enemy aerial activity would be conducted and therefore need to be contested. The greater number of aircraft employed on the land fronts, and the closer geographical proximity of their fields, also made for more frequent aerial encounters.

This is not to say that naval aircraft did not engage in combat. They tangled often over the Aegean Sea, the narrow reaches of the Adriatic, the Baltic littoral, the English Channel, the lower North Sea, and sometimes elsewhere. But the numbers engaged, and thus the losses, were far fewer than over land. During 1915, for example, only three Austro-Hungarian naval aircraft were downed in aerial combat, with the loss of three pilots; in 1916 the totals were twelve aeroplanes and twenty pilots.[1] Although these losses were relatively high as a percentage of the total number of *KuK* naval aircraft and aviators, they were minute in comparison with those sustained in nearly any given month by the opposing air services on the Western Front during 1915–18.

In the areas mentioned above, combat often (sometimes almost regularly) pitted naval aircraft against those of their foe's army aircraft flying from land bases — frequently, but far from entirely, seaplanes versus landplanes. Such combat should not be confused with the activity of naval fighter units assigned to the land fronts. Some navies, notably the British and German, formed such units to supplement army fighter squadrons; they were committed to support of land forces and had no association with naval aspects of the war.[2]

Formation of these units resulted in a good many pilots who wore naval uniform becoming aces — those who shot down five or more enemy aircraft.[3] But the number of the so-called seaplane aces — literally, those who flew seaplanes rather than landplanes — can probably be counted on the fingers of two hands. The most noted is Germany's Friedrich Christiansen, who is credited with downing twenty-one aircraft, including one of the only two British airships lost to aerial attack in the entire war. Impressive as this figure may seem, it merely tied Christiansen with two others for sixty-third place in the overall roster of German aces,[4] showing how little scope a naval pilot had for aerial combat. Austria-Hungary's top 'seaplane ace' was Gottfried Banfield, who is variously credited with nine or ten victories.[5]

All the 'seaplane aces' flew from harbour bases. There were a very few instances in which aircraft (either seaplanes or landplanes) flown from surface vessels tangled with enemy aeroplanes, and in all such cases the latter, as far as I can determine, were flying from harbour or land.

Control of the air over the sea, as far as it relates to aerial combat, must therefore be defined differently from control of the air over land. Maritime control of the air usually meant merely that a navy's aircraft could function at sea with slight fear, or none, of encountering opposition. If opposition *was* encountered, it might be overcome quantitatively, as when the *KuK* naval air arm was overwhelmed by numbers, or qualitatively, as when the German navy began operating the Hansa-Brandenburg floatplane fighters that could out-perform nearly any type thrown against them.

While aerial combat over the land fronts was fairly well constant after 1915, aeroplane-vs-aeroplane fighting at sea tended to be episodic — limited in duration, purpose and location. Nor did it generate the intense 'symmetrical response' competition noted in Chapter 1, although at least seventeen British and more than twenty German designs for naval fighter aircraft appeared, including landplanes, floatplanes and flying boats. None of the British types went into production or operational service; most never advanced beyond the prototype stage, with perhaps a few follow-on machines. They either performed unsatisfactorily, became outmoded by shifts in tactical thinking, or were developed too late to warrant production. A few of the German types did enter service, but in negligible numbers.

It can be concluded that aerial combat, although at times it might rage hot and heavy and at times prove influential, was a relatively minor function of Great War naval aviation. There has never been, and doubtless never will be, a novel or a film featuring a First World War naval aviator as its hero.

Notes

1. Schupita, *Die k.u.k. seeflieger.*
2. Both Britain and Germany formed fighter units composed of naval personnel for use on the land fronts. Probably the most famous such British unit was No. 10 (Naval) Squadron, which was credited with downing eighty-seven German aircraft during a three-month period in 1917. A comparable, but much larger, German formation was the *Marine-Feld-Jagdeschwader* of the *Marinecorps Flanders*, a combined-arms force that operated on the coastal flank of the Western Front.
3. The term stems from the French *l'as*, the highest card in a suit. It was first applied to French aviator Roland Garros after he had shot down five German aircraft. See Arch Whitehouse, *The Years of the Sky Kings* (New York: Doubleday, 1959).
4. Arguments about how many aircraft were shot down by whom, and when and where, continue to rage among First World War aviation buffs, regardless of the irrelevance of the disputes to aviation or military history. My figures are based on a consensus among various sources.
5. Banfield was the last surviving Austro-Hungarian naval aviator. He died in 1986 at the age of 96. For his First World War career, see his autobiographical 'Air War in the Adriatic: A Memoir of Gottfried von Banfield' (Peter Kilduff, trans), *Cross & Cockade*, Vol 14 No 1, 1973. For an obituary describing his later career, see Richard Bassett, 'Grounded at Last', *The Spectator*, 4 October 1986.

CHAPTER 6

Tactical Offence

Tactical offence by naval aircraft took many forms during the Great War; this chapter will discuss only attacks on surface vessels. The use of aerial devices against surface vessels was theorised long before such devices existed. As early as 1670 the Roman Jesuit scholar Francesco Lana de Terzi, proposing an aerial craft to be lofted by exhausting air from copper spheres, opined it could attack ships by means of grapnels or some sort of fireball. The introduction of the balloon in Europe in 1783 was followed over the next century by scores of ideas — some practical, some totally visionary — for 'aerial batteries' to rain shot, shell or fire on things below. Only once, in 1849 during the Austrian siege of Venice, was this carried into practice, utilising unmanned hot-air balloons. Some of these were lofted from the Austrian sidewheel steamer *Vulcano*, making her the first warship ever to employ aerial devices offensively.

Aerial bombardment, however, did not become a practical proposition until the advent of powered, controlled flying machines — first the airship, then the aeroplane — in the first decade of the twentieth century. This immediately spawned a host of proposals for offensive use of such craft. Dropping of objects against mock targets laid out or erected on the ground became a popular attraction at pre-First World War aviation exhibitions. These targets were often representations of ships. By the start of the war the belief that aerial attack could sink or at least badly damage surface craft was widespread, and argued for vehemently by many who were convinced that cheap, quickly-constructed aircraft could drive costly, elaborate warships from the seas.

Strangely, however, there were before the war no realistic tests in the form of dropping actual explosives on mobile floating targets. In 1910, Glenn Curtiss dropped lead weights on an area marked out on Lake Keuka, New York, and later that year tossed oranges at a yacht off Atlantic City, New Jersey. On 19 May 1912, two American aviators staged a stunt in which they dropped flour-sack 'bombs' on the battleships *New Jersey* and *Rhode Island* in Boston harbour.[1] The only examples I have found of use of live explosives were an unsuccessful Italian test in 1912 to ascertain if bombs from an airship could explode mines[2] and at least one inconclusive Russian experiment in 1914 in which bombs were dropped from a Curtiss seaplane of the Black Sea Fleet on barrels afloat off Sevastopol. In the absence of realistic tests, it was not appreciated how elusive a target a ship, especially a ship under way, would be.

The immediate pre-war period, however, did see the first offensive use in combat of aircraft against warships. In February 1913, as noted earlier, two Greek aviators dropped a few small bombs (probably converted grenades) on units of the Turkish fleet in the Dardanelles without scoring a hit. Their Farman floatplane was fired upon unsuccessfully, making this episode history's first verified aeronaval battle.[3]

On 30 May 1913, aviators flying for the Constitutionalist cause in the Mexican civil war attempted to bomb the Federal gunboat-cum-transport *Guerrero* at Guaymas on the Gulf of California. The extremely crude bombs missed and rifle fire from the ship failed to damage the Glenn Martin pusher biplane. A second attempt, utilising the same aircraft, was made against *Guerrero* on 14 April 1914 while that vessel was engaging the gunboat *Tampico,* a former Federal vessel whose crew had mutinied and taken her into Constitutionalist service. Again the bombs missed and again the ship's anti-aircraft rifle fire was futile.[4]

Despite the ineffectiveness of these pre-war demonstrations, the belief that aerial offence could become a factor in maritime combat nevertheless persisted as the great conflict began. Early operations, however, seemed to invalidate that belief. Not for several months was a ship struck by an aerial bomb. The Japanese seaplanes employed at Tsingtao were unable to hit their warship targets (although some Japanese sources persist in stating incorrectly that a German minelayer was sunk from the air). The first aerial attack on a warship in European waters, an attempt by an Austro-Hungarian flying boat to bomb the French armoured cruiser *Waldeck Rousseau* in the Adriatic on 17 October 1914, likewise failed.

The lack of success during this early period is hardly surprising in view of the state of aerial weaponry. Few true aerial bombs yet existed — many, such as those of the Japanese seaplanes, were improvised from artillery shells, usually fitted with fins or cloth streamers in an attempt at ballistic stabilisation. Bomb sights, racks and release mechanisms had been developed and demonstrated, and actually employed in the Balkans, North Africa and Mexico, but few aircraft were yet equipped with them; in the early months of the First World War bombs were often dropped by hand with eyesight estimation of where they would fall. True bombs, in addition to being crude, were in short supply — the Royal Naval Air Service went to war with a stockpile of fewer than thirty.

Bomb loads were light initially. They increased greatly in weight as aircraft grew more powerful, but accurate placement of aerial missiles continued to be a problem throughout the war. Although bomb sights saw considerable improvement, they remained inadequate for use at sea, where accuracy against a moving target demanded immediate and simultaneous solution of a host of variable factors involving speed, motion, altitude and wind. Dive bombing, which would prove so deadly to surface craft during the Second World War, had yet to be evolved — although it did make an embryonic debut in 1918.[5]

A telling demonstration of how inaccurate bombing could be under even the best of conditions was given after the German battlecruiser *Goeben* (nominally the Turkish *Yavuz Sultan Selim*) grounded in the Dardanelles on 20 January 1918 following her raid on Imbros island and was subjected to six days of unremitting aerial assault. Dozens of British aircraft flew more than 200 sorties against her, dropping 180 bombs with a total weight of 15tons. Despite the vessel's immobility she was struck only twice (although one bomb may have hit a tug alongside her). The attacks delayed refloating the ship, but the two hits inflicted only minor topside damage and wounded one crewman.[6]

* * *

Naval aircraft had flown with machine-guns and small-calibre cannon before the war, but only experimentally. The early wartime armament of most aircraft, exclusive of bombs, consisted of carbines, pistols or shotguns, although sometimes metal antipersonnel darts were carried.

Machine-guns had become standard by the end of the war. Cannon were more difficult to mount because of the strain their recoil placed on airframes. One solution to this problem was a gun devised by US Navy Commander Cleland Davis, in which a counterweight equal to the weight of the shell was discharged in the opposite direction, neutralising the force of the recoil. Davis guns were mounted on some US and British aircraft but apparently never were used in combat.[7] A recoilless cannon, the Becker 20mm, was experimentally mounted in some German seaplanes, but likewise did not see combat use.[8] The French SPAD XIV of 1917, a float version of the famous landplane fighter, featured a 37mm cannon firing through the propeller shaft; forty of these aircraft were ordered and a few may have been operational.[9] A number of French airships carried guns of 47mm and even 75mm calibre for use against submarines, but it is doubtful that these were ever fired in anger.

Some other innovative developments in naval air weaponry and tactics are worth noting. One of the lesser-known ones was the previously mentioned German aerial mine-laying campaign in the Baltic.[10] Even lesser-known were remotely controlled missiles developed by the Siemens Schuckert-Werke GmbH. They were unpowered gliders carrying an explosive warhead or a torpedo and controlled electrically through an unreeling wire, rather in the manner of the present American TOW anti-tank missile. Approximately 100 of these, of varying sizes and configurations, were built from and tested from January 1915 until the project was abandoned in late 1918. Many successful launches were made from naval airships, and controlled distances of nearly five miles achieved with considerable accuracy. The missiles, however, never became operational.[11]

A Siemens Schuckert weapon that did see service was the *Fernlenk*, a fast, remotely-controlled explosive-laden motorboat. These first were used in 1916; they were originally controlled, like the gliders, by wire from ship or shore with aerial observation helping to guide them to their targets. Later models were controlled entirely by wireless signals from aircraft. The only success of that technique, however, if success it can be called, came on 28 October 1917 when one of the air-guided craft struck the British monitor *Erebus* off Ostend. The monitor's anti-torpedo bulges easily absorbed the blast and damage was minimal. Continued failures caused the German navy to give up the idea.[12]

An even more advanced concept of remote control was investigated by the US Navy during 1917–18 — an unmanned explosive-laden aircraft utilising the combination of the gyroscope, as developed by Elmer Sperry, and wireless. This Sperry-Curtiss 'flying bomb' or 'aerial torpedo', as it was termed, was tested extensively with some slight degrees of success. Experiments continued for a time after the war, but then the idea was shelved for more than a decade.[13]

*   *   *

Retrospective assessments of the role of aerial tactical offence at sea during 1914–18 have produced two quite opposite views. Air power enthusiasts, such as Sueter, proclaimed that it could have achieved much if only it had not been hobbled by the 'Battleship Admirals'.

Most generalist historians, on the other hand, have dismissed it as trivial. 'The role of the airplane in the naval war', declared Bernard Brodie and Fawn Brodie, 'was deceptive in it gave no promise whatsoever of being the colossal threat to the warship that it proved to be in World War II' and 'it was never dreamed . . . that the airplane could threaten the existence of the battlefleet.'[14] The truth, as usual, lies somewhere between these two extremes.

The view that aerial offence would have been more effective if it had had been pursued more vigorously is refuted by the fact that it *was* pursued. There were, contrary to the Brodies, quite a number of persons, several previously mentioned, who believed that the aeroplane could indeed threaten the battlefleet. It failed to do so during 1914–18 due to the basic fact that aircraft and their armament had not evolved to the point at which they could seriously menace the armoured warship. That vessel, battleship or cruiser, remained highly resistant to aerial attack; although several armoured vessels were struck by bombs, none was sunk or sustained more than superficial damage.

But although armoured vessels were virtually immune to air attack, lesser craft were not. A bomb striking an unarmoured ship might inflict even greater damage than a shell, since a bomb, unlike a shell, need not be stressed to withstand firing from a barrel and so can contain a larger bursting charge. The RNAS nominally 20lb bomb of 1915, for instance, packed a 7lb bursting charge, nearly equal in explosive power to the much heavier naval 6in common shell. The 100lb RNAS bomb of the same period had a 40lb bursting charge, actually larger than that of the 9.2in naval shell, which weighed 380lbs.

Such missiles could be deadly to small craft, and they were — more often than is realised by the generalist historians who denigrate aircraft of the First World War because they were not the ship-killers they became during 1939–45.

To be sure, the losses of surface vessels caused by aerial attack are picayune, in terms of both numbers and tonnage, as compared with the tremendous air-inflicted losses of the Second World War. But there were a surprising number of instances in which aircraft, directly or indirectly, were responsible for sinking, permanently disabling, forcing into internment, capturing or otherwise neutralising warships and merchant vessels. The number would be even higher were it possible to compile the number of non-mechanically powered craft sunk by aircraft from Ostend to Pola to the Danube to Constanza to Trebizond to the Red Sea — lighters, barges, dhows, zebecs, coal schooners.

It is, of course, impossible to make such a compilation, but could it be done and the figures added to those for mechanically powered vessels, it is not inconceivable that, excluding the losses at Jutland, aircraft sent to the bottom more surface tonnage than all the capital ships of the world combined during the war.

Even if this is an exaggeration, it is a remarkable record for a weapon which in 1914 was barely more than a decade old. It contrasts favourably to that of the submarine, which (depending on how one defines 'submarine') had existed for at least a century but which did not achieve its first success (in the sense of a fully submerged craft employing an automotive torpedo) until 5 September 1914, when the German *U 21* sank HMS *Pathfinder*.

The losses inflicted, in one way or another, on surface vessels by aircraft can be verified as two destroyers (three if a loss during the Russian civil war is included), two torpedo-boats, six motor torpedo-boats, four naval auxiliaries and twelve merchant vessels (possibly fifteen). A breakdown is given in Appendix 2.[15]

Of the losses that can be attributed *directly* to aerial attack, six were caused by bombs, two (possibly four) by torpedo, one by combined bombs and torpedo, one by mine and three by machine-gun fire.

Some qualifications must be made. A number of these vessels were not specific targets of aerial attack but were struck by bombs aimed at harbour installations in general or at other ships. Only eight were attacked while under way at sea. Three were not permanently sunk but were salvaged, repaired and returned to service.

One might also quibble over whether losses to which aircraft contributed indirectly can be considered as air-inflicted. For example, the Russian torpedo boat *Stroini*, attacked by German seaplanes after she ran aground on Ösel Island in August 1917, was not sunk by their bombs, but the damage they inflicted delayed salvage work so long that she was later battered to destruction by storms. In such instances, my criterion has been whether the loss could reasonably have been expected to have taken place in the absence of aerial action. In the case of *Stroini*, it is reasonable to assume that the salvage would have succeeded had it not been for the aerial attack; *ergo*, she was an aerial-inflicted loss.

It might even be possible to argue that the German cruiser *Breslau* (nominally the Turkish *Midilli*, *Goeben*'s companion on the Imbros raid) was an indirect victim of aerial attack, for it was while manoeuvring to escape the bombs of British aircraft that she ran into the mines that sank her. This speculation, however, is probably going too far.

As far as direct sinkings are concerned, it is not possible to come up with a figure for total tonnage sent to the bottom by aircraft because warship tonnage is calculated in terms of displacement (avoirdupois weight) and that of merchant vessels in terms of gross register tons (internal volume of space). A second difficulty is that British warship displacement was measured by the English ton (2,240lbs) and that of continental European warships by the metric tonne (2,205lbs). Moreover, until a single standard for calculating displacement was established by the Washington Treaty, various navies used varying formulae.

*   *   *

Tactical offence by aircraft certainly did not in general affect the war at sea as directly and bloodily as it did on land. But neither was it as ineffective and trivial as so often supposed. It was influential to a considerable degree during the Gallipoli campaign, when RNAS aircraft joined submarines in interdicting Turkish sea lines of supply to the peninsula in 1915. These machines not only attacked Turkish supply vessels directly — the British official air history reports a total of seventy such attacks[16] — they also spotted for gunfire from warships against them in ports[17] and on one occasion guided a submarine to a concentration of shipping.

This aerial campaign, which caused serious concern in the Turko-German high command, marked the first use of torpedo planes in combat, and it has long and repeatedly been stated, on the basis of contemporary claims, that three Turkish vessels were sunk by them. The fact is that because no complete or accurate list of Turkish mercantile losses has ever been compiled, the identity of these ships remains a mystery. One had been stranded as the result of an attack by a British submarine and whether the aerial torpedo completed her destruction is unknown; another, although hit, may not actually have sunk.[18]

A prolonged torpedo-plane campaign, and one again in which aerial offence caused considerable alarm, began in April 1917 when torpedo-armed German seaplanes based at Zeebrugge started attacking British shipping in the Dover Straits. The campaign continued sporadically until September with fifteen attacks, and although only three vessels fell victim to it 'the moral effect was great',[19] producing a 'sense of anxiety'.[20] Anti-aircraft guns were placed aboard merchantmen passing through the straits in one direction, then transferred to others making the reverse passage; in mid-May, a special unit of fighter aeroplanes was stationed at Walmer to fly protection over ships anchored in the Downs, and anti-torpedo plane patrols were flown from existing air bases.

Even though the final attack, on 9 September, was successful, the Germans abandoned the campaign. Only three vessels had been sunk, and while on the other hand only three torpedo planes had been lost, all to AA fire, the large expenditure necessary to design and build the specialised aircraft and to train their crews did not seem worth the results.[21] Had the facts of the campaign's effect been known, a different conclusion might have been reached. The British air history attempts strongly to minimise that effect, but by describing the extensive protective measures taken shows that the torpedo planes threw quite a scare into the Admiralty.

The British and German experience pointed up the early problems of the torpedo plane, the greatest of which was the difficulty of lofting such a heavy missile from water. Only smaller types could be carried — at their largest the British 18in and the German 450mm (17.7in), both in the 1,000lb weight range and lacking the punch of larger models.

The British choice for the torpedo plane was the single-engine floatplane, and although several models were produced most were hard to get into the air even when flown with a single occupant and a reduced fuel load. Germany opted for larger, twin-engine seaplanes, but these were unwieldly and somewhat difficult to fly. The German experience also showed that because successful aiming and discharge of a torpedo required a low-altitude, straight-ahead run, the aircraft was vulnerable to AA fire — even low-angle guns could be brought to bear against it. Nevertheless, this pioneering work paved the way for development of the type of aircraft that would prove so effective in the Second World War.

* * *

A final example of effective offensive action by aircraft against surface vessels is significant as an omen of the future. It was an engagement on 11 August 1918 in which a squadron of six British motor torpedo-boats was wiped out by German seaplanes as it attempted to penetrate German waters in the Heligoland Bight. Sliced to ribbons by machine-gun fire, one boat, set afire, was blown up by its crew; two were scuttled; the remaining three, hopelessly adrift, were interned in Holland. As one writer has noted, 'The action was historic in that, during it, aircraft inflicted a greater loss on sea-going craft than at any time during the War.'[22] Indeed, one must look ahead a quarter of a century, to the Battle of the Bismarck Sea in 1943, to find a comparable example of virtual annihilation of a surface force by purely aerial action.

* * *

By November 1918 naval aircraft had flown with every weapon they would employ in the Second World War — some described above, some yet to be mentioned. Although, as the Brodies believed, aircraft had given no 'promise' during 1914–18 of becoming a threat to the surface warship, they had certainly dropped broad hints.

Notes

1. For a general survey of proposals and experiments from 1783 to the eve of the First World War, see Layman, *To Ascend.*
2. The experiment took place off Bengazi in north Africa on 7 August 1912. The targets were wooden blocks shaped in the form of mines and submerged a few feet under water. Not only did winds blow the bombs away from these targets, but, because they were impact-fused, they exploded on the surface instead of below it.
3. R D Layman, 'Moutoussis, Moraitinis and Muddle', *Small Air Forces Observer*, Vol 17 No 2, June 1993.
4. For a detailed account, see Manuel Ruiz Romero, *La aviacion durante la revolucion mexicana* (Mexico City: Soporte Aeronautico, 1988). See also James R Hinds, 'Bombs Over Mexico',

Aerospace Historian, Vol 31 No 2, September 1984, and Jose Villela Jr, 'Mexican Air Force', *Air Pictorial*, Vol 27 No 2, February 1965.

5. For early experiments in dive bombing, see Peter C Smith, *Dive Bomber: An Illustrated History* (Annapolis: Naval Institute Press, 1982).

6. Jones, *The War in the Air*, Vol 5, pp411–414; Martin H Brice, 'SMS *Goeben*/TNS *Yavuz*: The Story of the Oldest Dreadnought in Existence — Her History and Technical Details,' *Warship International*, Vol 6 No 4, 1969, and Richard T Whistler, 'The Imbros Raid — January 1918', *Cross & Cockade*, Vol 20 No 1, 1979.

7. This gun and its developments are described in D C Dwelle, 'The Davis Gun', *Cross & Cockade*, Vol 6 No 1, 1965.

8. Peter M Grosz, 'The 2cm Becker Aircraft Cannon — Development and Use', *Over the Front*, Vol 7 No 1, 1992.

9. J M Bruce, *Spad Scouts SVII–SXII* (New York: Arco Publishing Co, 1969).

10. The mines were planted between late June and early September 1917 in the Gulf of Riga by Friedrichshafen FF.41 seaplanes, which had been designed as torpedo planes. Each aircraft carried a single 750kg (1,654lb) mine. The torpedo-shaped mines had to be dropped at specific heights to prevent damage to their mechanisms, and to ensure this, as described in Alex Imrie, *German Naval Air Service* (London: Arms and Armour Press, 1989), 'a weighted line was extended . . . When the weight touched the surface, the drag of the water operated contacts that illuminated a light in the pilot's cockpit, indicating that the height was right for release'.

11. For descriptions and illustrations, see Egon Kruger and Peter M Grosz, 'A History of Siemens Schuckert Aircraft and Missiles, 1907–1919', *Cross & Cockade*, Vol 13 No 3, 1972.

12. See A[nthony] E Sokol, 'German Experiments With Remote Control During the Last War', *United States Naval Institute Proceedings*, Vol 70 No 2, February 1944. British encounters with the *F-booten* and the attack on *Erebus* (which killed two crewmen and wounded fifteen) are described by Admiral Sir Reginald Bacon in *The Dover Patrol 1915–1917* (London: Hutchinson & Co, nd), Vol 1, pp171–174. See also Georg Paul Neumann (J E Gurdon, trans), *The German Air Force in the Great War* (Bath: Cedric Chivers, reprinted 1969), pp74–75.

13. For details, see Lee Pearson, 'Developing the Flying Bomb', Adrian O Van Wyen, ed, *Naval Aviation in World War I* (Washington: Chief of Naval Operations, Government Printing Office, 1969).

14. Bernard Brodie and Fawn Brodie, *From Crossbow to H-Bomb* (New York: Dell Publishing Co, 1962), p180. This assessment parallels that of Bernard Brodie two decades earlier in *Sea Power in the Machine Age* (Princeton: Princeton University Press, 1941), p390: 'In the World War . . . the airplane could not become the great factor at sea that it quickly became on land.'

15. For detailed descriptions of the losses listed in the appendix, see R D Layman, 'Naval Warfare in a New Dimension 1914–1918', *Warship 1989* (London: Conway Maritime Press, 1989).

16. Jones, *The War in the Air*, Vol 2, p65.

17. At least two ships, and probably more, were sunk by air-directed gunfire, and at least one debarkation of troops and supplies was disrupted. See Layman, 'Over the Wine-Dark Sea.'

18. The best partial list of Turkish mercantile losses, which its author admits is far from complete, is P A Warneck, 'Pertes des marines marchands et de guerre turques survenues au cours de la periode 1911–1918', *The Belgian Shiplover*, No 79, May–June 1960. A recent work, Brend Langensiepen and Ahmet Güleryüz, (James Cooper, trans. and ed) *The Ottoman Steam Navy 1828–1923* (London: Conway Maritime Press, 1995), confuses the matter further. Ignoring the second two attacks, it identifies the stranded vessel as the 24,490grt *Mahmut Şevket Paşa*, incorrectly states she was attacked by two aircraft, claims the torpedo that struck her failed to explode and that she was eventually towed to Constantinople. This flies in the face of the report of the British pilot, Flight Commander Charles H K Edmonds, that the explosion of the torpedo 'sent a column of water and large fragments almost as high as her masthead' (Edmonds' report in Air/1665, document No 77 in Roskill, *Documents*). I find it hard to believe that the Turkish merchant marine of 1915 possessed a vessel of the tonnage reported. Edmonds' estimate of about 5,000 tons seems much more reasonable.

19. Jones, *The War in the Air*, Vol 4, p56.

20. Ibid, p57.

21. Germany was later off the mark than Italy and Britain in development of torpedo planes, but employed them more extensively. Nine types, including a training version, were designed and nearly 150 were built. They were first employed, although unsuccessfully, in the Baltic. For their technical details, see Peter Gray and Owen Thetford, *German Aircraft of the First World War* (London: Putnam, 1962).

22. C F Snowden Gamble, *The Story of a North Sea Air Station* (London: Oxford University Press, 1928), p419.

CHAPTER 7

Strategic Offence

Aerial bombardment of cities and civilians in wartime was predicted long before any means of such bombardment existed. The predictions multiplied after flying machines came into existence, and well before the First World War the prospect was almost universally accepted as inevitable.[1]

Early speculations on aerial bombardment, although rife with terrifying descriptions of death and destruction, were often vague about what it supposedly might accomplish as an instrument of war. During the immediate prewar years, however, a number of writers conceptualised how and why it could be carried out and what it could be expected to achieve. Probably the most seminal of these was the Italian army officer Giulio Douhet (1869–1930), although his influence was not felt until after the war.[2]

As put into practice during the conflict, the concept emerged eventually as the doctrine called strategic bombing, or strategic air warfare, or, more recently, 'deep interdiction'. As noted earlier, this became — and remains — a prime tenet of air power philosophy.[3]

Strategic aerial offence has been given many definitions; one of the most detailed describes it as a function 'directed against one or more of a selected series of enemy targets with the purpose of progressive destruction and disintegration of the enemy's war-making capacity and his will to make war. Targets include key manufacturing systems, sources of raw material, critical material stockpiles, power systems, transportation systems, communication facilities, and other such target systems. As opposed to tactical operations, strategic [air] operations are designed to have a long-range rather than immediate effect on the enemy and his military forces.'[4]

Thorough as this definition seems, it does not address some ambiguities.[5] It also ignores the most controversial aspect of the doctrine: the fact that strategic bombing inevitably results in civilian casualties, unintentional though they may be. It fails to note that indiscriminate bombing has often been advocated — and practiced, pious words to the contrary notwithstanding — as a means of terrifying a hostile population into surrender, under the rationale, as expounded by Douhet, that in twentieth-century total war there is no distinction between soldier and civilian, be the civilian a man, woman or child, and therefore aerial *Schrecklichkeit* is a legitimate weapon.[6]

However it is defined and however it has been practiced, the efficacy and morality of strategic bombing has been endlessly argued in a debate that still continues. It has raised a host of unresolved ethical, sociological, legal, military, technological, economic, political and even theological issues.[7] Avoiding such conundrums, this chapter will describe how the two largest European navies, although they did not conceive the idea, pioneered it during the early phases of the Great War.

* * *

It has frequently been stated, although sometimes disputed, that strategic air attack originated in Italy, due to the collaboration of Douhet, who provided the theory, and the aircraft designer Gianni Caproni di Taliedo, who provided the large, multi-engine, long-range bombers required to implement it.[8] Italy did indeed pursue strategic air offence during the Great War, but its late entry into the conflict denied it chronological primacy.

Such primacy might be credited to France on the basis of an order on 23 November 1914 that established the *Groupe de Bombardment No 1*. Composed of three squadrons totalling eighteen aircraft, this formation was under the direct control of the *Grand Quartier Général* and was intended 'as a means of striking far behind the enemy's front and inflicting severe material damage or upsetting the elaborate and complicated mechanism of the transport system'.[9] However, it did not become operational until early December.

Meanwhile, two days before the order creating this unit was issued, the Royal Navy had carried out what under any criterion can be termed the first strategic air attack of the war by raiding the Zeppelin airship works at Friedrichshafen on Lake Constance (Bodensee). The 21 November attack was made by the RN's first four Avro 504 single-engine aeroplanes, each carrying four 20lb bombs and flying from Belfort in southeastern France. The operation was planned and prepared by an aviator and Royal Navy Volunteer Reserve office, Lieutenant Noel Pemberton Billing — earlier the founder of the Supermarine aircraft firm and later a scathing parliamentary critic of British air policy.

Although one Avro was shot down and its pilot captured, the British were somehow deluded into believing that great havoc had been wrought, including severe damage to an airship and destruction of the hydrogen works.[10] Actually, only a few windows were blown out, although one bomb fell dangerously close to Zeppelin *L 7*.[11]

British strategic air efforts lapsed for many months after this episode; the next would be made by Germany.

* * *

The rigid airship, as perfected by Ferdinand *Graf* von Zeppelin, created two sets of vastly differing national perceptions during the immediate prewar years. To the German populace and press it was an example of Teutonic technological and scientific triumph; to the British populace and press it was a looming menace.

British apprehension had been heightened by periodic Zeppelin panics when airships were reportedly seen in British skies; newspapers and magazines were replete with scare stories about German mastery of the air; it became almost a foregone conclusion that a war with Germany would bring a devastating assault by what was widely believed to be a huge fleet of Zeppelins.[12]

There was some justification for the German perception; there was none at all for the British. The German army began the war with only a handful of airships and the navy, as noted earlier, had only one operational ship, unequipped for combat. There had been only one prewar experiment with bombing by an airship, and aerial bombs and their associated gear had to be improvised. This feeble strength was soon to be augmented by an ambitious programme of construction of airships and their bases (to be discussed later), but by the end of 1914 the navy had only six Zeppelins.

It is remarkable then, perhaps astonishing, that agitation for airship attack on Britain began in naval circles before the war was a month old. Its initially stoutest and most persistant exponent was *Konteradmiral* Paul Behncke, Deputy Chief of the Naval Staff. On 20 August 1914, in a memo to Admiral von Pohl, chief of that staff, Behncke urged aerial attacks on London and the main British naval bases. In addition to inflicting material damage, he argued, such attacks 'may be expected, whether they involve London or the neighborhood of London, to cause panic in the population which may possibly render it doubtful that the war can be continued'.[13]

Von Pohl, acutely aware of how few airships the navy possessed, sensibly believed they should be reserved for fleet reconnaissance, but as the year wore on Behncke's continued suggestions for an aerial assault on Britain were supported by *Konteradmiral* Philipp, chief of fleet aviation, *Fregattenkapitän* Peter Strasser, commander of the Naval Airship Division and its driving force until his death in the air in 1918, and *Grossadmiral* von Tirpitz.

Von Pohl finally gave in, and on 7 January 1915 in a submission to Kaiser Wilhelm recommended airship attacks on Britain although stipulating that the Zeppelins' primary function should remain scouting for the High Seas Fleet. The monarch gave his approval, although apparently somewhat grudgingly, with the stipulation that targets were to be restricted to coastal areas and the lower Thames. London was to be off-limits because Wilhelm, as a grandson of Queen Victoria, was concerned over the possibility of harming his relatives in the British royal family. Von Pohl transmitted the Emperor's decision to the High Seas Fleet on 10 January, and that same day Strasser prepared plans for raiding a select number of naval bases and maritime centres.

The next day Behncke drew up a far more extensive and ambitious list of targets of which many, regardless of the Kaiser's strictures, were in the City of London, the heart and nerve centre of the British Empire. The list included, in addition to the obvious military and naval bases and installations (such as Woolwich Arsenal), the Admiralty, War Office, Foreign Office, Bank of England, Stock Exchange, Mint, Central Telegraph Office, principal railway stations, water works, gas and electric plants and textile warehouses. It was a programme as well calculated to ruin a nation's social, political and economic infrastructure as any promulgated by any strategic air power planner ever since.

The first raid, on some of the sites selected by Strasser, was made the night of 19–20 January by two ships (a third, with Strasser aboard, was forced back by engine failure). This was the faltering start of a campaign that was to last much of the rest of the war, gaining in intensity as more and higher-performance airships entered service and in scope as the Kaiser's restrictions were gradually relaxed until by the end of 1915 virtually any spot in Britain could become a target. It reached an apogee in 1916 but diminished thereafter as British defence measures started to become effective.[14]

Although army airships sometimes took part (they were, in fact, the first to bomb London), this sustained strategic air campaign, history's first, was primarily a naval effort until, starting in 1917, emphasis shifted to bombardment by army aeroplanes.[15]

The history of the airship raids is far beyond the scope of this book.[16] An assessment of their effects and value may be attempted, although there can be no final verdict. If precision bombing of the sort of targets listed by Behncke is a criterion of success, the campaign was a failure. Only rarely were these hit; probably the two most successful raids in this respect were those of 15–16 June 1915 when Zeppelin *L 10* severely damaged two engine-manufacturing works and also hit a chemical plant, and 8–9 September 1915 when *L 13* touched off a huge and costly fire in the London textile warehouse district.

The failure to hit what the airshipmen were trying to attack was due largely to faulty navigation, which employed dead reckoning over water and pilotage over land. Time and again landfalls were made far from those planned, and airship commanders often literally did not know what city or area they were over. The problem was exacerbated by the fact that because the airships were highly vulnerable in daylight hours, the raids had to be made at night; this, of course, hindered visual observation — especially after the British adopted blackout measures — and made bomb sights, which were inadequate anyhow, even more unreliable.

Navigation by means of bearings transmitted by wireless — one of the German naval innovations mentioned earlier — was attempted, but in the infancy of electronic technology often proved unreliable. (On the other hand, wireless transmissions from the airships could be intercepted by British stations, which by cross-bearings could determine a Zeppelin's position and probable course; this led to the destruction of at least one airship.)

The result of all this was that although the airship crews were trying to attack the type of legitimate targets specified by Behncke and Strasser, their bombs too often fell far and wide, inflicting many civilian casualties. Consequently, to the British press and populace, it appeared the bombing was indiscriminate, and the aerial assailants were condemned as 'pirates', 'murderers', and (in probably the most popular epithet) 'baby-killers' (the airships did indeed, albeit unintentionally, kill children, as well as women, pensioners, theatre-goers, pub-crawlers and other innocents).

Although there was no deliberate policy of *Schrecklichkeit* in the bombing campaign, a byproduct was expected to be the 'panic' predicted by Behncke and others. Here, too, they were to be disappointed. True, thousands of Britons (especially in London) nightly sought shelter in subway tunnels or basements, or even hied to open fields, but 'panic' would be too strong a term to describe this activity — the air attacks certainly did not cause public outcry for surrender and peace.

In statistical terms as given in the British air history,[17] there were fifty-one airship raids (including those by army craft) in which 5,806 bombs, including explosive and incendiary and totalling about 196 tons, were dropped, killing 557 persons and injuring 1,358 (fewer casualties than normal 'wastage' on the Western Front in nearly any given month).

In monetary terms, again according to the British history, property damage came to a value of £1,527,585. This invites evaluation of the airship bombing campaign under the latter-day criterion of cost-effectiveness, *ie*, whether the expense of mounting it was worth what it accomplished in monetary terms. The total cost of the German effort is unknown, but sample figures collected by Douglas H Robinson show that as early as 20 February 1915 the equivalent of £1,550,292 had been spent on construction of airships and their bases.[18] Additional random figures bring the total by the end of the war to more than £4 million, but actual expenditure was obviously far more than that amount.

However, not all the German expense can be charged to the bombing campaign, for the primary mission of the airships remained maritime reconnaissance. An assessment under cost-effective criteria must also take into account the indirect monetary losses the campaign inflicted. The British air historian declares that 'had the Zeppelins been built and maintained solely for the raids . . . they would more than have justified the money and ingenuity that went to their building. The threat of their raiding potentialities compelled us to set up at home a formidable organisation which diverted men, guns, and aeroplanes from more important theatres of war'.[19] By the end of 1916 air defence involved 17,341 officers and men and 110 aircraft. It also drew heavily upon personnel of the civilian police, fire, telephone and medical services. Additionally, quite a number of Royal Navy ships and aircraft were assigned to anti-Zeppelin operations.

The cost must also take into consideration the incalculable, because mainly unquantifiable, losses in industrial production caused by the raids. During danger periods rail transport was interrupted, factories ceased operation, worker absenteeism soared and steel production was reduced when fear of bombing caused blast furnaces to be shut down.

In the long run, however, the bombing campaign, while certainly a hindrance to the British war effort, fell far short of achieving the decisive results its naval planners had expected. Aware of British prewar apprehension about the Zeppelin, they vastly overestimated the psychological effect that bombing would have, and also apparently shared a delusion common early in the war — that 'If . . . explosive was to be dropped from the air, it was accredited with a thousand times the effect of the same explosive propelled from a cannon.'[20] The leading historian of the Naval Airship Division concludes flatly: 'As strategic bombers, the hydrogen-filled rigid airships of 1914–1918 failed.'[21]

* * *

Air power historians have frequently ignored, perhaps because it is unpalatable to them, the fact that the seed of British strategic air doctrine was planted by the Admiralty, which also initiated development of the type of aircraft required for it. Churchill and Sueter played major roles. In 1914 the First Lord instigated an anti-Zeppelin bombing offensive of which the attack on Friedrichshafen was one result. His vision soon embraced a much broader aerial effort; at a conference of senior RNAS officers on 3 April 1915 he 'pointed out the necessity of developing a very large fleet of aircraft, capable of delivering a sustained series of "smashing blows" on the enemy; more in the nature of a "bombardment" by ships than the present isolated "dashing exploits" of individual or two or three aeroplanes dropping a few bombs only. The object to aim at was so to harass the enemy and destroy his works as to effect [sic] very materially his ability to continue the war.'[22]

Such a campaign would require long-range, heavy-payload aircraft. Such aeroplanes did not yet exist in the British air arms, but their development had been anticipated by Sueter's Air Department. In 1914 its design section produced a large seaplane, designated AD-1000, as a long-range naval scout and torpedo-bomber. This three-engine craft, the largest built in Britain up to that time, was directly inspired by Igor Sikorsky's four-engine *Ilya Mourmetz*, a floatplane version of which had flown earlier in 1914.[23]

The AD-1000 was not a success and never entered production or service, and it may have been with reservations about it in mind that in December 1914 Sueter laid before aeroplane designer Frederick Handley-Page naval requirements for a large, long-range craft that should be a 'bloody paralyser'. The eventual result was the twin-engine Handley-Page O/100, followed by the improved O/400 and ultimately the huge four-engine V/1500, which, had the war continued a few days longer, would probably have bombed Berlin. The O/100 took considerable time to develop; the prototype did not fly until December 1915 and the first production models did not enter service — and then only piecemeal — until late 1916.

While the Handley-Page was struggling into existence, two other aircraft of significance were acquired by the RNAS: the Short Bomber, pretty much a landplane version of the Admiralty Type 184 floatplane, and the Sopwith 1½ Strutter. The latter came in two versions — a single-seat bomber and a two-seat fighter.[24] Neither type could be termed a strategic bomber, but both were available when a strategic bombing programme finally began. In fact, the air history implies it was their existence that enabled the programme finally to be put into effect more than a year after Churchill had proposed it. However, its implementation was delayed not only because of a lack of suitable aircraft but, perhaps more significantly, by a dispute between the Admiralty and the War Office over bombing policy. The War Office and the army high command in France opposed strategic bombing as a diversion of aircraft from what they deemed the more important task of supporting the army on the Western Front, yet at the same time they wanted — perversely in the navy's view — to share or even monopolise the big new bombers.[25]

The dispute might have been settled earlier had Churchill and Sueter remained in positions of authority. Churchill, who left office in May 1915 under the cloud of the Dardanelles failure, probably would have acted more decisively than his successor, the less-resolute Arthur Balfour. In September, during an RNAS reorganisation, Sueter was in effect downgraded, becoming the Air Department's superintendent of aircraft construction — a post he was eminently qualified to fill, but which removed him from the realm of operational policy-making.

The impasse was finally broken by a decision of the Joint Air War Committee, which was formed in February 1916 'to collaborate in and to co-ordinate the question of supplies and design of *matériel* for the Naval and Military Air Services'.[26] This stated 'it is considered that the destruction of dockyards, arsenels and other centres of production, which would affect the enemy's naval productive capacity as a whole, should be undertaken by the RNAS.'[27] The phrase 'naval productive capacity as a whole' provided a rationalisation opening a wide range of targets to RNAS bombs.

So chartered, the Admiralty began formation of a strategic bombing force, designated No 3 Wing RNAS, in May 1916 after first receiving French approval and assurance of French co-operation. It was to base near Belfort, which placed a variety of targets in Alsace-Lorraine within its range. There, and elsewhere later, No 3 Wing was to share a base with, and act in conjunction with, French bombardment squadrons. It was to be equipped initially with fifty-five aircraft — fifteen Short Bombers, twenty Sopwith 1½ Strutter bombers and an equal number of the two-seat fighters. An eventual strength of 100 aircraft was projected.

Hardly had formation of the wing begun, however, when it was retarded by a plea to the Admiralty from Major General Hugh Trenchard, commander of the Royal Flying Corps, for aircraft to assist in the forthcoming Somme offensive. Responding, the Admiralty diverted aircraft intended for No 3 Wing, a total of sixty-two Sopwiths being handed over by mid-September. Thus the wing's first operation, in July, was a mere three-machine raid. By late August it possessed only twenty-two aircraft; the figure rose to forty-seven by the end of December, fewer than half of the projected number.

The first major operation, in conjunction with French units, was an 12 October attack on the Mauser arms factory at Oberndorf by sixty-two aircraft including escorting fighters. Although 135 bombs were dropped, they succeeded only in causing a partial disruption of work at the plant for two days and killing five persons, two of them prisoners of war. The allies lost six aircraft and twenty-one aviators.[28]

Subsequent strategic raids by No 3 Wing were primarily on blast furnaces and associated facilities of the southern German steel industry — eleven attacks through April 1917. Emphasis was changed from day to night bombing, the new Handley-Pages began arriving, and to acquaint the Franco-British aviators with the nature and vulnerability of their targets they were given a tour of a blast furnace and a smelter.

In early 1917 the British strategic effort was disrupted by another call for help by the RFC, which had been depleted by attrition during the drawn-out Somme struggle. The navy responded by gradually dissolving No 3 Wing, assigning its personnel to RNAS squadrons working alongside the RFC; by the end of May the Wing had been officially disbanded.

Throughout the Wing's existence, the Admiralty, to circumvent War Office objections to its operations, maintained the almost fictional rationale that they were directed against the 'naval productive capacity as a whole'. This was evident in a reply in February 1917 to a request from Admiral Beatty for clarification of air policy that he coupled with a plea for more aircraft, aviation vessels and aviators to counter the High Seas Fleet's Zeppelins. The Admiralty's answer spoke, *inter alia*, of 'A RNAS Wing of long distance bombing machines, operating against blast furnaces and munition factories in Alsace-Lorraine, with a view to impeding the production of steel and munitions to the High Sea Fleet and for the attack of Zeppelin bases.'[29]

This smacks strongly of sophistry, for it was obvious that an attack on southern German industry could have no immediate or direct effect on the North Sea naval war. The mention of attack on Zeppelin bases is plainly an untruth; No 3 Wing never made such an attack, and the Zeppelins that concerned Beatty were based far outside the wing's operational area.

In reality, the bombing was directed at industry *qua* industry; it mattered not whether the products of the steel mills were to be used for armour plate, shells, field guns or locomotives. The attacks were exactly what Churchill had proposed them to be: Blows against an enemy that would affect 'very materially his ability to continue the war'.

* * *

There was a hiatus in British strategic air operations after the demise of No 3 Wing, but they resumed later in 1917 with formation of the composite RFC–RNAS 41st Wing and increased in tempo after creation in 1918 of the Royal Air Force and the Inter-Allied Independent Air Force — although the latter was barely forming before the Armistice.

These units, however, could do little but repeat the operations of their predecessor. As one former commander of No 3 Wing has noted: 'When the RAF Independent Command was formed . . . it was stationed in the same general neighbourhood in France in which No 3 Wing had conducted its strategical operations. It often occurred that the targets selected for attack . . . were the same targets earlier assaulted by No 3 Wing.'[30] Moreover, many of the aircraft were those that had been developed at naval behest or those descended from them.

It remains to be asked what the Royal Navy's pioneering venture into strategic air offence accomplished. The answer would seem to be that it mirrored the effects the German navy's similar venture had on Britain. As the British air history puts it, without drawing parallels or offering statistics, the 'bombing attacks went some way to shake the morale of the industrial population and had an adverse effect on the output of munitions of war, but chiefly they compelled the Germans to divert aeroplanes, labour, and materiel to the beginnings of widespread schemes of home defence'.[31]

Otherwise, it is doubtful that the raids had any really serious impact on German war production. Field Marshal Sir Douglas Haig declared in February 1917 his belief it was 'highly improbable' that German steel output had been 'seriously affected'. However, he had already gone on record as opposing the strategic attacks.

*　*　*

In retrospect, it is apparent that the navies of both nations, far from undervaluing aviation, as so many air power historians would have us believe, in fact *overvalued* it, placing too much faith in how decisive it would be as a strategic weapon. And it is instructive to note that the doctrines and the operations springing from that faith — which was to become the bedrock of Royal Air Force policy — were developed independently by both navies long before anybody outside of Italy (and very few in that country) had ever heard of Douhet.

Notes

1. There is a vast literature on the subject, including an entire fictional genre of which the best-known example is probably H G Wells' 1908 novel *The War in the Air.* See I F Clarke, *Voices Prophesying War: Future Wars 1763–3749,* (Oxford University Press, new ed. 1992); Michael Paris, *Winged Warfare: The Literature and Theory of Aerial Warfare in Britain, 1859–1917* (Manchester and New York: Manchester University Press, 1992), and Michael Paris, 'Fear of Flying: The Fiction of War 1886–1916', *History Today,* Vol 43, June 1993. Paris lists more than forty English-language works of 'predictive fiction', and more than twenty on theories of aerial warfare, published between 1859 and the pre-war months of 1914, and this is only the tip of the iceberg. I am grateful to Thomas F Tefft for calling Paris' work to my attention.

2. How, when or even if Douhet influenced doctrinal thinking in the Royal Air Force and/or the US Army Air Corps (later the US Army Air Forces) is a matter of controversy. For one discussion, see Higham, *The Military Intellectuals in Britain*. Douhet's book *The Command of the Air* was published in 1921; revised editions appeared in 1927 and 1932. Translated excerpts of various length were published or circulated in the 1930s in France, Britain and the United States. A translation of the 1927 edition by Dino Ferrari (New York: Coward-McCann, 1942) seems to be the only full-length edition of the book available in English. For an exposition and analysis of views expressed in *The Command of the Air*, see Louis A Sigaud, *Douhet and Aerial Warfare* (New York: C P Putnam's Sons, 1941).

3. Literature on the history of strategic air offence is immense. Among works I have found useful are Neville Jones, *The Origins of Strategic Bombing: A Study of the Development of British Air Strategic Thought and Practice Up to 1918* (London: William Kimber, 1973); Max Hastings, *Bomber Command* (New York: Dial Press/James Wade, 1979); Lee Kennett, *A History of Strategic Bombing* (New York: Charles Scribner's Sons, 1982); Ronald Schaffer, *Wings of Judgment: American Bombing in World War II* (Oxford University Press, 1985); Michael S Sherry, *The Rise of American Air Power: The Creation of Armageddon* (Yale University Press, 1987), and Conrad C Crane, *Bombs, Cities and Civilians: American Air Power Strategy in World War II* (University Press of Kansas, 1993).

4. John Quick, ed, *Dictionary of Weapons and Military Terms* (New York: McGraw-Hill, 1973).

5. As in the case of strategic versus tactical reconnaissance, the line between strategic and tactical bombing is often blurred. Bombing of a railway marshalling yard, for instance, could be considered 'strategic' if intended as part of a long-range programme to disrupt an enemy's transportation system in general, but could be construed as 'tactical' if intended to prevent immediate transfer of infantry reinforcements to a particular location at a particular time.

6. Douhet is one of those theorists such as Marx, Freud, Mahan and Clausewitz who are more talked about than studied. A reading of *The Command of the Air* reveals that Douhet did not so much advocate indiscriminate terror bombing (in fact, he deplored it) but simply accepted it as inevitable and reasoned pragmatically from there.

7. These issues are discussed in the works cited in note 3 above. For an extended discussion of the moral/theological questions, see Louis A Manzo, 'Morality in War Fighting and Strategic Bombing in World War II', *Air Power History*, Vol 59 No 3, 1992.

8. See Frank P Donnini, 'Douhet, Caproni and Early Air Power', *Air Power History*, Vol 37 No 2, 1990. This article also advances a revisionistic view of Douhet's international influence.

9. Cuneo, *The Air Weapon 1914–1916*, p371.

10. Walter Raleigh, *The War in the Air*, Vol 1 (Oxford University Press, 1922), pp399–400.

11. Douglas H Robinson, *The Zeppelin in Combat*, p43.

12. So pervasive had this belief become that in his 1913 novel *When William Came*, depicting a fictional German occupation of Britain, H H Munro ('Saki') made several references to aircraft as an important factor in the British defeat that led to the occupation, alluding to 'the Zeppelin air fleet' and the Teutonic 'mastering of the air and the creation of a scientific aerial war fleet, second to none in the world'. For factual discussions of the British perception, see John R Cuneo, *Winged Mars*; Alfred Gollin, *No Longer an Island: Britain and the Wright Brothers, 1902–1909* (Stanford University Press, 1984) and the same author's *The Impact of Air Power on the British People and Their Government, 1909–14* (Stanford University Press, 1989).

13. Quoted in Robinson, *The Zeppelin in Combat*, p50.

14. The most effective of these was the explosive and incendiary ammunition introduced in 1916 for the machine-guns of defending aircraft. Eleven airships (ten naval, one army) were downed by aeroplanes using such ammunition.

15. See Raymond H Fredette, *The Sky on Fire: The First Battle of Britain 1917–1918 and the Birth of the Royal Air Force* (New York; Holt, Rinehart and Winston, 1996).

16. For this story, see Jones, *The War in the Air*, Vol 3; Robinson *The Zeppelin in Combat*, and Raymond Laurence Rimell, *Zeppelin!: A Battle for Air Supremacy in World War I* (London: Conway Maritime Press, 1984).

17. Jones, *The War in the Air*, Vol 3, p147, and *Appendices*, Appendix XLIV, p164.

18. Robinson, *The Zeppelin in Combat*, p349.

19. Jones, *The War in the Air*, Vol 3, pp243–244.

20. Cuneo, *The Air Weapon 1914–1916*, p384.

21. Robinson, *The Zeppelin in Combat*, p350.

22. 'Extracts from Minutes of a Conference held in the Admiralty on 3 April 1915,' ADM 1/8497, Public Record Office (hereafter cited as PRO), in Stephen W Roskill, ed, *Documents Relating to the Naval Air Service*, Vol 1, *1908–1918* (London: Navy Records Society, 1969), p199. It should be noted that some PRO file numbers of documents as given in this book (hereafter cited as Roskill, *Documents*) have been changed since its publication.

23. For the influence of the *Ilya Mouromets* on the AD-1000, see Harald Penrose, *British Aviation: The Pioneer Years 1903–1914* (London: Putnam, 1967). The AD-1000 is also described in J M Bruce, *British Aeroplanes 1914–1918* (London: Putnam, 1957).

24. These aircraft were officially the Admiralty Type 9700 (the two-place version) and Admiralty Type 9400S (the single-seater). The nickname stemmed from the arrangement of the cabane struts.

The Type 9700 was the first British aircraft to be fitted with both a flexible rear-cockpit machine-gun and a fixed forward gun equipped to fire through the propeller.

25. So perverse did the army's objections seem that a memorandum of an Admiralty meeting of 21 March 1916 could seriously state 'It seemed to be generally agreed that one of the main reasons for the Army's objection to the Navy undertaking Long Range Bombing was that they were not in a position to do it themselves, and did not wish the Navy to have the honour of doing it before them.' ADM 1/8449, in Roskill, *Documents*, p335.

26. 'The Constitution, Functions and Procedure of the Joint Air War Committee,' Air 1/270 *et alia*, in Roskill, *Documents*, p307.

27. 'Joint Air War Committee. Extracts from Paper Air 4, dated 3 March 1916,' Air 1/270, in Roskill, *Documents*, p310.

28. This was probably the largest air raid of the war to that date. For details, see H D Hastings, 'The Oberndorf Raid,' *Cross & Cockade*, Vol 5 No 4, 1964, and Gustave Bock, 'Additional Information on the Bombing Raid on the Mauser Factory in Oberndorf', *Cross & Cockade*, Vol 8 No 1, 1967. For the formation and operations of No 3 Wing, see Jones, *The War in the Air*, Vols 2 and 4; Raymond Collishaw, '1916 Strategic Bomber Command: No 3 Wing, Royal Naval Air Service', *Cross & Cockade*, Vol 4 No 1, 1963; Chaz Bowyer, '3 Wing, RNAS — Britain's First Strategic Bombers', *Aircraft Illustrated Extra No 12: Naval Aviation, 1912–1945*, (London: Ian Allan, nd), and Richard Bell Davies, *Sailor in the Air: The Memoirs of Vice Admiral Richard Bell Davies* (London: Peter Davies, 1967).

29. 'Extracts from Letter No. 164/H.F. 0036 from Admiral Sir David Betty to the Admiralty . . . dated 21 January 1917, and Admiralty reply thereto M.0812 dated 14 February 1917,' ADM 1/8475 and 1/8478, in Roskill, *Documents*, p462.

30. Collishaw, '1916 Strategic Bomber Command'.

31. Jones, *The War in the Air*, Vol 4, p122. The German defensive measures were probably not as extensive as the British, but did absorb a fairly large number of men and much material. Some indications of its scope are given in Ernest von Hoeppner in *Germany's War in the Air: The Development and Operations of German Military Aviation in the World War*, reprint ed., J. Hawley Larned, trans. (Nashville: Battery Press, 1994). pp61–66 and pp127–131. General von Hoeppner was commander of the German army air service from its reorganisation in October 1916 to the end of the war.

CHAPTER 8

Defending the Sea Lanes

———————— · ————————

The submarine quickly became the dominant factor in the 1914–18 war at sea, drastically restricting fleet movements and sending to the bottom far more tonnage than was sunk by all other means combined. By, in effect, blockading the British isles, submarines very nearly won the war for Germany, in the process revolutionising naval warfare as it had been known for centuries and refuting Mahan's dictum that *guerre de course* could never be decisive. The *Unterseebooten* were defeated only after enormous efforts by the Allied and Associated Powers in which aviation played an important role.[1]

* * *

Most major navies had experimented before the war with aerial detection of submarines, as well as mines. Results were varied, depending upon the opacity of the water and the state of the sea. In the Mediterranean, for instance, it was found that in a calm sea a submarine could often be seen at periscope depth or even deeper, but this was not true in the more opaque waters around the British Isles.[2] However, even if an aircraft could spot a submerged craft, there was no way of attacking it, for no form of anti-submarine weaponry yet existed.

In March 1912 a Royal Navy submarine officer, Lieutenant Hugh Williamson, who had recently qualified as an aviator, conceived an aerial weapon for use against submarines in response to an Admiralty committee's request for thoughts on how to combat the underwater menace. In a remarkably prescient paper titled 'The Aeroplane in Use Against Submarines',[3] he first spelled out the requirements for an anti-submarine aircraft (good visibility, long endurance, a reliable engine and a large payload) and then described its weapon. It would be a double-fused bomb; upon impact with water the first of these would activate a time fuse set to explode the charge under the surface. This may well have been the first proposal for the depth charge.

The threat of aerial attack, Williamson reasoned, would cause a surfaced submarine to submerge, and here, it has been noted, he 'put his finger on precisely the manner in which the aircraft was to exert its greatest pressure on the submarine . . : by forcing a boat to submerge, in other words by denying it free use of the surface, the submarine would temporarily be neutralised'.[4]

To understand why this should be so, it must be remembered that the submarine of 1914–18 was for all practical purposes simply a submersible torpedo-boat. Its underwater propulsion was by electric motors relying on batteries with limited capacity. When that capacity was exhausted the boat had to surface to recharge the batteries from its diesel engines. Electrical propulsion severely limited a submarine's underwater performance. Maximum submerged speed of German First World War submarines never exceeded 9kts, and this could be maintained for only about an hour before the batteries went dead. Even at the average submerged cruising speed of 4kts, the craft could travel scarcely more than sixty nautical miles before having to surface to recharge.

German submarine skippers therefore spent as much time as possible on the surface, using the superior surface speed (the larger German boats averaged 16kts) to manoeuvre into position for underwater attack. Thus it was by forcing them to submerge, not by sinking them, that aircraft contributed most significantly in helping to defeat the U-boats.

This deterrent factor gained in importance after the introduction of the merchant convoy in 1917. Now a submarine could no longer simply loiter on a main trade route awaiting individual, unprotected merchantmen. Instead, it encountered a cluster of vessels, which, although presenting a tempting target, was guarded by warships armed with depth charges and beginning to be equipped with underwater detection devices.

The addition of aircraft heightened deterrence by forcing the U-boats down further away from the convoy than would have been the case otherwise; moreover, they could direct warships to the location of a sighted submarine, giving its commander another reason for staying underwater.

Parenthetically, it should be noted that toward the end of the conflict some British aircraft were equipped with hydrophonic listening devices. These were fitted to flying boats for use while alighted on the surface, and to airships which lowered them into

A Gotha WD 14, the German torpedo plane constructed in the greatest number (sixty-nine) and the first to see operational service. (*Cross & Cockade Journal*)

The wrecked Russian torpedo boat *Stroini*, destroyed by winter storms after bombing by German seaplanes prevented her salvage and repair. (Boris P Drashpil collection)

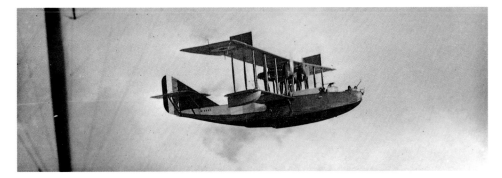

A Felixstowe F 2A, typical of the flying boats of the 'Spider Web' anti-submarine patrol. This particular aircraft, N 4297, was forced down by four Hansa-Brandenburg W 29s on 4 July 1918 but survived to fly again, as proved by this photo taken on 20 August 1918. (J M Bruce/G S Leslie collection)

A Short Admiralty Type 184 torpedo plane, No 184 itself, slung from HMS *Ben-my-Chree* at the Dardanelles in 1915. Shorts from *Ben-my-Chree* carried out the world's first aerial torpedo attacks there, but the results have been exaggerated and what they accomplished is still not really known. (*Cross & Cockade Journal*)

An Italian Caproni bomber aboard a Hickman-Mustin sea sled on 15 November 1918 during tests at Hampton Roads, Virginia. Mustin proposed building thousands of these hydroplaning boats for mass aerial attacks on German U-boat bases, but only a handful were constructed. (US Naval Historical Center)

A British SS-class airship (probably *SS 19*) and its ground handling party on the Aegean island of Imbros in August or September 1915. This type and its successors, built in large numbers, were ubiquitous in the hunt for U-boats. (Brian P Flanagan collection via August G Blume)

A Blackburn Kangaroo. Produced in small numbers and too late to see much operational service, this type was the finest anti-submarine aircraft of the war, superior in several respects to comparable aeroplanes of RAF Coastal Command in 1939. (J M Bruce/G S Leslie collection)

The commerce raider *Wolf* upon her return to Germany, displaying on deck the seaplane that was instrumental in several of her captures. (Courtesy of Peter M Grosz)

Three of the four main vessels of the Russian Black Sea Fleet's 'carrier striking force' anchored at Sevastopol—from right, *Rominia, Imperator Nikolai II* and *Imperator Akexsandr I.* (Boris P Drashpil collection, US Naval Historical Center)

the sea while hovering. No operational success was achieved, but it was a harbinger of the air-dropped or air-towed sensors of the Second World War and later.

The deterrent effect of aircraft was used to good advantage in early 1918 after the U-boats, frustrated by convoy in the Western Approaches, turned their attention to British coastal waters, where mercantile losses grew alarmingly. To counter this, a system of aerial 'scarecrow' patrols was established, using De Havilland DH 6s. The DH 6, a simple and ungainly landplane designed as a trainer, had been superseded in that role and a large surplus of the type was at hand. These patrols were pure bluff — the performance of the DH 6 was so limited that it could carry only a 100lb bombload and then had to be flown without an observer — based on the correct belief that a submarine would submerge immediately when its lookouts spotted *any* type of aircraft.[5] And once under water, the submarine commander was in a quandary as to when to surface again, for until the development of sky-search periscopes late in the war his aerial foe was invisible to him and might still be lurking.

The 'scarecrow' tactic thus took advantage of the fact that submergence was the U-boat's only sure protection. It was ill-equipped to fight it out against an aerial assailant, having only a machine gun or two as anti-aircraft armament. The standard deck gun could not ordinarily be elevated high enough or trained quickly enough to use against an aeroplane. An airship, however, presented a much larger and slower target, and one French airship was shot down and one American airship damaged by deck gun fire. Some of the large 'cruiser' U-boats of 1918 mounted a pair of 88mm AA guns to supplement their large deck guns, but there was never an opportunity to employ them against aircraft.

* * *

As the aerial anti-submarine effort developed, the greater became the need for aircraft with greater endurance and radius — qualities which also, of course, made them valuable for oceanic scouting. The large flying boat seemed to meet the need admirably. The first such type in the Royal Navy was the American Curtiss H 4, designed before the war for transatlantic flight. It was followed by the bigger Curtiss H 12, after which they were nicknamed 'Small America' and 'Large America', respectively. Both proved to be underpowered, and an improvement on their design was undertaken by RNAS Squadron Commander John Cyril Porte, commander of the Felixstowe naval air station, who had worked with Glenn Curtiss before the war. He produced a series of twin-engine flying boats, all generically designated Felixstowe, that served to the end of the war and beyond. Highly seaworthy, with endurance of up to six hours, well-armed for self-defence and able to carry two 230lb bombs, they took a prominent part in anti-submarine operations and frequently tangled with German seaplanes.[6] Flying boats were employed on the so-called Spider Web patrol established in April 1917 to monitor the lower North Sea area most frequented by U-boats from the Belgian ports. It is described as 'an imaginary octagonal figure, sixty sea miles in diameter. There were eight radial arms (each thirty miles in diameter) and chords, joining the arms, ten, twenty, and thirty miles from the center. The web . . . enabled about four thousand square miles of sea to be searched systematically . . .'.[7]

Another aircraft prominent in British anti-submarine operations was the small non-rigid (technically, pressure-rigid) airship. Its use in this role was a brainstorm of Lord Fisher after he 'had fully satisfied myself that small airships with a speed of fifty miles an hour would be of inestimable value against submarines and also for scouting purposes near the coast'.[8]

His proposal, put forward on 28 February 1915,[9] was acted on with remarkable speed, and a prototype flew within weeks. Given the class designation SS (Submarine Scout) and soon to be nicknamed 'blimp',[10] the type was built in large numbers, followed by ever-improved classes of differing designations, equipped with wireless and able to carry a small bombload and a machine-gun or two.[11] Their advantage over aeroplanes for anti-submarine work was their greater endurance. Because, as noted earlier, an airship does not depend on its lifting element to propel it, the time it can stay in the air is limited only by the amount of engine fuel it can carry and its rate of consumption (although crew fatigue is also a factor). Some classes of British non-rigids could remain aloft for up to 24 hours depending upon the speed at which they flew, which dictated how much fuel they burned.

More than 200 British non-rigids were built during the war, and more than 100 were still in service at the time of the Armistice, operating from more than thirty bases in the United Kingdom alone.[12]

British anti-submarine operations were not, of course, confined to seaplanes and airships. In addition to the DH 6s, many other landplane types were pressed into service. One specifically tailored for the role was the Blackburn Kangaroo, a twin-engine machine originally designed as a floatplane. Although smaller and lighter than the Felixstowe flying boats, it could carry a heavier bombload, had a longer endurance, was faster and cost less to manufacture. As several writers have pointed out, it had a greater endurance and a heavier bombload than the Avro Anson, the RAF Coastal Command's principal anti-submarine aircraft in 1939. However, the Kangaroo entered service too late and in too small numbers to demonstrate its potential.[13]

By far the greatest burden of the aerial anti-submarine effort was borne by the Royal Naval Air Service and (later) the Royal Air Force for most of the war. France and the United States did join in, however. The French contribution had been slight until establishment of the *Direction de la Guerre Sous-marine* on 18 June 1917. This command operated mainly small flying boats and non-rigid airships, the latter including those transferred from the army after it gave up airship operations. The United States Navy started lending belated assistance in early 1918, also employing small flying boats (almost entirely French) and airships (entirely French).[14]

The Allies, of course, were not unique in using aircraft to combat submarines. Aircraft of the Central Powers harried Allied submarines in the Heligoland Bight, Adriatic, Sea of Marmora, Baltic and elsewhere. In fact, what was probably the first aerial attack on a submarine during the war was made by Zeppelin *L 5* when it tried unsuccessfully to bomb the British *E 11* on 25 December 1914 during the so-called Cuxhaven Raid.[15] Austro-Hungarian seaplanes sank the British *B 10* at its moorings in Venice harbour on 16 August 1916[16] and a few weeks later fatally damaged the French *Foucault* — the first submarine to succumb to aerial attack while submerged in the open sea.[17]

But because their merchant marines never — except briefly in the Baltic and the Sea of Marmora — had to be protected from the sort of immense threat posed by the U-boats in the Atlantic and the Mediterranean, Central Power aerial anti-submarine efforts were far more limited in scope and importance than those of the Allies.

* * *

The hours and mileage flown by Allied aircraft on anti-submarine patrol reached astronomical figures. Overall statistics are hard to come by, but some select figures give an idea of the magnitude.

During the period 1 July–30 September 1918, three groups of anti-submarine aircraft based in England (each composed of landplanes, seaplanes and airships) flew a total of 24,309 hours.[18] Between June 1917 and October 1918, British airships were aloft for 59,703 hours, carrying out 9,069 patrols.[19] French airships spent 16,300 hours in the air during 1917–18.[20] Incomplete figures show that even the late-coming USN made at least 5,170 flights covering at least 506,784 miles, although it is unclear how much of this effort was on actual anti-submarine patrol.[21]

The aerial war against submarines was not confined to the sea, but also waged with strikes against their bases and support facilities where geography and range of aircraft permitted. Such offensive action, if successful, could have both short-term tactical and long-term strategic effects. An example was the Italian attempt to bomb the building slips at Fiume where pre-fabricated submarines were assembled after rail shipment from Germany. The Fiume site of the Whitehead torpedo works was also attacked, one big raid in 1916 dumping four tons of bombs on it — an exercise, however, in futility, for unbeknowst to the Italians the factory had been moved far inland the previous year.[22]

German shipbuilding yards were beyond the reach of aircraft and the main North Sea U-boat bases too heavily defended to be approached, but German-occupied Belgian ports presented targets after submarines began to be based at them in late 1914. These were Zeebrugge and Ostend, on the coast, and Bruges, eight miles inland. Their proximity to shipping lanes in the English Channel and adjacent waters inspired the construction of the small UB (coastal) and UC (coastal mine-laying) boats that formed the Flanders flotilla established in mid-1915,[23] replacing the larger boats that had previously been based at Zeebrugge. The flotilla was a thorn in the Allied side almost to the end of the war, and to seize its ports was at least one reason for the bloody Passchendaele offensive of 1917.

Bruges, beyond the range of enemy naval guns, became the flotilla's main base, connected by canals to Zeebrugge, eight miles to the northwest, and Ostand, eleven miles still farther to the northwest (and twelve miles from Zeebrugge). These ports also sheltered small torpedo-boats and on occasion were visited by High Seas Fleet destroyers temporarily detached for raids into the English Channel.

All three were within easy aerial reach, and raids on them began in early 1915, increasing in frequency and intensity as the war continued, by British, French and eventually American machines. No major results were achieved, but the persistant infliction of minor damage to ships and their facilities kept repair crews constantly busy.[24] So annoying did this become that as early as 1915 the Germans began construction of bombproof shelters for the U-boats at Bruges. By the end of the war these had grown into ferro-concrete structures of massive size and impressive architecture. 'The design was, in effect, a roofing over, with bombproof covering, of a large stretch of the [harbour] basin, the rows of columns on which the roof rested forming separate bays in which the submarines could lie.'[25] These were the forerunners of the so-called U-boat pens that would dot the coasts of Europe in the Second World War.

In early April 1917 the United States authorised formation of a land-based naval air unit to join the attack on the Zeebrugge-Ostand-Bruges triangle, a plan heartily endorsed by Admiral Sims. Designated the Northern Bombing Group, it was to consist of a Day Wing operated by the Marine Corps and a Night Wing manned by navy personnel. Because the US Navy lacked American aircraft of adequate performance, the unit was to be equipped with the British de Havilland DH 4 (some built in the United States) and DH 9A, single-engine two-seaters, for the Day Wing, and the large multi-engine Italian Caproni Ca 5 for the Night Wing.

By the time the Day Wing came into existence, after delays in training, acquisition of aircraft and completion of bases, the Germans had begun abandoning the Belgian ports, and the Northern Bombing Group was assigned other targets. The Night Wing never really got off the ground; production of the Capronis lagged and the few delivered proved unserviceable — only one raid was ever made by one of them.[26]

Suggestions for attacking the German bases by aircraft carriers or airships also were broached in the USN but came to nought. A more ambitious — although fantastic might be the more accurate adjective — plan was advocated by Commander Henry C Mustin, a pioneer USN aviator who had been investigating a powered, high-speed, aircraft-carrying lighter based on a hydroplaning hull. He proposed a fleet of 5,600 such vessels, each carrying one aeroplane, for an offensive against German mainland ports as well as the Belgian bases. *Outre* as this scheme seemed, a few of these 'sea sleds' were built, but testing was incomplete at the time of the Armistice.[27]

* * *

As mileage flown on anti-submarine work mounted, so did reports of U-boats sighted and attacked. During the high period of unrestricted submarine warfare through the first quarter of 1918, British aircraft reported 202 sightings (138 in home waters) and 125 attacks (101 in home waters). For the entire war, France's *Aéronavale* listed 246 attacks, all but sixteen during 1917–18. US aircraft were credited with thirty-two attacks.

These statistics, although inscribed in the pages of official histories and elsewhere, are open to suspicion. At the height of the submarine campaign there were never more than seventy U-boats at sea in all theatres of war, and usually fewer. Thus, for example, it seems highly improbable that aircraft could have sighted eighty-five and attacked forty-eight in British home waters alone during the period July–September 1918, as officially recorded. It is safe to conclude that the majority of supposed sightings were false — caused by tricks of sun and wave on the human eye, floating debris or even schools of fish — and likewise that most of the reported attacks were on imaginary targets.

The number of U-boats believed to have been sunk by aerial attack was greatly exaggerated during the war. British estimates of these ranged as high as 100, and the *Aéronavale* claimed seventy-nine 'probable successes', although it is unclear whether this referred to boats believed sunk, believed damaged or a combination of both. (In reality, the only French success, if such it can be called, was the destruction of the British *D 3* in a mistaken-identity attack by an airship.)[28] The US Navy thought it may have sunk two, and was officially, but falsely, credited with one.

Postwar investigation soon demolished these claims. By 1934, the year of publication of Volume 4 of *The War in the Air*, the British claim had been winnowed to six and the French to a probable four.

Even these figures were too high. It was not until after the Second World War, with publication of the final volumes of the official German First World War submarine history[29] and the researches of American historian Robert M Grant,[30] that the truth emerged. Of the four submarines of three nationalities sunk by unassisted aerial attack, only one was German.[31] Three (two German, one British) were permanently disabled. Four, possibly five, German boats were lost to combined air-sea action (see Appendix 2).

The number of submarines damaged by air attack cannot be determined, but it was certainly greater than the number sunk. A submarine damaged could be placed as effectively out of action, if only temporarily, as one sunk. Aerial bombs bursting close enough could shatter depth gauges or other instruments, jam hydroplanes, rupture high-pressure air pipes, distort periscope housings or, worst of all, start leaks allowing entry of sea water that would generate a cloud of deadly chlorine gas if it reached the batteries.

Some of the exaggerated wartime claims of destruction can be blamed on propaganda or wishful thinking, but most were probably based on honest errors of observation. An aviator seeing a submarine dive just after he aimed bombs at it could well be deceived into thinking it was sinking. Fuel leaking from a damaged but unsunk vessel could lead to the same conclusion.

The rapidity with which a U-boat could submerge, requiring no more than 30 to 45 seconds in some classes, probably accounts for many cases of survival under actual aerial assault. Despite its immense superiority in speed, an aircraft could need perhaps two minutes or more to reach a position for attack once it spotted a submarine, and if it and its prey sighted each other at the same time there was little chance of it reaching that position before the U-boat was under the surface.

* * *

Its help in defeating the U-boats is the one respect in which most general historians have acknowledged the worth of First World War aviation at sea. Sometimes, however, the concentration has been too heavily on its role in offence, with writers retroactively bestowing upon aircraft the destructive capability they demonstrated during the Second World War, when Axis submarine losses were inflicted in almost equal number by aircraft and surface vessels. The truth about how few and uninfluential were aerial sinkings of submarines in the earlier war has not been widely diffused, and one continues to read that 'a number of' or 'several' U-boats were lost to aircraft.

The real contribution of aviation to the defeat of the submarine campaign can be summed up in a sentence from the British air history which, although speaking specifically of airships, is applicable to all types of aircraft: 'Not by "doing," but by "being" they saved many vessels.'[32]

How many it is impossible to say. One reported figure gives a clue: Of 257 convoyed merchantmen sunk by submarines during the final eighteen months of the war, only two were lost from convoys that had aerial escort.[33]

Basically, however, the aerial contribution cannot be quantified. There are no overall statistics to tell us precisely how many times aircraft deterred U-boat attacks or were able to divert convoys from submarine-laid mines.

To appreciate fully the role played by aviation in this most crucial aspect of the naval war, it is necessary to view the submarine and anti-submarine campaigns of 1917–18 as a clash of strategic aims. The initial German strategic aim was to knock Britain out of the conflict by severing its vital sea lines of supply; the decision to attempt this, in the form of unrestricted submarine attack, was made at the famous meeting of military and political leaders at Pless on 9 January 1917. The decision was taken even with the almost certain knowledge that it would bring the United States into the war as a foe.[34] The prospect of American hostility had been hinted at in early 1915 during the first period of unrestricted U-boat warfare, which had been called off in the face of strong US diplomatic pressure. In 1917 most German leaders saw a US declaration of war as inevitable, but believed or were led to believe that Britain would succumb to the submarine campaign before American resources could be mobilised in the Allied cause.

After the first result was not achieved, the next strategic aim was to prevent the arrival of American forces in Europe, at least in sufficient number to become influential.

The Allied strategic aims were first to keep the sea lanes to Britain open to sustain its economy and war effort, then to permit the safe transport of a mass American army.

The means of achieving the German aims was the submarine. The means of achieving the Allied aims took various forms, but the most important was mercantile convoy. Convoy in the First World War must be considered a strategy, not a tactic — just as blockade was a strategy, not a tactic.[35] Convoy was intended not as a means of provoking combat but as a way of achieving unhindered movement of goods essential to sustain an economy as well as transport of troops and military material. Convoy thus may be likened to the movement of an army and its logistical train in accordance with a strategic plan before battle is joined.

Viewed in this light, aviation's role in defence of the sea lanes can be seen as an element of strategy rather than as a tactical weapon. As a tactical weapon at sea, it displayed much less offensive capability than it did on land. As a component of naval strategy, however, it was equally as influential on a higher level as it was on the land fronts, exerting that influence in much the same way as described in Chapter 1. The counterpart of seeing what was beyond the other side of the hill was seeing what was beyond the next wave.

Notes

1. For a good general survey of the development and use of aircraft in anti-submarine warfare, see Alfred Price, *Aircraft versus Submarine: The Evolution of the Anti-submarine Aircraft 1912 to 1972* (London: William Kimber, 1973).
2. For descriptions of some of these early experiments, see Price, op cit, and Layman, *To Ascend From a Floating Base*.
3. The original manuscript is held by Churchill College, Cambridge University. I am grateful to Ian M Burns for a copy. Williamson later transferred to the RNAS, served on the seaplane carrier *Ark Royal* at the Dardanelles, where he was severely injured in a crash, later became an exponent of the flight-deck aircraft carrier, and ended the war, appropriately, as commander of an RAF anti-submarine group. For a sketch of his career, see R D Layman, 'Hugh Williamson and the Creation of the Aircraft Carrier', *Cross & Cockade (Great Britain) Journal*, Vol 13 No 2, 1982.
4. Price, *Aircraft versus Submarine*, p8.
5. For a discussion of the DH 6 patrols, see Price, op cit, and Bruce, *British Aeroplanes*.
6. The Felixstowe craft are described in Bruce, op cit, and Kenneth M Molson, 'The Felixstowe F5L', *Cross & Cockade (Great Britain) Journal*, Vol 9 No 2, 1978. Various improved versions of the F5L were flown by the American and Japanese navies for several years after the war.
7. Jones, *The War in the Air*, Vol 4, pp53–54. The work of the Spider Web patrol is discussed in this volume and in Snowden Gamble, *The Story of a North Sea Air Station*. For an informal account, see 'P.I.X.' [T D Hallam], *The Spider Web: The Romance of a Flying-boat War Flight* (Edinburgh and London: William Blackwood and Sons, 1919 (reprint ed., London: Arms and Armour Press, 1979)).
8. Admiral of the Fleet Lord Fisher [Sir John Fisher], *Memories and Records*, Vol 1, *Memories* (New York: George H Doran, 1920), p130.
9. Fisher, ibid, indicates he advanced this idea 'Soon after I became First Sea Lord on October 31st, 1914,' but all other sources agree on the later date.
10. This is an onomatopetic word coined by Flight Lieutenant A D Cunningham after he playfully flipped a finger against a non-rigid airship's envelope and imitated the sound it made.
11. Technical details of all classes can be found in Patrick Abbott, *The British Airship at War, 1914–1918* (Lavenham, Suffolk: Terence Dalton, 1989).
12. Ibid.
13. For details of the Kangaroo, see Bruce, *British Aeroplanes*, and O G Thetford and E J Riding, *Aircraft of the 1914–1918 War* (np: 1954).
14. A few US-designed and built airships were used to patrol American home waters, but all those employed operationally overseas were French. One British ship was used for training. For further information, see Roy A Grossnick, ed, *Kite Balloons to Airships . . . The Navy's Lighter-than-Air Than Air Experience* (Washington: Deputy Chief of Naval Operations [Air Warfare] and the Commander, Naval Air Systems Command, Government Printing Office, nd).
15. See R D Layman, *The Cuxhaven Raid: The World's First Carrier Air Strike* (London: Conway Maritime Press, 1985).
16. This incident is described in Richard T Whistler, 'Raider Alarm!: Notes on the Air-Sea War, 1914–1918', *Cross & Cockade*, Vol 19 No 3, 1978. This article also describes other aerial-inflicted losses listed in Appendix 2. Another description of the destruction of *B 10* can be found in Paul Kemp and Peter Jung, 'Five Broken Down B Boats: British Submarine Operations in the Northern Adriatic, 1915–1917', *Warship International*, Vol 26 No 1, 1989.
17. For a first-hand description of the attack by one of the Austro-Hungarian airmen involved, see Walter Zelezny, 'The Sinking of the French Submarine *Foucault*', *Cross and Cockade*, Vol 4 No 1, 1963.
18. Jones, *The War in the Air, Appendices*, Appendix XVIII.
19. Abbott, *The British Airship at War*.
20. Charles Christienne and Pierre Lissarrague (trans Francis Kianka), *A History of French Military Aviation* (Washington: Smithsonian Institution Press, 1986).
21. These statistics were compiled from official records by Noel C Shirley, to whom I am grateful. For USN aviation activity overseas, see Turnbull and Lord, *History of United States Naval Aviation*; Van

Wyen, *Naval Aviation in World War I*, and Thomas G Miller Jr, ed, 'Naval Aviation Overseas, 1917–1918', *Cross & Cockade*, Vol 4 No 1, 1963.

22. Edwyn Gray, *The Devil's Device: The Story of Robert Whitehead, Inventor of the Torpedo* (London: Seeley, Service, 1975) p190.

23. For how the occupation of the Belgian ports led to the genesis of these boats, see Eberhard Rössler (trans Harold Erenberg), *The U-boat: The Evolution and Technical History of German Submarines* (Annapolis: Naval Institute Press, 1981).

24. Noted in Lowell Thomas, *Raiders of the Deep* (New York: Doubleday, Doran, 1928). Bruges itself sustained so much damage that, according to an American flier in the RAF who visited the town after the war, children who grew up there during the occupation regarded the British, not the Germans, as the enemy. Anon., *Extracts From the Letters of George Clark Moseley* (privately printed, 1923).

25. Jones, *The War in the Air*, Vol 4 p104. For further descriptions of these structures, see *idem*, pp103–5, and Keith Mallory and Arvid Ottar, *The Architecture of War* (New York: Pantheon Books, 1973), p69.

26. The organisation and operations of the Northern Bombing Group are described in Van Wyen, *Naval Aviation in World War I*; Turnbull and Lord, *History of United States Naval Aviation*; Roger M Emmons, 'The First Marine Aviation Force', Part 2, *Cross & Cockade*, Vol 6 No 3, 1965, and Edward C Johnson, *Marine Corps Aviation: The Early Years 1912–1940* (Washington: History and Museums Division, Headquarters, US Marine Corps, Government Printing Office, 1977). For the failure of the Caproni programme, see Noel C Shirley, 'La Guardia, Caproni Bombers, and the US Navy', *Cross & Cockade*, Vol 25 No 2, 1984, and R D Layman, 'Les Caproni Ca-5 de l'US Navy', *Avions*, No 4, June 1993.

27. Various of these proposals are outlined in Turnbull and Lord, *History of United States Naval Aviation*. For some details of the sea sleds, see R D Layman, 'The Hickman Sea Sled', *Warship International*, Vol 11 No 2, 1974, pp204–205.

28. This incident is described in detail in Eric Brothers, 'Airship Sinks "Friendly" Sub', *Buoyant Flight*, Vol 41 Nos 4 and 5, 1994.

29. *Der Handelskreig mit U-Booten*, Vols 4 (1965) and 5 (1966).

30. Robert M Grant, *U-Boats Destroyed: The Effect of Anti-Submarine Warfare 1914–1918* (London: Putnam, 1964) and *U-Boat Intelligence 1914–1918* (London: Putnam, 1969). The information in these volumes supersedes that in earlier studies by Grant as published in the *United States Naval Institute Proceedings* in 1938 and 1939.

31. This was *UB 32* (see Appendix 2). Actually, there is some residual doubt that it was a victim of aerial attack, but the evidence seems overwhelming. It has been claimed that one other boat, *UB 7*, which disappeared in the Black Sea in October 1916, may have been sunk by a Russian seaplane but there is no confirming evidence. For an analysis and refutation of other claims, see R D Layman with Peter K Simpson and E J L Halpern, 'Allied Aircraft vs German Submarines', *Cross & Cockade*, Vol 11 No 4, 1970.

32. Jones, *The War in the Air*, Vol 4, p60.

33. Price, *Aircraft versus Submarine*.

34. For a thorough discussion of this decision and its consequences, see Marder, *From the Dreadnought to Scapa Flow*, Vol 4.

35. Although the strategic aim of convoy remained the same in the Second World War, the convoy experience differed widely from that of 1917–18. Greatly improved submarine and anti-submarine weaponry, new electronic and acoustic detection devices, U-boat 'wolf pack' tactics, attack by aircraft (which no First World War convoy ever had to endure) and a number of other factors turned the passage of many a Second World War convoy into a running aeronaval battle of a kind never seen in the earlier conflict.

CHAPTER 9

Attacking the Sea Lanes

In the struggle for control of the sea lanes aviation proved a more effective gamekeeper than a poacher, but when it did take on a role as predator it exercised influence on a few occasions — notably during the German torpedo plane offensive of 1917, the RNAS operations at the Dardanelles, and to a certain extent in Russian activity in the Black Sea (which this chapter will discuss). And although this function was not significant in terms of sinking vessels, if, as noted earlier, an accounting could be made of the toll inflicted on minor sail-powered and non-powered surface craft, the tonnage sent to the bottom would unquestionably reach a considerable figure.

* * *

What was probably the first use of aviation in this role began in early 1915 with assaults by German aircraft from the Belgian bases against Allied shipping in the North Sea and English Channel in 1915, and these continued throughout the war. There was an unfortunate early incident when a German seaplane, whose pilot was unable to identify the ship as neutral, bombed and damaged the US tanker *Cushing* off the Dutch coast on 29 April 1915. An apology was made for this 'unintentional accident', but the incident was cited in the later US diplomatic protest over the sinking of the *Lusitania*.[1]

The first British merchant vessel to be sunk from the air was for some years believed to have been the 970 ton collier *Franz Fischer* (a captured German ship), supposedly bombed by a Zeppelin in coastal waters on the night of 2/3 February 1916. Later investigation, however, established that there were no airships anywhere near the site of the sinking that night. The vessel was most likely struck by a drifting mine.[2]

In fact, no British merchantmen were lost to air attack until the three ships sunk by torpedo or torpedo-*cum*-bomb in 1917. How little the German effort availed is shown in the official listing of 'British Merchant Vessels Damaged or Molested by the Enemy but not Sunk'.[3] This records forty-three aerial attacks — by bomb, torpedo, machine-gun, darts or a combination of these weapons — but in only eleven cases was damage, mostly minor, inflicted. Of these eleven ships, only one was damaged at sea; the others were bombed while in French ports and were most likely hit by happenstance during general raids rather than being deliberately targeted.

An innovative and probably more useful function of Belgian-based seaplanes was their employment in monitoring neutral shipping that might be bound to or from British ports. The aircraft would alight alongside a suspicious vessel to ascertain its cargo and destination. If anything seemed amiss, the ship would be ordered to proceed to a German or German-occupied port for search that could result in seizure. Most such ships were small sailing craft, but on at least one occasion a larger vessel was involved — the 1,877 ton Dutch steamer *Gelderland*, stopped while en route to the Tyne, ordered into Zeebrugge, and interned after found to be carrying contraband goods.

A unique episode occurred in April 1917 when Zeppelin *L 23* intercepted the 688 ton Norwegian schooner *Royal* off the Danish coast, ascertained she was carrying pit props (legally contraband) to Britain, and placed aboard a prize crew that sailed her to the Elbe.[4]

Even more innovative was the use, for the first time in the history of *guerre de course*, of an aircraft by the German commerce raider *Wolf*, which, disguised as an innocent merchantman, prowled the South Pacific and Indian Ocean during much of 1917. Of the fourteen merchant vessels that fell prey to her (exclusive of those sunk by her mines), her seaplane was instrumental in the capture of at least four. In addition to reconnaissance that located or helped track her victims, the aircraft sometimes assisted more directly by bombing or threatening to bomb them. The usual procedure was to let fall a warning bomb, then drop a surrender demand on deck. When the American schooner *Winslow* ignored the warning, the seaplane alighted alongside and the aviators compelled surrender at pistol-point.

The Allied search for the raider in the Indian Ocean also employed shipboard aircraft. The British seaplane carrier *Raven II* took part. Her aircraft searched the Maldive Islands, and one was lent for a time to the cruiser *Brisbane*. Another of the *Wolf*-hunters, the Japanese auxiliary cruiser *Chikezen Maru*, carried two seaplanes.

The aerial searches, however, were no more successful than the surface hunt, and the wily *Wolf* returned to Germany in triumph with the aircraft, a Friedrichshafen FF 33e floatplane nicknamed *Wölfchen* ('Wolf Cub' or 'Little Wolf'), proudly displayed on deck. It had made more than fifty flights, often under harrowing conditions — undoubtedly the most achieved by any shipboard aircraft during the war.[5] In doing so, it was directly or indirectly responsible for inflicting greater losses on Allied commerce than the entire rest of the German naval air service. There can be little doubt but that the *Wolf* experience influenced the decision to equip the German surface raiders of the Second World War with aircraft.[6]

A German naval air staff analysis, issued in March 1918, less than a month after *Wolf*'s return, concluded that the seaplane 'proved itself useful and valuable in many instances',[7] but recommended that a sturdier and handier machine, with a better armament than the *Wölfchen*'s hand-dropped bombs, be developed for any future surface raider. A prototype of such an aircraft was indeed built and test-flown.[8]

The work of *Wolf*'s seaplane also revived interest in a proposal, broached the previous year, to place small scouting aircraft aboard the large *U-kreuzer* submarines under construction or projected.[9] Design and construction of a small seaplane, suitable for use by both submarines and surface raiders, was undertaken, but not completed until after the war.[10]

This small, unarmed single-seater was intended purely as a scout, but Allied intelligence reports about it, coming just as the large U-boats were beginning to operate in North American coastal waters in 1918, may have been in part responsible for speculation that these submarines were carrying aircraft to bomb US cities.

Far-fetched as this notion seems in hindsight, it was taken quite seriously at the time and 'brought about drastic action in New York, where the police authorities issued an order forbidding all display lights at night until further notice. Manhattan, the Bronx, Brooklyn, Staten Island and Coney Island went dark on the night of June 4 [1918] and stayed dark for thirteen nights. Several nearby New Jersey towns adopted similar measures. . . . On June 5 New York placed siren horns at intervals of thirty blocks and controlled them electrically so that twenty-minute signals would herald the coming of enemy aircraft. . . . Stringent fire regulations were also issued.'[11]

* * *

Due to Allied naval control of Mediterranean waters and the entrances to the Atlantic, Allied aircraft had little opportunity to attack Central Power merchant shipping, which simply evaporated outside the Adriatic, Baltic, Marmora and Black Sea. Russia lacked the bases as well as aircraft of sufficient range to interfere with German trade routes in the western Baltic. Seaplanes from bases in the Åland Islands kept some track of German vessels carrying ore from northern Swedish ports in the Gulf of Bothnia, but seem never to have taken offensive action against them.[12]

It was a different story in the Black Sea, where Russian seaplane carriers took a highly active part in attempts to sever Turkish sea lanes. The most vital of these was the route along the northern Anatolian coast. Its importance lay in the fact that Constantinople and the Turko-German fleet were heavily dependent upon coal from eastern Anatolian mines. Because there was no direct rail link between the coal-producing area and the metropolis, and transportation over an inadequate road system was lengthy and laborious, the bulk of this essential fuel was carried by sea from ports of which Zonguldak was the most important.

Coal was transported almost entirely by sailing craft plus some small steamers, and it was against these that the Russian effort was directed, accompanied by bombardment of the ports. This campaign, in which the seaplane carriers began to take a hand in early 1915, was so successful that at times the *Goeben* and *Breslau* were virtually immobilised by lack of reserve fuel. If Russian sources can be believed, the Black Sea Fleet sank, burned or captured more than 1,000 Turkish coastal craft during 1914–17.[13] How many of these fell victim to aircraft cannot be known, but only 5 per cent would represent a considerable number.

The carriers' aircraft on several occasions joined warships in bombarding ports, and at Zonguldak in February 1916 sank (albeit temporarily) the largest merchant vessel lost to air attack during the entire war — the 4,211 ton ex-German collier *Irmingard*.[14] They also put the port's electrical generating plant out of operation for a time.

Here again the influence of aviation was exerted more on the strategic than the tactical level under the previously quoted definition of strategic air operations as 'designed to have a long-range rather than immediate effect on the enemy and his military forces'. The German torpedo planes and the RNAS aircraft at the Dardanelles disrupted shipping movements not in terms of sinking or damaging ships, but by forcing changes in sailing times and routes, and the Russian aircraft helping to interdict Turkish coal shipments were certainly performing as 'strategic' a function as those attacking the smelters of Alsace-Lorraine.

Notes

1. Thomas A Bailey and Paul B Ryan, *The Lusitania Disaster: An Episode in Modern Warfare and Diplomacy* (New York: The Free Press, 1975), p61.
2. See Layman, 'Naval Warfare in a New Dimension'.
3. In *British Vessels Lost at Sea 1914–1918* (Cambridge, 1977). This is a one-volume reprint of two documents, *Navy Losses* and *Merchant Shipping (Losses)*, first published in 1919 by His Majesty's Stationery Office.
4. This incident is described in August Dobert, 'The One and Only Time an Airship Captured a Ship at Sea', *Buoyant Flight*, Vol 41 No 3, 1994.
5. For a highly detailed account of aerial aspects of *Wolf*'s operations, see Peter M Grosz, 'The Cruise of the *Wölfchen*', *Cross & Cockade*, Vol 14 No 1, 1973. See also Roy Alexander, *The Cruise of the Raider Wolf* (Yale University Press, 1939).
6. For use of these aircraft, see August Karl Muggenthaler, *German Raiders of World War II* (Englewood Cliffs, NJ: Prentice-Hall, 1977).
7. Quoted in Grosz, op cit.
8. Because *Wolf* had to maintain the guise of an ordinary merchantman, the seaplane could not be carried above deck but had to be stowed below except when needed. This required removal of its fixed wings, and reassembly could take up to four hours. The type designed for use by future surface raiders, the Friedrichshafen FF 64, was given folding wings, permitting it to be hoisted into and out of a cargo hold quickly and easily. It also featured a machine-gun for the observer. In all other respects, Grosz notes, it 'was basically a cleaned-up, more robust version of the *Wölfchen* with minor refinements in design'.
9. A small flying boat for this purpose, the Hansa-Brandenburg W 20, intended for disassembled carriage in a deck container, was designed by Ernst Heinkel but proved unsatisfactory. For details of this craft, see Nowarra *et al*, *Marine Aircraft of the 1914–1918 War*.
10. This was the Luftfahrzeug Gesselschaft LFG Roland V 19, a tiny twin-float monoplane unusual in being one of the first aircraft of all-metal construction. It too was designed for disassembled stowage in deck containers. For a general discussion of German investigation of submarine-borne aircraft, including a bibliography, see the 'Ask INFOSER' column in *Warship International*, Vol 28 No 1, 1991, pp84–86; for a detailed description of the LFG V 19 see Gerrard Terry, 'The LFG Roland V 19', *Cross & Cockade International Journal*, Vol 18 No 2, 1987. A floatplane similar in size and concept to the LFG craft, the Arado AR 231, likewise designed for U-boats, was developed in 1941 but was never used in its intended role. Two of these were embarked on the surface raider *Stier* and proved useless, managing 'only a few feeble flutters' (Muggenthaler, op cit, p12). For details of the AR 231, see William Green, *War Planes of the Second World War*, Vol 6, *Floatplanes* (Garden City, NY; Doubleday and Co, 1963).
11. William Bell Clark, *When the U-Boats Came to America* (Boston: Little, Brown and Co, 1929), p79.
12. Activity of these air bases is described in Kenneth Gustavsson, *Granboda flygstation: Ryskt marinflyg pa Åland under första världskriget* (Mariehamm: Ålands Museum, nd).
13. A number compiled from figures given in George Mekrasov, *North of Gallipoli: The Black Sea Fleet at War 1914–1917* (Boulder, Colo: East European Monographs, 1992).
14. This sinking is disputed in Langensiepen and Güleryüz, which states the ship was only damaged and later sailed to Constantinople.

CHAPTER 10

Ships for Aircraft

_____ · _____

While the submarine was coming to dominate naval warfare during 1914–18, another type of ship was evolving that in a few decades would equally revolutionise conflict at sea — the flight-deck aircraft carrier. From the moment heavier-than-air flight became feasible, the type had been predicted. It was obvious that if an aeroplane were to take off from and alight on a ship the vessel would require a long, unobstructed flat surface atop its hull. Forecasts of what remain the basic principles of the flight-deck carrier were made well before the Great War by, among others, the French aviation pioneer Clément Ader, American aero historian Victor Loughhead and British Rear Admiral Mark Kerr.

Simple as the idea seemed, translating it into reality was quite another matter. One is reminded, although it is not exactly apropos, of Clausewitz's dictum that 'Everything in war is very simple, but the simplest thing is difficult.'

The design of the carrier confronted the naval architect with a myriad of problems. Some were obvious; for instance, if the flight deck were to be unobstructed the aircraft would have to be housed below it, requiring large, open interior spaces that could threaten hull strength. Other problems were unforeseen; of these, the greatest was how dangerous to an alighting aircraft would be the buffeting air turbulence created by the torrent of engine room gasses streaming from a funnel. Even a normal centreline superstructure created potentially perilous air currents — but how could a vessel lacking such a superstructure be conned and navigated?[1] Also unforeseen was the need for some kind of apparatus to slow an alighting aircraft to a stop on deck. Development of such arresting gear constitutes in itself a complex chapter in the aircraft carrier story.

How unrecognised some obstacles were is shown in the first formal proposal for a British aviation vessel, a design submitted to the Admiralty in 1912 by the shipbuilding firm of William

Beardmore & Company. It featured a clear fore-and-aft flight deck, but this was flanked on both sides by parallel superstructures complete with funnels and masts and connected by an overhead gallery.[2] The concept was not merely unrealistic but positively deadly, yet it was to recur for several years in proposed carrier designs.

Fortunately for any aviators who might have been called upon to risk landing on such a ship, the Beardmore proposal was rejected, the Admiralty deciding to withhold judgment on what an aviation vessel should be until experience had been gained with operation of seaplanes by the cruiser *Hermes* during 1913 manoeuvres. The aviation ship authorised in 1914 as a result of this experience — the *Ark Royal*, to be described fully later — differed completely from the Beardmore design.

* * *

If by 1914 the aircraft carrier was an idea whom time had come, there were those who questioned the need or practicality of such a vessel. Instead of putting all one's aerial eggs in one floating basket, they argued, aircraft should be dispersed on individual conventional warships (such was the view of the USN's Captain Chambers). The goal of adopting conventional vessels to operate aircraft generated many wild and weird schemes.[3] In the long run, both approaches were taken, and virtually every major conventional warship of the 1930s and early 1940s was equipped with aircraft. The controversy did not really end, however, until the later years of the Second World War saw the demise of the shipboard seaplane.

In the interim between the two World Wars, a third approach was advocated — creation of a ship that would combine the functions of a gunnery vessel and a carrier in one hull, the progenitor of which was the British *Vindictive* of 1918. This chimera was pursued for decades, but only a handful of such so-called hybrids were built and all were unsuccessful.[4]

Returning to 1914, by the start of the Great War the conventional wisdom was, as described earlier, that the seaplane for obvious reasons constituted the ideal shipboard aircraft. This turned out to be not so simple a proposition. It was found that the seaplane placed many demands on a warship, some of which were detrimental to its employment as a fighting vessel. A seaplane required stowage space, which on a cramped vessel was often difficult to find. It needed some form of shelter to protect it from the ravages of wind and wave as well as from salt-air corrosion of its engine and other metallic parts. Stowage room had to be found for its fuel, lubricants and items essential to its main-tenance. Launching structures such as ramps or platforms tended to hinder normal shipboard activity and restrict training arcs of guns.

The major handicap of the seaplane, it must be repeated, was the unreliability inherent in its total dependence on the whims of the water from which it had to ascend (until development of the shipboard catapult) and alight; it could never be counted on to function when and where it might be needed. As this problem became increasingly apparent, the case for a specialised vessel from which landplanes could operate gained strength, reinforced by the growing superiority of the landplane's performance.

* * *

There can be no doubt that the flight-deck carrier would have come into existence eventually — it was too logical a concept to have been ignored. But it was the exgencies of Britain's Royal Navy during 1914–18 that caused it to appear when it did. It did not, of course, spring Aphrodite-like from the foam, but was the product of an evolutionary process.[5] It is one of the oddities of history that the process was accelerated by two Germans — Ferdinand von Zeppelin and Alfred von Tirpitz.

Zeppelin's rigid airship possessed qualities that made it emi-nently suitable as a naval scout. It was far superior to the aero-plane in range and endurance, had an equally wide field of oceanic vision, could achieve higher altitudes, could more easily lift the heavy and space-consuming wireless apparatus of the period, possessed high speed relative to surface vessels, and en-joyed an early virtual immunity to attack in the air.

The German navy, however, belying British fears, was ill-equipped with airships when the war began. Tirpitz had resisted introduction of the type. For one thing, he doubted its reli-ability: 'As a naval officer who had got to know the force of the wind and the malice of squalls on sailing ships', he was to write later, 'I never promised myself much from the airships.'[6] He also resented diversion of funds for construction of the battleships and torpedo boats that were the fundamentals of his naval strategy.

As recounted in Chapter 4, Tirpitz was finally pressured into accepting airships, and an ambitious programme of construction of them and bases for them was undertaken. Bases were equally as important as the ships themselves, for these giant craft — longer than most battleships and ocean liners afloat — required equally huge structures to shelter them from the elements; Tirpitz was correct in his belief that the airship was highly vulnerable to the malice of the wind.

The newly-formed Naval Airship Division got off to a rocky start. Its first two ships were destroyed in mid-air accidents, killing most of the division's experienced cadre, and recovery from these disasters was barely under way when the war began. There was only one operational Zeppelin in August 1914 and only four by the end of the year, divided equally between the North Sea and Baltic fleets.

The Phoenix-like rise of the Naval Airship Division, resulting in Germany creating by 1918 the largest fleet of rigid airships in history, was a consequence of the interplay of German and British naval strategies. The *Admiralstab* expected the Royal Navy to attempt a classic nineteenth-century close blockade in the German coastal shallows, where British superiority in dreadnoughts could be nullified by mine and torpedo. The High Seas Fleet, which contrary to its name had no plans for high-seas operations, therefore initially adopted a posture that Admiral Scheer described as 'awaiting the enemy's offensive'. There was, however, no offensive to await, for the British Admiralty, having studied the lessons of the Russo-Japanese War, in which mines inflicted severe losses on vessels investing Port Arthur, had decided on a policy of distant blockade, choking off entrances to the North Sea far from German shores.

Baffled by the failure of the enemy to appear and constrained by the Kaiser's order that losses of his beloved capital ships were to be avoided, the German fleet turned to what Scheer frankly termed a guerrilla policy — attempts to whittle down the Grand Fleet by traps and ambushes, overwhelming isolated segments of it until numerical equality or superiority in dreadnought strength was achieved. Then a fleet action could be fought on advantageous or at least equal terms.

Such a policy demanded continual and efficient reconnaissance — the ambushes could not be laid without knowledge of the location and activities of the British. But the High Seas Fleet was woefully deficient in scouting vessels as the result of a policy decision by Tirpitz when in 1897 he set about creating the modern German navy. He deprecated the value of scout cruisers under his 'risk theory' (*Risikogedanke*), in which a strong battle fleet was to be concentrated in the North Sea as a potential threat to Britain. The theory was that 'The ultimate strength of the [German] fleet would deter an eventual opponent [*ie*, Britain] from risking an all-out naval encounter with Germany because even if he emerged victorious from battle, such an enemy might then find himself at the mercy of a third strong naval power, or even coalition.'[7]

In an influential memorandum of June 1897, 'General Considerations on the Constitution of Our Fleet According to Ship Classes and Designs', Tirpitz declared: 'Against England, indeed against any fleet penetrating our home waters, the value of scouting vessels is much reduced . . . such vessels represent in a sense a reduction from the forces needed for the ultimate outcome.'[8]

Tirpitz later had second thoughts and eventually proposed building a total of forty light cruisers, but the damage had been done. Just as the High Seas Fleet was badly in need of scout cruisers, its table of organisation upon the outbreak of war listed only six of them.

Fortuitously, the airship was there to compensate for the lack — not, of course, immediately, but a 'crash' programme of airship and airship base construction was quickly undertaken. An airship could be produced far more cheaply and quickly than a cruiser. Construction cost of six light cruisers built during 1909–12 averaged £405,494 per vessel,[9] while the cost of eight airships constructed by 20 February 1915 averaged £50,875 apiece.[10] Building time for the same six cruisers ranged from 24 to 33 months; some of the early airships were churned out in as little as five weeks, and only six or seven months were required for construction of later, larger craft.

As the airships began to become available in greater numbers, they not only provided the High Seas Fleet with the scouting craft it needed but permitted the bombing campaign against Britain. But even earlier, they had stimulated development of aviation vessels by the Royal Navy. This started on the eve of the Battle of the Marne, when Churchill agreed to a request by Lord Kitchener, Secretary of State for War, that the RNAS assume responsibility for the aerial defence of Britain, freeing the RFC for field operations on the continent. Still under the belief (unjustified as it was in 1914) that the major aerial threat would come from airships, Churchill inaugurated an aggressive policy toward them. Realising that a proper buildup of defences in Britain itself would take considerable time, he concluded that 'it was no use sitting down and waiting for a year while these preparations were completing. Only offensive action could help us. I decided immediately to strike, by bombing from aeroplanes, at the Zeppelin sheds wherever these gigantic structures could be found in Germany.'[11]

Consequently, attacks were made by land-based RNAS aircraft on German army Zeppelin hangars at Cologne and Düsseldorf — only one of which was successful — as well as the raid on Friedrichshafen previously described. The German advance through Belgium and northern France, however, soon placed such targets beyond aerial range, which had been the case from the start of the German fleet's airship bases. If the latter were to be attacked, it could be accomplished only by aircraft taken by sea to within striking range.

The means for this were at hand in the form of three vessels taken over in August for use as seaplane carriers — the cross-channel passenger ships *Engadine*, *Riviera* and *Empress*. They were selected because of their relatively high speeds — 18 to 21kts — which permitted them to keep pace with battleships, although not with cruisers and destroyers. Crudely converted by addition of fore and aft canvas shelters and seaplane-handling booms, they were originally to have gone to Jellicoe's Battle Fleet at Scapa Flow but as a result of the Churchillian anti-airship offensive were dispatched instead to Commodore Tyrwhitt's Harwich Force. After several false starts, they mounted an attack on Christmas Day 1914 at an airship base the British believed was at Cuxhaven on the German mainland but which was actually some distance from that city. The attack was unsuccessful, but resulted in the first open-water naval battle in which aircraft were the sole striking weapons employed by both sides. Opposing surface warships failed to exchange a single shot, and although both British and German submarines were present they proved ineffective.[12]

A secondary motive for the attack was the hope that the presence of a small surface squadron deep in German waters would lure elements of the High Seas Fleet out to a position where they could be engaged by the Grand Fleet, which sortied in distant support of the raiding force — although too far distant to have intervened had Tyrwhitt's ships been subject to surface action. The Germans, however, failed to rise to the bait, responding only with aircraft and U-boats.

This so-called Cuxhaven Raid set the tone and tactics of British carrier operations in the North Sea and adjacent waters for nearly the entire rest of the war — attempts to attack land objectives, with airship bases ranking high on the target list, coupled with efforts to intercept the Zeppelins in the air.

The winter of 1914–15 demonstrated that something more substantial than canvas was needed to protect the carriers' aircraft from the elements, so in early 1915 all three were fitted with large aft hangars. The same treatment was given to the next converted vessel, the Isle of Man packet *Ben-my-Chree*. These slab-sided structures made the vessels somewhat tricky to handle in strong winds, especially at slow speeds, but served their purpose admirably.

*   *   *

Meanwhile, Jellicoe had finally received an aviation vessel, the former record-setting ex-Cunard liner *Campania*. She had been purchased by the Admiralty in 1914 literally off the scrap heap, for she had been sold for breaking up after long years of hard service on the Atlantic run. She was originally to have become an auxiliary cruiser, but at Sueter's recommendation was converted instead into a seaplane carrier. Her choice for this role reportedly was because she was the best available ship of the requisite size and speed. *Campania,* although old and tired, with defective machinery that made her a very hard-luck lady, is worthy of note because she contributed considerably to the development of British shipboard aviation and was the first vessel to be termed a 'fleet carrier'.[13] As converted, she mounted a platform stretching from bridge to prow from which seaplanes were to take off on trolleys. Using this technique, successful flights by Sopwith Schneider single-seat floatplanes were made in August and November 1915. However, the platform was not long enough for take off by the larger, heavier, two-place seaplanes needed to carry the wireless equipment essential for reconnaissance work. An ingenious solution to this problem was devised: The ship's forward funnel was replaced by two parallel stacks, leading from split boiler uptakes, and the platform extended between them, permitting its use by the larger craft.

By this time the virtual uselessness of the seaplane as an anti-airship weapon had become apparent. Even when a seaplane could get into the air, it could not match the Zeppelin in rate of climb or altitude. But it could seldom get into the air. Repeated attempts during 1915–16 to attack Zeppelins, on the ground or in the air, by seaplanes from the carriers supplemented by others from cruisers, met with failure. Floats broke up, engines failed, propellers splintered, ship wakes caused capsizing, rough seas or fog prevented take-off.[14]

In late July 1915, shortly before the first flights of trolley-mounted seaplanes from *Campania*, Jellicoe, fearing airships might be used to spot for German gunfire in a fleet action, lamented to the Admiralty that 'our seaplanes are incapable of engaging the Zeppelins owing to their insufficient lifting power, and our guns will not be able to reach them. . . . I regret that I am unable to propose any means of meeting this menace, unless it be by the use of aeroplanes [*ie*, landplanes], rising from the deck of *Campania*, capable of climbing above the Zeppelins, and able to land on the water and be supportedly sufficiently long by air bags to allow rescue of the pilots'.[15]

Jellicoe's suggestion was exactly the path that was followed, not only on *Campania* but on the next four vessels in the evolutionary process, which have retroactively been termed 'mixed carriers'.[16] These retained the aft hangar for seaplanes but were fitted with forward ramps for take-off by aircraft with wheel undercarriage. Commissioned at various times between November 1915 and August 1917, the first two, *Vindex* and *Manxman*, were converted from merchantmen already afloat, while the second pair, *Nairana* and *Pegasus*, were modified during construction as merchant vessels.

The ultimate along these lines was the 'large light cruiser' *Furious*, one of Lord Fisher's brainstorms of 1914. She was originally intended to mount two 18in guns, the largest naval ordnance in the world, but while on the stocks was redesigned with an aircraft 'flying-off' platform replacing the forward turret. Many successful take-offs were made from *Furious*, but the problem of how aircraft could return to her remained. Two landings were achieved by an aircraft side-slipping onto the platform, but in a third try the aeroplane, a Sopwith Pup, went over the side and the pilot was killed.[17]

An attempted solution to this problem was replacement of the aft 18in gun with a 'landing-on' platform, but this proved unworkable because the centreline superstructure and funnel were retained, creating extreme air turbulence. Of thirteen landing attempts by Sopwith Pups, their wheel undercarriages replaced by skis, only three were successful — in all the others the aeroplanes were wrecked, lost over the side or damaged in varying degree.

The *Furious* experience, plus wind tunnel tests on various ship models at the National Physical Laboratory, proved conclusively that landing on a platform aft of a centreline superstructure was totally unfeasible. Unfortunately, this knowledge came too late to prevent completion of another vessel featuring the *Furious* configuration of separated take-off and landing areas — HMS *Vindictive*, a redesigned unit of the *Birmingham* class originally named *Cavendish*. She retained a gun armament that placed her in the hybrid category. Use was made of her take-off platform during postwar service in the Baltic, but only one attempt at landing on the aft platform was made — astonishingly, it succeeded.

From the early months of the war, Jellicoe had repeatedly asked the Admiralty to provide him with aviation vessels, requests that grew more urgent as *Campania*'s unreliability became apparent. There had been a spate of proposals for conversion of various warships and/or merchant vessels to the role, but this had been carried out only on those named above. At least one specialised vessel had been designed,[18] but there was reluctance to lay down such a ship, not because the need was unrecognised but, as the air history puts it, 'the demands for cruisers, destroyers, and other . . . classes of warships and the difficulties connected with the evolution of a satisfactory type of vessel for a service as yet in its infancy, prevented any definite programme of construction being embarked upon'.[19]

Finally, probably as a result of one more plea from Jellicoe after Jutland, the Admiralty on 22 September 1916 authorised construction of a carrier, but on a compromise basis: the vessel would not be built from the keel but from an incomplete hull. There were two candidates: liners that had been building for Italy on which work was suspended at the start of the war. The choice, because her machinery was in a more advanced state of completion, was the *Conte Rosso* on the stocks at the Beardmore firm. Thus came into being the world's first flight-deck carrier, HMS *Argus*.

Her construction, however, did not proceed smoothly. Probably as a carry-over from Beardmore's 1912 scheme, the firm's original design featured two parallel superstructures connected over the flight deck. These were about to be emplaced when the experience aboard *Furious* and the wind tunnel tests showed the folly of such a configuration. So it was back to the draughting board for a redesign, featuring a completely flush deck, that delayed the ship's completion until nearly the end of the war.

To the credit of *Argus'* design was the solution, at least partially, of two problems. Engine room gasses, instead of being exhausted through a vertical funnel, were routed through long ducts, parallel to port and starboard, for venting aft on each side of the vessel, and a retractable charthouse was fitted forward, lowered during flight operations.[20]

An experiment aboard *Argus* shortly after her completion led to a lasting feature of carrier design — the offset superstructure that came to be called the 'island'. This configuration had been suggested in 1915 by Hugh Williamson, whom we last encountered as the exponent of use of aircraft against submarines. He carved a crude wooden model of a ship with a starboard island that he showed to John H Narbeth, the Assistant Director of Naval Construction, and the idea was considered on 25 August 1915 by the Admiralty Airship, Aeroplane and Seaplane Subcommittee.[21]

Nothing came of the proposal then, but wind tunnel tests in 1918 indicated that an island would not impede deck landing. To confirm this, Narbeth, then involved in the design of the next flight-deck carrier (the vessel that became HMS *Eagle*, built on the hull of the incomplete Chilean battleship *Admirante Cochrane*), had a large wood-and-canvas dummy island erected on *Argus*. Several take-offs and landings proved the feasibility of the concept, after which the structure was removed.

Subsequently, *Eagle* was completed with an island, as was the next carrier, *Hermes*, the first purpose-designed flight-deck vessel. The island was to starboard, as had been the one on Williamson's model and the mock-up on *Argus*. Williamson wrote later that this location was purely arbitrary,[22] although one might suspect he could have been subconsciously influenced by the right-hand steering position of British motor vehicles. Whether Narbeth was influenced by the Williamson model is debatable. The designer implicitly denied it several years later in his explanation for the choice of position: 'Before setting the island on the starboard side of the *Eagle*', he stated, 'I inquired of many flying men what would happen, and how they would steer, if on approaching a ship they decided that after all they would not land, and in all cases they said they would turn away to the left. This is the reason why the island was placed on the starboard side of the ship.'[23]

Although Narbeth made no mention of it, the choice of turn was dictated by the fact that by 1918 all deck flying had been done by aircraft powered by rotary engines. The whirling mass of a rotary imparted torque that tended to nose an aircraft down in a right-hand turn and up in a left-hand turn. An aviator wanting to abort a landing would naturally seek to turn up and away from the ship rather than down and toward it. Thus starboard placement of the island became a convention that has continued to this day.

Partly because of the perceived threat of the Zeppelin and partly because of its far-flung responsibilities, the British navy created and operated the war's largest and most active fleet of aviation vessels. The navies of Britain's allies and enemies, having little or nothing to fear from airships and functioning generally in more restricted geographical areas, had less need for such ships. These facts resulted in contrasting approaches to shipboard aviation. With a few minor and one major exceptions, the British vessels were employed far more aggressively.

The difference was exemplified in the German approach to aviation vessels. Germany was actually faster off the mark than the Royal Navy, requisitioning two ships for conversion to seaplane carriers eight days before the three British channel packets were acquired. These cargo-passenger vessels, *Answald* and *Santa Elena*, were much more extensively and elaborately remodelled than the British ships but proved unstable, had to be further modified and did not enter service until early 1915. In contrast, the British vessels, although only crudely converted, began operations almost immediately, months earlier than the German. And while the Royal Navy chose relatively speedy ships able to keep up with battleships, the 11kt German vessels were suitable to act only as floating depots for seaplanes performing passive reconnaissance. The same was true for three other merchantmen converted to seaplane tenders.[24]

Only in the Baltic did more aggressive action take place, when *Santa Elena*'s aircraft flew bombing missions against Russian shore installations and ships along the Courland coast. She also helped support aircraft during Operation Albion, the seizure of Oesel, Moon and Dago Islands at the entrance to the Gulf of Riga in October 1917.[25]

It was not until late 1917 that the High Seas Fleet command asked for more capable aviation vessels. Consideration was given to the conversion of one or more of six light cruisers and/or six various merchantmen, but in the end the conversion of only the light cruisers *Stettin* and *Stuttgart* was authorised. Work was completed on only the latter, which commissioned in May 1918 and took part in support of a few minesweeping operations in the Heligoland Bight.

Conversion of the old armoured cruiser *Roon* was broached in August 1918, but construction of submarines took priority over the materials needed for the scheme. Proposals for flight-deck vessels were advanced in October 1918, and a naval officer, *Leutnant zur See* Jürgen Reimpell, came up with a plan to convert the incomplete liner *Ausonia* to that configuration, but the war ended before any serious consideration could be given to it.[26]

* * *

Roles equally as passive as those of the German ships were played by the only two principal French aviation vessels, *Foudre*, the converted torpedo-boat carrier alluded to previously, and the ex-merchantman *Campinas*, both of which operated in the Mediterranean. *Foudre*, after an unproductive foray or two into the Adriatic in 1914, was dispatched to Port Said, where her seaplanes but not the ship herself gave valuable service. Likewise undistinguished were the careers of Italy's sole seaplane tender, *Europa*, and the only one in Russia's Baltic Fleet, *Orlitza*, both converted merchantmen. In both the Adriatic and the Baltic, the relatively short geographical distances in which naval operations were conducted obviated the need for truly sea-going carriers.

Such was not the case in the Black Sea, where, in the major exception mentioned above, the Russian navy emulated and in some respects exceeded the Royal Navy in aggressive use of shipboard aviation. The Black Sea Fleet's principal seaplane carriers were two nearly brand-new British-built cargo-liners, *Imperator Nikolai I* and *Imperator Alexandr I*, converted after being taken over for service as auxiliaries, and a hybrid cruiser-yacht, *Almaz*, built originally as a viceregal yacht for service in the Far East. The three were speedy enough to keep abreast of the pre-dreadnoughts that initially formed the Russian battle line, and even with the two dreadnoughts that entered service in 1915.

The two *Imperator*s were rated as 'hydro-cruisers' (*gidrokresiesera*) and formed a separate division in the fleet, although they did not always operate in company but often independently or in co-operation with other aviation vessels. They and *Almaz* were augmented by five Romanian vessels after Romania entered the war in August 1916. Four of these, all ex-merchantmen, became auxiliary cruisers but all operated seaplanes from time to time. The fifth, *Rominia,* was rated as a 'hydroplane transport' (*gidroviotransport*) but functioned as an active carrier.[27]

The carriers were active from early 1915 to the end of Russia's participation in the war. Their part in the attacks on the Turkish coal ports has been mentioned. Their aircraft also took part in operations off the Bosporus and, after Bulgaria entered the war, the Bulgarian coast and ports. The seaplanes bombed shore installations, ships in port or in coastal waters, spotted for bombardment by battleships and cruisers, flew extensive reconnaissance missions over land and sea, escorted troop convoys, and screened mine-laying operations.[28]

The Black Sea Fleet's aircraft initially were largely Curtiss floatplanes and flying boats, and the latter continued in operational service until well into 1915, making them the first American-designed and American-built naval aircraft to see combat. They were augmented and finally replaced entirely by Grigorovich flying boats.

The 'hydro-cruisers' were able to accommodate as many as eight aircraft, and in conjunction with other carriers on at least two occasions put eighteen or more into the air — the largest number ever flown from shipboard anywhere during the war. Crews became highly adept and skilled at launching techniques — an American observer reported seeing one of the vessels getting seven seaplanes aloft in 15 minutes.

On the tactical level, shipboard aviation was tightly integrated into fleet structure, even more so than in the British navy. Rarely was a Black Sea naval operation undertaken without the presence of a carrier. In some operations against the Anatolian and Bulgarian coasts the carriers were the sole or principal striking units, with battleships relegated to screening. It is no exaggeration to say that the Black Sea fleet pioneered the 'battleship-carrier task force'.

This fact was totally forgotten, if indeed it were ever known in the West, during the interwar years. Russian shipboard aviation ceased to exist for all practical purposes, save for riverine operations during the Civil War. Most of its exponents, including Admiral Kolchak, the last commander of the Black Sea Fleet, and those with the greatest expertise in it, either met death during that conflict or fled far afield, some turning up in the naval air arms of Poland, Spain and the United States. It did not revive in the Soviet Union for many decades, and its First World War achievements were submerged under the myth accepted and propagated by Western historians that the Russian navy of 1914–17 was an inept force whose operations were trivial and irrelevant.

Notes

1. For a thorough discussion of the problems involved in carrier design, see Sir Arthur W Johns, 'Aircraft Carriers', and following comments on it in *Transactions of the Institution of Naval Architects*, Vol LXXVI (London: 1934).
2. The design is described in Johns, op cit, Layman, *Before the Aircraft Carrier*, and Dick [R C] Cronin, *Royal Navy Shipboard Aircraft Developments 1912–1931* (Tonbridge: Air-Britain, 1990).
3. For a survey of many of these schemes, see R D Layman and Stephen McLaughlin, 'Flights of Fancy: Unusual Aircraft Launch and Recovery Systems', *Warship 1993* (London: Conway Maritime Press, 1993).
4. See R D Layman and Stephen McLaughlin, *The Hybrid Warship: The Amalgamation of Big Guns and Aircraft* (London: Conway Maritime Press, 1991).
5. The complete story of the evolution of the British carrier is beyond the scope of this book. The most detailed study is Norman Friedman, *British Carrier Aviation: The Evolution of the Ships and Their Aircraft* (London: Conway Maritime Press, 1988). Among many other useful references are Norman Polmar, *Aircraft Carriers: A Graphic History of Carrier Aviation and Its Influence on World Events* (Garden City, NY: Doubleday & Co, 1969); W G D Blundell, *British Aircraft Carriers* (Hemel Hempstead, Herts: Model & Allied Publications, 1969), and Layman, *Before the Aircraft Carrier*. A good non-technical survey is in Hugh Popham, *Into Wind: A History of British Naval Flying* (London: Hamish Hamilton, 1969).
6. Alfred von Tirpitz, *My Memoirs*, Vol 1 (New York: Dodd Mead, 1919), p181.
7. A definition given in Holger H Herwig, '*Luxury Fleet': The German Imperial Navy 1888–1918* (London and Atlantic Highlands, NJ: George Allen & Unwin and Ashfield Press, rev ed 1987), p36.
8. Quoted in Jonathan Steinberg, *Yesterday's Deterrent: Tirpitz and the Birth of the German Battle Fleet* New York: Macmillan, 1965), p211. The full text of the memorandum is given in this volume in both German and English.
9. Selected at random, these were the *Regensburg, Graudenz, Stralsund, Strassburg, Kolberg* and *Augsburg*. I am grateful to Stephen McLaughlin for supplying the cost figures. Construction times are taken from the 1919 edition of *Jane's Fighting Ships*.
10. Robinson, *The Zeppelin in Combat*, p349.
11. Winston S Churchill, *The World Crisis 1911–1918*, Vol 1 (New York: Barnes & Noble, rep ed 1993), p260. The pagination of this reprint differs from those of previous editions.
12. For a full description of the Cuxhaven Raid, see Layman, *The Cuxhaven Raid*.
13. This term was applied to *Campania* by her commanding officer, Captain (later Air Vice Marshal Sir) Oliver Schwann. In 1917 he anglicised his name to Swann. He is credited with creating the first successful British seaplane in 1911.
14. The long list of failures is detailed in Jones, *The War in The Air*, Vol 2.
15. Quoted, ibid, p364.
16. This was not a contemporary term. It seems to have been used first by Maurice Prendergast in 'Wings and Wheels: Wood and Wire — British Aircraft Carriers, 1914–1924', *United States Naval Institute Proceedings*, Vol 58 No 2, February 1932.
17. The pilot was Squadron Commander Edwin H Dunning. The most detailed description of the incident is in W Geoffrey Moore, *Early Bird* (London: Putnam, 1963), pp99–102. Moore was a pilot aboard *Furious*.
18. The proposed vessel was designed jointly by Lieutenant Gerard Holmes, a former assistant naval architect for the Cunard firm, and Sir John H Biles, a civilian naval architect, in 1915. It was a competitor against the design finally adopted for *Argus*. For details, see Friedman, *British Carrier Aviation*, p62.
19. Jones, *The War in the Air*, Vol 2, pp335–336.
20. For *Argus*' genesis, design, particulars and history, see Friedman, *British Carrier Aviation*; Layman, *Before the Aircraft Carrier*, and Keith McBride, 'The Hatbox': HMS *Argus*', *Warship 1994* (London: Conway Maritime Press, 1994).
21. Reports and Minutes of the Airship, Aeroplane and Seaplane Subcommittee, Adm 116/11140, PRO.
22. Williamson Memoirs, Churchill College, Cambridge University. See also Layman, 'Hugh Williamson and the Creation of the Aircraft Carrier'.
23. From Narbeth's comments on Sir Arthur Johns' paper, *Transactions of the Institution of Naval Architects*, Vol LXXVI, op cit.

24. For details and histories of these and other German aviation vessels, see Dieter Jung, Berndt Wenzel and Arno Abendroth, *Die Schiffe und boote der deutschen seeflieger* (Stuttgart: Motorbuch, 1977), and Layman, *Before the Aircraft Carrier*.
25. For *Santa Elena*'s role in this operation, see Brian P Flanagan, 'Operation Albion', *Cross & Cockade*, Vol 8 No 2, 1967.
26. For details, see Layman, *Before the Aircraft Carrier*.
27. For particulars and capsule histories of these vessels, see Layman, *Before the Aircraft Carrier*.
28. These operations are described in R D Layman, 'Euxine Wings'; Nekrasov, *North of Gallipoli*; René Greger (Jill Gearing trans), *The Russian Fleet 1914–1917* (London: Ian Allan, 1972) [translation of *Die russische flotte im ersten weltkrieg 1914–1917*, Munich: J F Lehmanns], and N B Pavlovich, ed, C M Rao trans, *The Fleet in the First World War*, Vol 1, *Operations of the Russian Fleet* (New Delhi: Amerind Publishing Co, 1979) [translation of *Flot v pervoi mirovoi voine*, Moscow: Ministry of Defence, 1964].

CHAPTER 11

Aircraft for Ships

Although prewar speculation had often concluded that the operation of aircraft at sea would require a special type of surface vessel or modification of conventional warships, it was not at first generally realised that equally specialised or modified aircraft would be needed. The first inkling of this was apprehended when aircraft wingspans began to exceed the beam of many warships. The wings of an aircraft embarked with its fuselage parallel to the ship's fore-and-aft axis could overhang each beam, exposing them to damage from sea or wind, while deck space was usually insufficient to allow carriage with wings stretching fore and aft.

The solution to this problem was the folding wing. In early 1913 the Short Bros aviation firm patented a mechanism permitting wings to be swung back horizontally parallel to the fuselage. The first to feature it was a floatplane introduced later in 1913 that became known as the Short Folder and was active in many early aeronaval operations.

Rights to the patent were purchased by the Sopwith Aviation Company (for a mere £15) and the mechanism was used in its Admiralty Type 807 floatplane, worthy of note because it apparently figures in the layout of the first warships to incorporate aircraft accommodation from the initial design stage. These were the four *Abercrombie* class 14in gun monitors, which featured after-deck stowage space for two seaplanes tailored to almost the exact folded-wing dimensions of the Type 807.[1]

Folding wings were incorporated on nearly all models of Short floatplanes, including the Admiralty Type 184, which, built in large numbers from mid-1915, became the Royal Navy's workhorse two-seater seaplane for the rest of the war. In the 184, folding reduced its wingspan of more than 63ft to slightly more than 16ft, and thus it could be accommodated on light cruisers, most of which averaged around 40ft in beam, and fit into the seaplane carriers' hangars. These vessels had no difficulty in carrying the other principal shipboard seaplanes, the small and nearly identical Sopwith Schneider and Sopwith Baby,[2] which had a roughly 25ft wingspan.

Some other refinements and modifications were necessary for the efficient handling, launching and recovery of seaplanes. Open deck space on conventional warships was often at a premium, making unfolding of the wings difficult while the aircraft was aboard. This led to development of devices by which unfolding could be done from the cockpit after the seaplane was in the water.

Careful attention had to be paid to the placing of spots for attachment of lines from hoisting devices, to keep the aircraft stable while being lowered; otherwise it might pitch into the water at an angle, flooding the engine or damaging the wings, as the Russian navy discovered during experiments with a Curtiss floatplane aboard the Black Sea Fleet collier *Dnepr* in August 1913.[3] Again, it was a case of 'the simplest thing is difficult.'

In general, however, the seaplane did not undergo fundamental changes during the war. The German floatplanes and the small flying boats favoured by the French, Austro-Hungarian and Russian navies required only minor modifications to fit them for shipboard accommodation. Consequently, only slight attention was paid by these navies to design of specialised shipboard aircraft, and only a few prototypes were produced.

The British navy found the Schneider/Baby and the Short 184 quite adequate for shipboard use, but a few more specialised seaplanes were introduced. The first, and the first to be ordered in number, was the Fairey Aviation Company's F 16/F 17, called the Campania because it was intended for employment on the carrier of that name. For that reason, although it was a perfectly conventional two-place floatplane, it has often called the first specifically-designed shipboard aircraft. Actually, this meant principally that its dimensions were tailored to those of *Campania*'s hatches.[4] Three improved Fairey seaplanes, the IIIA, IIIB and IIIC, arrived so late in the war as to see little or no operational service.

*   *   *

Once it had been demonstrated that landplanes could take off from decks or platforms, the question in the Royal Navy was what type of aircraft should be embarked. Initially, the single-seat

The British seaplane carrier *Engadine* after remodelling that fitted the large aft hangar. This configuration was typical of British carriers, although the later 'mixed carriers' featured a forward aircraft launching platform. (J M Bruce/G S Leslie collection)

HMS *Furious* as completed, with her 'flying-off deck' forward and retaining the aft 18in gun. (Author's collection)

HMS *Hector* at the Dardanelles, with an attendant destroyer and trawler, typical of British balloon vessels converted from merchantmen. (P H Liddle from J M Bruce/G S Leslie collection)

A skid-equipped Sopwith Pup alighting on the aft deck of *Furious*. The landing at this stage appeared to be successful . . . (Imperial War Museum)

. . . but it was not. A few moments after the preceding photo was taken the Pup smashed into the crude crash barrier aft of the vessel's centreline superstructure. This was only one of the many unsuccessful attempts to alight aboard the ship. (J M Bruce/G S Leslie collection)

A Fairey F 17 Campania, named for the ship it was intended to operate from. It has often but incorrectly been termed the first aeroplane designed specifically for shipboard operation. (J M Bruce/G S Leslie collection)

A Beardmore WB III shipboard fighter. This aircraft was based on the Sopwith Pup airframe but extensively modified for ease of shipboard accommodation. Although embarked on a number of Royal Navy vessels, it was not a particularly successful type. (J M Bruce/G S Leslie collection)

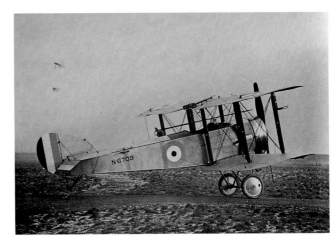

The rear fuselage flotation bag of a Sopwith 2 F1 Camel, a variant of how bags were stowed. This particular aircraft, N 6603, saw service (when it was wearing its fabric) aboard four light cruisers, a battlecruiser and a 'mixed' carrier. (J M Bruce/G S Leslie collection)

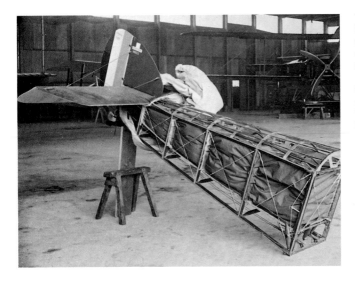

A typical hydrovane installation on a Sopwith fighter, designed to prevent noseover in a touchdown at sea. (J M Bruce/G S Leslie collection)

An aerial photo that was crucial to the operations against the *Königsberg*. The cruiser is visible in the centre foreground, in the first bend in the river. (Author's collection)

The wrecked *Königsberg* in an aerial photo taken after her destruction by air-directed gunfire. Her guns have been removed; they would provide the heavy artillery for the German East African army. (Courtesy of Frank A Contey)

A Nieuport floatplane aboard a British light cruiser in 1915. Nieuports carried by cruisers and a pair of merchant vessels were instrumental in charting the route of the Turkish advance on the Suez Canal in early 1915. (P H Liddle from J M Bruce/G S Leslie collection)

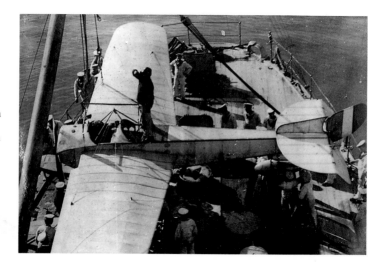

Bristol Scout Model C was employed for anti-airship work, but it lacked performance and armament adequate for the role. The principal Zeppelin fighter remained the Sopwith Baby seaplane.

The question was studied early in 1917 by the Grand Fleet Committee on Air Requirements, appointed by Beatty not long after he took over the fleet command from Jellicoe when the latter was named First Sea Lord. Among the conclusions the committee reached, as stated in a report of 5 February 1917, was: 'There are two distinct duties to be performed by heavier-than-air machines carried with the Fleet which cannot be performed by airships, viz. — Close reconnaissance and attack on enemy Zeppelins. . . . The machines for these two duties are necessarily of totally different design, and after consideration and consultation with technical experts the Committee are definitely of [the] opinion that any attempts at the present time to combine the two duties would only result in impairing their efficiency for either duty, whilst for the purposes of this war it is useless to consider a new design.'[5]

The committee recommended that the Sopwith Pup landplane replace the Sopwith Baby on the carriers *Campania* and *Manxman* 'as this will greatly increase the number of occasions when the anti-Zeppelin type can be flown from the decks of these ships . . .'.[6] The Pup, due to the rapid evolution of the fighter aeroplane as noted in Chapter 1, was becoming increasingly outmoded on the Western Front, but was considered adequate for work at sea, where enemy aerial opposition was less likely to be encountered. The committee's recommendation was accepted, and the Pup became the standard anti-airship machine on *Campania*, the 'mixed' carriers, light cruisers, capital ships and initially on *Furious*.

The shipboard Pup was only slightly modified, mainly by substituting a free-firing Lewis machine gun for the synchronized Vickers. After the advent of the 'landing-on' deck, however, a number, as noted in the previous chapter, had their wheel undercarriages replaced by skids.[7]

Despite the committee's stricture against attempts to develop new types of aircraft for fleet work, some were produced, either at Admiralty behest or as private ventures. The first, a variant of the Pup, appeared later in 1917 — the Beardmore WB III, which, more than the Fairey Campania, may lay claim to be the first aircraft designed specifically for shipboard use. The Beardmore shipbuilding firm had become an aircraft-manufacturing subcontractor for the Admiralty, building Pups and other machines under licence, and eventually set up its own aircraft design section. The WB III's structure was basically a Pup, but there were differences major enough to classify it as a distinct and separate type.

To facilitate shipboard carriage, the WB III had folding wings, a feature made possible by eliminating the Pup's stagger between upper and lower wings. Landing wheels on early models could be tucked up into the bottom of the fuselage; later versions featured a jettisonable undercarriage.

Although a number of the Beardmore aircraft saw operational service, 'the drastic modifications of the Pup design impaired its handling qualities; and it inspired little confidence in aerobatics. It did not distinguish itself in any war-like way although HMS *Furious* had as many as fourteen . . . at one time'.[8]

Two other strikingly original shipboard fighter designs were produced by Beardmore — the WB IV and WB V, the latter initially intended to carry a 37mm gun, and both featuring folding wings and flotation devices. Neither advanced beyond the prototype stage.

The ultimate and most successful shipboard fighter of the war years was the Sopwith 2F 1 Camel, the 'navalised' version of the famous F 1.[9] Although it did not have folding wings, its rear fuselage could be detached to facilitate shipboard stowage, and some versions had a jettisonable undercarriage. Because anti-airship work was the 2F 1's *raison d'etre*, the second synchronised Vickers gun of the F 1 was omitted in favor of a wing-mounted Lewis gun, firing over the propeller arc, 'owing to the danger of firing explosive and incendiary ammunition . . . through the propeller'.[10] The 'Ship's Camel,' as the 2F 1 became known, was superior in all areas of performance to the Pup and the WB III and eventually almost entirely superseded them in the Grand Fleet.

For the 'close reconnaissance' role as described in the Grand Fleet committee's report, the choice fell upon the Sopwith 1½ Strutter. An example of advanced aeronautical technology when it entered service in 1916, it was totally outclassed by 1918 but, like the Pup, quite adequate for work at sea. Not only did it serve aboard *Campania* and *Furious*, but experiments on the battle-cruiser *Australia* proved it could be flown from a turret platform. By the end of the war nearly every Grand Fleet capital ship carried a Strutter for observation and spotting and a Pup, Camel or WB

III as a Zeppelin fighter. Some of the naval Strutters were fitted with detachable wings for handier stowage.

Two fleet reconnaissance/spotter aircraft, both two-seater landplanes, were developed or under development by the end of the war. The first, the Grain Griffin, was a product of the RNAS Experimental Construction Depot at Port Victoria, Isle of Grain. The few Griffins built saw no operational service before the armistice but some were employed in the Baltic during the period of British intervention in Russia.

The second of the specifically designed craft, the Parnall N 2A Panther, was too late for wartime use but was later produced in quantity and served until 1924 on carriers and elsewhere. Like the Griffin, it had folding wings; also, in a unique feature, the rear fuselage could be folded sideways.

* * *

As we have seen, the trend as the war progressed was to replace the seaplane with wheeled aircraft. Not only were these capable of higher performance, they could generally be relied upon to get into the air under conditions when seaplanes could not, without the complications of launching trollies, and, in the case of the small fighters, after extremely short take-off runs permitting shorter and thus lighter flying-off platforms.

Until the arrival of the full flight deck, however, these advantages were offset to a considerable degree by the fact that if the aircraft were out of range of land or suffered engine failure it had no choice but to come down at sea, with inevitable damage to the machine or its complete loss. The light aircraft of the period could usually stay afloat for a time after a controlled splashdown, permitting salvage of the aeroplane and rescue of its pilot if a friendly ship were nearby, but that time was often short. Even in a successful ditching the weight of the engine naturally tended to submerge the nose, sometimes overturning the machine completely. A typical photo of a 1914–18 landplane down at sea shows the engine well below water, the empennage elevated at a high angle and the pilot perched on the rear fuselage awaiting rescue.

All this spurred a quest for methods of minimising damage to the aircraft, lessening injuries to the pilot and lengthening his chances for survival. The jettisonable undercarriage mentioned above was one step in this direction; dropping it lessened the shock of impact and helped keep the machine from overturning.

Another innovation was the hydrovane, a V-shaped, plough-like, one- or two-bladed device jutting forward of the propeller, also intended to prevent overturning as well as keeping the nose from digging too deeply into the water. A smaller version was often fitted to the aft fuselage.

To help prevent an aircraft from sinking and to keep it on an even keel, flotation bags were developed. Usually mounted on the lower forward fuselage, they were inflated by compressed air. Some aircraft were given a combination of bags and jettisonable undercarriage. The bags were generally quite successful; in one experiment a Pup was kept afloat for six hours.[11]

All these devices, in varying combinations, were sported by Pups, Camels, Strutters and WB IIIs as well as other aircraft during the final months of the war. As deck landing experiments demonstrated that means of retarding aircraft were necessary (both to keep them from swerving and to shorten their braking distances), other devices made their appearance — skids (as mentioned above), hooks on undercarriage axles to grasp fore-and-aft lines and/or fuselage-mounted hooks to engage athwartship lines.

*   *   *

Such was the beginning of a process that would eventually differentiate shipboard aircraft sharply from their land-based brethren, a process that would intensify as time passed. The continuing lesson of 1914–18 was that both surface and aerial craft had to undergo transformations to allow them to form a mutually beneficial partnership.

Notes

1. Ian Buxton, *Big Gun Monitors: The History of the Design, Construction and Operation of the Royal Navy's Monitors* (Tynemouth: World Ship Society and Trident Books, 1978), p26. These vessels were also probably the first to be designed from the outset with anti-aircraft guns as standard armament. They never did carry the Sopwith 807, but some of them embarked single Short seaplanes from time to time to spot for shore bombardment.
2. These types differed principally in their engines, although some early Schneiders had wing warping instead of ailerons. The Schneider was often called the 'Schneider Cup Seaplane' because the prototype was built to enter the 1914 Jacques Schneider International Trophy competition for seaplanes. Later versions of the Baby built by sub-contractors incorporated features not found in the original craft.
3. Andrei Alexandrov, 'They Flew in the Russian Sky: The Russian Career of the Early Curtiss Seaplanes 1912–1916', unpublished manuscript.
4. Even so, the combined length of the fuselage and floats required seaplanes to be 'tilted' in carefully, a procedure described in an unpublished manuscript by B G Blampied, an RNAS/RAF officer who served aboard *Campania* in 1918. I am grateful to Phil Tomaselli for a copy.

5. Air 1/648, PRO, in Roskill, *Documents*, p471.

6. Ibid.

7. Various types of skids, some flexible, some to fit into troughs, even one set intended to make magnetic contact with a metallic deck, were experimented with.

8. J M Bruce, *War Planes of the First World War*, Vol 1, *Fighters* (Garden City, NY: Doubleday, 1965), pp70–71. How the modifications to the Pup spoiled its excellent 'performance and handiness' is noted in Moore, *Early Bird*, p99. Moore flew WB IIIs from *Furious*.

9. This aircraft began life as the Sopwith N 5, an improved version of the Baby seaplane, but de-evolved into a modified F 1. For its confusing history, see Bruce, *War Planes*, op cit, Vol 2, *Fighters* 1968.

10. Jones, *The War in the Air*, Vol 5, pp148–149. One Lewis and one Vickers was the standard armament, but there were variations: Some 2F 1s carried twin Vickers (as did a few F 1s used at sea) and at least one was equipped with twin Lewises.

11. David Collyer, 'In and Over "The Drink": Experimental Work at the Isle of Grain', *Air Enthusiast*, March/May 1993.

CHAPTER 12

The Rise and Fall of the Naval Balloon

Although observation balloons had been used in military operations for more than a century before the First World War, that conflict was the first to see them employed in large numbers, not only on land but at sea, where the British navy became their greatest exponent. While the large-scale use of the naval balloon was unique to the First World War and had no lasting influence on the development of naval aviation, it rendered important service at the time, warranting a discussion.

*   *   *

The generally spherical shape of the balloon was maintained for more than a century after its inception. A spherical balloon rode smoothly when floating free, but could be highly unstable when tethered. This eroded its value for military purposes, for except in calm wind it would 'oscillate, bounce and twist in a manner too violent for the strongest of stomachs to withstand'.[1]

The kite balloon, developed in Germany during the 1890s, remedied this through a series of fins and vents that kept it stable in all but the strongest of winds and thus made it a far more reliable observation platform. It was quickly adopted by the armed forces of several nations. The British army, however, clung to the spherical type, mainly because the kite required more elaborate ground equipment and larger handling crews.

Despite their handicaps, the sphericals rendered highly useful service during the Boer War — but the lesson, for inexplicable reasons, was almost immediately forgotten.[2] Practically on the eve of the Great War, the army turned all its lighter-than-air (LTA) craft, including airships, over to the Admiralty — no beneficiant gift, for the small airships had limited range and the balloons were the weary leftovers from the Boer War. Before this, the navy had had virtually no experience with balloons, although it had experimented with man-lifting kites lofted from warships to test the value of aerial observation.[3]

The navy's real association with balloons began in early October 1914 when a balloon section was formed to assist the Royal Naval Division defending Antwerp, but the city had fallen before it could be dispatched. Later that month, Rear Admiral Sir Horace Hood, commanding a naval force supporting the left flank of the Allied forces in Belgium and France, requested balloons to help spot gunfire for his vessels against targets obscured by coastal dunes. In response, a Naval Balloon Section was formed and, equipped with some of the old Boer War sphericals, was sent to Dunkirk. Its work was far from successful; visibility was often poor, the sphericals demonstrated once again their instability and communication was complicated and lengthy, observations of the balloonists being sent 'by telephone to the Belgian Headquarters, thence by messenger to a field wireless station, and thence by wireless to the fleet'.[4]

The British balloonists were quick to note the superiority of the kite types used by the Germans and Belgians, and recommended the adoption of similar craft. The recommendations were heeded, and by March 1915 development of a kite balloon had been undertaken and the RNAS had established a balloon depot and training centre.

The balloon ship entered Royal Navy history shortly thereafter. The first was created at the behest of Major-General Sir William Birdwood, reporting on the army force being massed to occupy the Gallipoli Peninsula should it be required to support the planned naval assault through the Dardanelles. On 4 March he suggested to Kitchener that 'a man-lifting kite or captive balloon would be of great use to the navy not only for spotting long-range fire, but also for detecting . . . concealed batteries'.[5]

'When this request was placed before the Board of Admiralty immediate action followed, and the tramp steamer *Manica* . . . was acquired and hurriedly prepared to take a balloon . . .'[6] In the remarkably short time of seventeen days *Manica* was fitted for her new role by 'fitting a long sloping deck from forecastle to waist, fixing a dynamo to drive a hydrogen compressor, installing [a] winch and connecting it to the main engines, building a wireless telegraphy house [and] building quarters for [aeronautical] officers and men'.[7] Her balloon, since no British type had yet been produced, was French, as was the winch.

Manica arrived in the Aegean on 9 April and proceeded to perform valuable service before, during and after the troop landings that month, especially for spotting naval gunfire against land targets (this and other aerial aspects of the Dardanelles/Gallipoli campaign will be discussed later).

Manica, first of her short-lived breed, was followed by four other balloon ships, *Menelaus, Hector, City of Oxford* and *Canning*, all converted merchantmen that entered service between May 1915 and September 1916.[8] Like *Manica*, their forte turned out to be direction of warship fire against land installations — another example of the use of the air to project sea power ashore. Not long after *Manica* had demonstrated this ability at Gallipoli, Rear Admiral Reginald Bacon, newly named commander of the Dover Patrol, began using balloons to assist bombardment by monitors of the German-occupied Belgian coast.

He was assigned *Menelaus*, but this vessel was too large to venture near the shoreline, where she could come under fire from coastal batteries. Experiments therefore were made in transferring the balloon to the trawler *Peary*, which could approach shore more closely, and this technique was used in a bombardment in September 1915.[9] In early 1917 a steel barge, named *Arctic*, was equipped to operate a balloon and employed for several months, towed by a monitor or trawler.

Such operations, however, were sporadic. As Bacon noted later, 'The general condition of the coast altered so rapidly, and observation by aeroplane improved so vastly, that little opportunity occurred for the use of the balloons. They, however, filled in a gap in the transition stage . . .'[10]

*   *   *

Reports of *Manica*'s work at Gallipoli stirred the Admiralty to suggest to Jellicoe in May 1915 that a similar vessel could be useful to the Grand Fleet. He was initially skeptical, preferring to wait until a practical demonstration of its utility, and proposing that tests be conducted by *Campania*.

Meanwhile, the balloon had not escaped the attention of Beatty. He saw it as a means of nullifying, at least partially, the advantage that airships supposedly gave the High Seas Fleet. Balloons, he wrote in a memorandum of 20 August 1915, 'could often be sent up in weather where it would not be possible to launch a seaplane; probably in weather that would be prohibitive for Zeppelins.'[11]

He repeated this argument on 23 September and succeeded in having a balloon section sent to Rosyth for sea-going experiments under the personal supervision of Rear Admiral Hood, who as noted above had first suggested the use of balloons in 1914 and who now commanded the 3rd Battle Cruiser Squadron. Tests carried out by seaplane carrier *Engadine* proved a balloon could be towed successfully at speeds up to 22kts and could easily reach a height of 3,000ft.

In an enthusiastic report to Beatty on the tests, Hood wrote: 'I think I have proved the value of the kite balloon for reconnaissance purposes; in a suitable vessel the strategic and tactical value will be very great; at 3,000ft there will be a radius of vision of 60 miles and the communication will not be of the sketchy kind in use from aeroplanes, but will be conversation by telephone from a skilled observer sitting comfortably in a basket, to a responsible officer in the balloon ship, who with efficient W/T and all signal books and codes at hand, will rapidly signal by the most efficient method the information . . .'[12]

Here Hood pinpointed the great advantage the balloon had over the aeroplane before aerial wireless had been perfected — the fact that information could be transmitted far more reliably, securely and speedily via a telephone line.[13] It was this advantage that made balloons so useful in shore bombardment.

'I hope', Hood wrote, 'that a proper [balloon] ship may be fitted without delay and if possible one that may have the speed to accompany the Battle Cruiser Fleet.'[14] This echoed the opinion, expressed in April by Squadron Commander J D Mackworth, in charge of *Manica*'s balloon section, that her successes 'warrant the question of properly designed kite balloon ships to be taken up'.[15]

Hood's enthusiasm was shared by Beatty, who in forwarding Hood's report to the Admiralty declared 'the advantage that the enemy has hitherto possessed by the aid of his Zeppelins in obtaining information of the position, composition, disposition, and course and speed of our Fleet will by the use of the kite balloons be in a great measure nullified'.[16] (This was in fact a great exaggeration of what the German airships had actually accomplished.) He proposed that balloons replace some of the seaplanes aboard *Campania*.

Jellicoe, too, now joined in the request for a special balloon ship, preferably of high speed, but the Board of Admiralty, despite its earlier such suggestion to the admiral, turned a deaf ear; 'the demands of large fast merchant ships for other war purposes had first to be met.'[17] Implicit in the refusal was an apparent determination that designing a specialised ship and building it from the keel would be too lengthy a process. The upshot was that during her second remodelling, in which the take-off platform was lengthened, *Campania* was fitted to operate a balloon — as had been advocated by Beatty.

Before this decision had been reached, Rear Admiral Frederick Tudor, the Third Sea Lord, had advanced a compromise proposition — that the existing balloon ships be used as depot vessels to supply balloons to light cruisers. The air history comments that 'This suggestion, which recognised that the real function of the balloon at the time was to extend the range of vision of the scouting screen of the fleet, was not taken up; many tides were to wash against Heligoland before it was finally adopted.'[18]

Before the last of those tides had washed, the role of the specialised balloon ship had ended as a consequence of the course of the war. Valuable as it was to direct naval gunfire against land targets, once activities ashore had moved beyond the range of vision of its observer — which, although considerable, was finite — its utility vanished. *Manica's* balloon, for instance, although it had rendered useful service off East Africa following the abandonment of the Gallipoli campaign,[19] was superfluous after the German coastal enclaves there had been seized. *Canning*, dispatched to Salonika, could do nothing but disembark her balloon section for service on the distant land front.

Moreover, in-shore operation threatened the ships (*Manica* was once hit by an enemy shell off Gallipoli) and their balloons were large, inviting and, because of their hydrogen contents, highly vulnerable targets — although it seems that no shipboard balloon was ever destroyed by either shellfire or aerial attack. Finally, the existing balloon ships could not assist the fleet in high-seas operations; none was capable of more than 13kts — they could not keep pace even with battleships.

Assessing these factors, the Grand Fleet Committee on Air Requirements in its February 1917 report opined that the balloon vessels were tying up more than 400 officers and men 'practically doing nothing' and, since the ships were 'of considerable mercantile value', three of them 'should be paid off as soon as possible'.[20]

Subsequently, *City of Oxford* was converted into a seaplane carrier, *Canning* was retained as a balloon depot vessel, the others reverted to merchant service, and Mackworth's 'properly designed' ship never came into being.

* * *

This was far from the end of the balloon in the Royal Navy. Beatty remained convinced of its value. In May 1917 Vice Admiral Sir John M de Robeck was put in charge of balloon matters, and balloons were used in fleet manoeuvres in July. During the course of these, however, the balloons were spotted by 'enemy' ships before they themselves were seen, and critics charged that balloons would simply reveal the presence of the fleet prematurely. What the air history characterises as 'a lively controversy' arose, but Beatty was adamant, stating in a report to the Admiralty 'the consensus of opinion, 'in which he concurred,' was that the functions of the balloons were sufficiently promising to warrant their retention. They were wanted in the advance line for reconnaissance, and although they might be seen by the enemy, the value of the information which the balloon observers could give would far outweigh the disadvantage of disclosing the presence of the British ships. Balloons would also, when experience had been gained, have a further value as spotting media for guns of the Battle Fleet.'[21]

Moreover, balloons had not only the advantage of superior communications, they could function when sea conditions made seaplane operations impossible, and during a period when land-planes could not return to the ships that launched them.

Beatty's view prevailed, and balloon winches were ordered to be installed on nine battleships, two battlecruisers, the 'large light cruisers' *Glorious* and *Courageous*, four light cruisers and three destroyers. By the end of the war nine more battleships, another battlecruiser and three more light cruisers in the Grand Fleet proper had been equipped to operate balloons, and balloon direction of capital ship gunfire — as Beatty had predicted — had been practiced.

The operational procedure was for the balloon to be inflated ashore, then towed out to the ship. Only a winch was required on board, for it was found that a balloon could be towed aloft for long periods unmanned and need be hauled down only to permit the observer to enter or leave the basket. This eliminated the danger to the vessel of thousands of cubic feet of hydrogen parked on deck and obviated the need for hydrogen generation equipment, stowage space for the gas and screens to shelter the balloon.

* * *

The balloon entered the anti-submarine campaign in 1917, again at Beatty's instigation. By the early months of that year British wireless intelligence had gained considerable knowledge of the routes used by the U-boats in their surface traverses of the North Sea, and in June 'hunting' patrols of destroyers were sent out in attempts to intercept them. There were many sightings and several attacks, but no sinkings. Beatty, believing aerial observation could give greater chances for success, organised a 'Kite Balloon Force' of six destroyers, five fitted to operate balloons, which carried out two 'sweeps' in July. The first accomplished nothing; during the second *U 69* was sunk by the destroyer *Patriot* after her balloon observer guided her to the submarine's submerged site.[22] This first success, however, was also the last — it became apparent that such needle-in-a-haystack searches were unrewarding, even with the assistance of aerial eyes.

A more useful employment of balloons against submarines came after the advent of the convoy system. Lofted from escorting vessels, balloons joined powered aircraft in maintaining surveillance of the sea. There were objections that a balloon would simply serve as a highly visible marker to guide U-boats to convoys, but their prominent presence turned out to be an asset. Submarine commanders apparently quickly learned that their boats could be seen by a balloon observer during the surface approach, even at considerable distances (*Patriot*'s observer spotted *U 69* at a distance of 28 miles).

Thus the balloon, although it posed no threat to a submarine, added to the deterrance that was the greatest contribution of aircraft to the defeat of the U-boats. Like the contribution of airships, that of balloons cannot, in the absence of verifiable statistics, be quantified. It has been claimed that only two ships in balloon-escorted convoys were lost to U-boats; that is probably an underestimate, but it does seem true that few successful attacks were made on convoys possessing balloons.

The faith that the Royal Navy placed on balloons for ASW is indicated by the large number of ships fitted to operate them — destroyers, sloops, P-boats, trawlers and other craft. The exact total is impossible to determine, but by the end of the war it numbered at least 152 vessels, exclusive of those in the Grand Fleet proper.[23] Most ships required little modification to permit balloon operation, but a number of sloops had their mainmasts, gallows and sometimes the after gun removed to facilitate balloon towing and to allow installation of a handling platform.

* * *

No other navy employed seagoing balloons on such a scale. The French navy also began using them for convoy escort in 1917; no official figures are available, but unofficial sources indicate that about 200 balloons were acquired, with at least twenty-four ships equipped to operate them.[24]

The Italian navy, which had been innovative in use of balloons before the war, was laggard by 1918. Official statistics list only sixteen captive balloons by the end of that year.[25] The only specialised balloon vessels were two powered lighters.

The US Navy, which had steadfastly ignored lighter-than-air craft since the Civil War, had exactly two balloons in early 1917 but by the Armistice had acquired more than 200, many furnished by allies but more than half manufactured domestically. However, they equipped very few ships — four battleships, five destroyers and two (perhaps three) patrol vessels.[26] They would have been joined by four other destroyers and three more patrol ships, but a decision to change the type of winches they were to receive delayed installation until too late for them to see service.[27]

Many more shipboard balloons would have been seen had the war continued, for a number of destroyers laid down during the conflict but completed too late for service were fitted with balloon winches. These became objects of mystery in 1939 when two of these ships were being recommissioned from reserve, their purposes having been long forgotten. Much correspondence was required to establish what they were for, and even then it was erronously supposed the balloons were to have been for defence against aircraft.[28]

* * *

The involvement of the US Navy (and to a lesser extent the army) had a far-reaching consequence — the development of means to produce helium on a huge scale. This element, although heavier than hydrogen and thus possessing somewhat inferior lifting strength, had the enormous advantage over hydrogen of being non-flammable. Discovered on the sun in 1868 and on earth in 1895, helium was an exceedingly rare and expensive commodity in early 1917. Only three flasks of it existed, in a chemical laboratory at the University of Kansas, and their contents were valued at $2,500 per cubic foot.

In less than two years, starting from August 1917, a crash programme of scientific and industrial development had made possible its production by millions of cubic feet at a cost of only a few cents per cubic foot. Serendipity played a part, for it is by a geological quirk of chance that the bulk of the world's helium is contained in natural gas deposits in the southwestern United States, but nevertheless the American achievement in so short a period was spectacular.[29] Even so, it came just a bit too late; on Armistice Day 750 cylinders of helium were awaiting overseas shipment from New Orleans.

This was sufficient for only about a single airship inflation, but had the war continued there is no doubt that helium would have replaced hydrogen in Allied airships and balloons, as it has largely in LTA craft since 1918 — including the large fleet of airships operated by the US Navy during the Second World War.

Not only did mass production of helium make lighter-than-air travel far safer than it had ever been before, but more importantly it permitted its use for a host of industrial, commercial and scientific purposes that have benefitted countless millions of human beings. Would this have occurred if the First World War had not generated a demand for airships and balloons, especially naval airships and balloons? That is a question impossible to answer; that it did occur is an example of how attempts to advance aeronautics/aviation could result indirectly in consequences unimaginable at the time.[30]

The shipboard observation balloon was, as noted above, very much a phenomenon of the First World War and did not outlast it long, lingering for only a few years in a few navies. The balloon ship followed it into oblivion; the US Navy completed only one such vessel, the USS *Wright,* of a planned three, but quickly converted it into a seaplane tender.

The balloon's demise can be attributed partly to operational difficulties — mooring lines could snap in rough weather and lightning was a threat[31] — but principally because it became outmoded with the advent of the flight-deck carrier, the shipboard catapult and the long-range flying boat. Aeroplanes, possessing the independent mobility and range the tethered balloon lacked, could carry out fleet functions far more efficiently, especially as aerial wireless communication became more reliable. Useful as the balloon was for a time, it was simply a stop-gap during the formative years of naval aviation.

Notes

1. Cuneo, *Winged Mars*, p13.
2. This use of balloons is described in Percy B Walker, *Early Aviation at Farnborough*, Vol 1, *Balloons, Kites and Airships* (London: Macdonald & Co, 1971).
3. For a survey of the British kite experiments and others in other navies, see R D Layman, 'Naval Kite Trials', *Warship 1994* (London: Conway Maritime Press, 1994).
4. Conrad Cato, *The Navy Everywhere* (London: Constable, 1919), p141.
5. Jones, *The War in the Air*, Vol 2, p33.
6. Ibid.
7. Cato, *The Navy Everywhere*, pp144–145.
8. For details of these vessels, see Layman, *Before the Aircraft Carrier*.
9. The Dover Patrol's balloon operations are described in Jones, *The War in the Air*, Vol 2, and Admiral Sir Roger Bacon, *The Dover Patrol 1915–1917*, Vol 1 (London: Hutchinson & Co, nd).
10. Bacon, *The Dover Patrol*, Vol 1, pp35–36.
11. Quoted in Jones, *The War in the Air*, Vol 2, pp336–337.
12. Quoted, ibid, p368.
13. Before the introduction of the telephone, information had often been transmitted by a telegraph line linking the balloon observer to the ground, a technique first used in the American Civil War.
14. Quoted in Jones, *The War in the Air*, Vol 2, p368.
15. Ibid, p34.
16. Ibid, pp368–369.
17. Ibid, p369.
18. Ibid.
19. *Manica*'s African operations are described in Cato, *The Navy Everywhere*.
20. Air 1/648, PRO, in Roskill, *Documents*, p472.
21. Jones, *The War in the Air*, Vol 4, p38.
22. These operations, and the destruction of *U 69*, are described in Jones, *The War in the Air*, Vol 4, pp63–64. Another account of the submarine's loss can be found in Alan Morris, *The Balloonatics* (London: Jarrolds, 1970), pp96–97. The first of the balloon-assisted sweeps is described in Newbolt, *Naval Operations*, Vol 3, but strangely there is no mention of the second.
23. The total of 152 is deduced from figures given in Air 1/2103, PRO.
24. Jean Labayle Couhat, *French Warships of World War I* (London: Ian Alan, 1974).
25. *The Italian Navy in the World War, 1915–1918: Facts and Figures* (Rome: Office of the Chief of Staff of the Royal Italian Navy [Historical Section]), 1927.
26. The armoured cruiser *Huntington* was also fitted with a balloon but lost it in a squall during her first voyage as a convoy escort in September 1917. The balloon observer was rescued by a ship's crewman who thereby received the war's first Medal of Honour, the highest US military award.
27. Untitled and unpublished manuscript by Noel C Shirley, to whom I am indebted for sharing information from his extensive research into early US naval aviation.
28. John D Alden, *Flush Decks and Four Pipes* (Annapolis: Naval Institute Press, 1965), p21.
29. For a definitive history of this achievement, see Clifford W Seibel, *Helium, Child of the Sun* (Lawrence, Kan, and London: University of Kansas Press, 1968).
30. It is possible, if fanciful, to push this hypothetical question even further: if the German campaign of unrestricted submarine warfare, the proximate cause of US entry into the war, had not been undertaken, would the search for helium have occurred?
31. A harrowing description of how bad weather could affect balloons is given by Admiral of the Fleet Sir Roger Keyes in *Scapa Flow to the Dover Straits: The Naval Memoirs of Admiral of the Fleet Sir Roger Keyes*, Vol 2 (London: Thornton Butterworth, 1935), pp127–128. The frequent loss of balloons to gales and lightning is noted by a First World War aviation ship veteran, Commander R Moore, in 'SS *Campania*,' *Model Maker & Model Boats*, Vol 14 No 168, December 1964. A balloon being lofted by the US battleship *New York* was destroyed by lightning in July 1918 while the King and Queen of Belgium were visiting aboard, giving the royal couple an unscheduled fireworks display. The incident is described in Francis T Hunter, *Beatty, Jellicoe, Sims and Rodman: Yankee Gobs and British Tars, as Seen by an 'Anglomaniac'* (New York: Doubleday, 1919), pp62–63.

CHAPTER 13

The Suez Canal and the *Königsberg*: Reconnaissance and Strategic Success

—————— · ——————

Just as reconnaissance was the most important function of aviation on land during 1914–18, so it was as employed at sea. Equally, that function was more influential on the strategic rather than the tactical level. Strategic reconnaissance by naval aircraft resulted in two major British successes in 1915. The first, and more important, was the repulse of the Turkish assault on the Suez Canal.

* * *

Inklings of preparations for such an attack became apparent almost immediately upon the British declaration of war on Turkey on 5 November 1915, and by the end of the month an offensive was firmly expected. Consequently, 'Air reconnaissances of the Turkish bases and lines of communication to give warning of the enemy intentions would, it was recognised, be essential.'[1] RFC aircraft dispatched from Britain began operations on 27 November, but Turkish staging points across the Sinai Peninsula were beyond their range. Means of overcoming this handicap came in the form of French seaplanes.

To explain this, we must backtrack to the early days of the war, when the seaplane carrier *Foudre* had been attached to the main French fleet, the *armée navale*, which was originally based at Malta. She had accompanied the fleet on a foray or two into the Adriatic but had been unable to accomplish anything useful — nor had two seaplanes that attempted to operate from Lake Scutari in Montenegro. Despairing of finding a role for either the ship or the aircraft, the fleet commander, Vice Admiral Augustin Boué de Lapeyrère, dispatched them in early December 1914 to Port

Said, to be placed at the disposal of Lieutenant-General Sir John
G Maxwell, commander of the British Suez forces. The five aircraft aboard *Foudre*, two-seater Nieuport float monoplanes, were
reinforced by three more the next month.[2]

It was at once realised that if these aircraft were carried by ships
cruising off the Mediterranean coast they would be able to reconnoitre sites beyond the range of landplanes operating from Suez,
and the first such operation off the Sinai Peninsula was carried out
on 10 December by the cruiser *Doris*. Also during December, similar reconnaissances on the right flank of the Suez defence line
were made from cruisers *Diana* and *Minerva* in the Gulf of Aqaba.
All three cruisers also used their aircraft to assist in raids against the
hostile coasts, but these, while disrupting Turkish supply lines to
some extent, were far less significant than the preliminary information gained by aerial observation of the locations and movements
of the forces being concentrated for the attack on the canal.

The most important discovery was that the Turks were abandoning the traditional invasion route along the Mediterranean
coast, where their forces could be observed from the sea and
subject to interdiction by warship gunfire, and instead planned to
advance inland across the Sinai Desert. This would have been a
daunting venture for any 1915 army, but 'towards the end of the
year the Sinai Peninsula was swept by heavy rainstorms which
filled the wells and pools of the desert, thus bringing . . . the gift
of water [and] plans for an early attack on the Canal were thereby
greatly helped'.[3]

This vital information was gleaned in January mainly by the
French aircraft operating from two improvised carriers — the
former German freighters *Aenne Rickmers* and *Rabenfels*, seized at
Port Said in August 1914. They originally retained their German
names and flew the British mercantile flag, until ten months later
they were commissioned into the Royal Navy and were re-
christened respectively *Anne* and *Raven II*, which they will hence-
forth be called.[4]

It was apparently General Maxwell's idea to employ them as
carriers, and in operational (although not nautical) command of
Anne, the first to enter service, he placed Captain L B Waldon of
the Dublin Fusiliers, who had been serving as the general's map
officer. It was a sage choice, for Waldon had spent fourteen years
with the Egyptian Survey Department and had a thorough knowledge of the Sinai Peninsula's topography (after the war he became Egyptian surveyor-general).

Neither *Anne* or *Raven II* received any modifications to fit them for their new role; the Nieuports were stowed on hatch covers (not easily accomplished because of their fixed wings), sheltered by simple canvas covers and handled by standard cargo booms. Initially the ships were not even armed, and *Anne* retained her prewar cargo of timber and antimony. Crude and improvised as they were, both vessels rendered valuable service for many months, eventually becoming units of the East Indies and Egypt Seaplane Squadron (to be described later) and we shall encounter them again in these pages.

Anne, which began her first scouting operation on 18 January 1915, was a vessel of polyglot personnel: the aircraft pilots and mechanics were French, the observers British (some from the topographical service), the crewmen (who proved highly unreliable) were mainly Greek, and there was a sprinkling of Royal Navy seamen and Royal Marines.[5]

Waldon was also charged with landing spies on enemy shores, a task that was carried out, but whatever information they may have obtained was insignificant compared with that gathered by the aircraft. Sustained flights from the two carriers during the rest of January located with precision the movements of the main and subsidiary Turkish columns and obtained fairly accurate estimates of their strength, enabling the British to predict where and approximately when the attack would occur. As a result, troops, as well as the French and British warships that provided the defenders with mobile heavy artillery, were placed in positions well-calculated to repulse the assault when it took place on 3 February.

Repulsed it was, and remarkably easily: 'The climax of the Turkish invasion, so long and elaborately organised, was the passage across the Suez Canal of three pontoons whose occupants were killed or taken prisoner.'[6] A Turkish withdrawal began the next day, a fact revealed by aerial observation. Aircraft tracked the retreat for a time, but the supply of information soon came to a halt 'largely due to the break-down of the hard-worked French seaplanes'[7] which 'for over a fortnight . . . had been flying practically from dawn to dusk.'[8] It has been suggested that their unserviceability at this juncture was one reason for the British failure to pursue the retreating enemy.

The aircraft certainly had seen hard usage — battling adverse winds, struggling (sometimes unsuccessfully) to climb over mountain peaks and plagued by engine-clogging sand, they had nevertheless 'carried out reconnaissance flights which were remarkable, particularly in view of the fact that the forced descent of a seaplane on land meant almost certain death for pilot and observer'.[9] And indeed, a few did become casualties.

The combination of French pilots and British observers proved quite successful, and the latters' reports, according to the Air History, 'for fullness and accuracy compare well with any among official records [and] gave much information of military value'.[10] That judgement is confirmed in many sources, including even the British naval history, which usually scants aerial activity.

In passing, it should be noted that the aircraft occasionally made bombing attacks during the Turkish advance and retreat, but the missiles were too few, too light and too inaccurate to have had any appreciable effect — the seaplanes' bomb sight has been described as 'a barbaric affair consisting of two nails driven into the fuselage as reference, and a sandglass'.[11]

With hindsight, the Turkish assault was a forlorn venture as far the aim of obtaining permanent occupation of the canal may have been intended. Logistical difficulties alone, in light of Allied dominance of coastal waters from Smyrna to Port Said, would inevitably have forced a withdrawal. It seems, rather, to have been more in the nature of a large-scale raid, 'to get command of a part of the Suez Canal for long enough to allow of ships to be sunk and such other action to be taken as might close the Canal permanently.'[12]

That a permanent closing could have been effected is highly improbable, but the severance of only a few weeks of the aorta to India, the 'crown jewel' of the British Empire, would certainly have had considerable repercussions. It would have been a severe blow to Allied prestige, disheartened the British populace and government (with possible political consequences), and probably have caused changes in dispositions of British naval and military forces, perhaps disrupting preparations for the Dardanelles campaign. Conceivably, such a *coup* by an Islamic nation could have stiffened resistance to British Empire rule among its millions of Moslem subjects, possibly even to the point of revolt — a possibility long of serious concern at Whitehall, where memories of the Great Mutiny had not faded.

Such speculation is otiose, of course, for none of these things happened. But that they did not is due in large measure to a handful of seaplanes and two nondescript merchant ships. It was the first demonstration of how surface vessels and aircraft could form a symbiotic relationship allowing them to exert in combination an influence on strategy that neither could have exerted independently.

* * *

The second major success in 1915 was the elimination of the German light cruiser *Königsberg* as the final threat to the Indian Ocean trade routes. This vessel, stationed at Dar-es-Salaam in German East Africa at the outbreak of the war, had sunk a merchant vessel and the British cruiser *Pegasus* and then, sustaining engine trouble, had taken refuge in the Rufiji River delta until repairs could be made (accomplished by having native labourers haul the defective machinery to Dar-es-Salaam and back again, a process that took several weeks).

Although not as successful or notorious as her near-sister, *Emden, Königsberg* was deemed an equal menace to merchant shipping as well as troop convoys from India and Australia, and her disappearance after mid-September only heightened apprehension. Fear of her caused the French *Messageries Maritimes* to hold seven vessels at Diego Suarez for two months[13] and Churchill to direct that even individual troop transports be given warship escort.

Responsibility for locating and neutralizing *Königsberg* fell upon Vice Admiral Herbert G King-Hall, commander-in-chief of the Royal Navy's Cape Station. It was a formidable task; even had he known she was in the Rufiji delta, that area was an admirable hiding place — a muddy maze thirty miles wide, with eight mouths to the river, innumerable small waterways, large swamps and masses of confusing vegetation. *Königsberg* had the advantage that shortly before the war the area had been charted by the German survey ship *Möwe*, while to the British it remained *mare incognita* until by chance copies of German charts were found aboard the liner *Präsident* when she was seized on 19 October. These gave the British some hydrographical information on the delta but more importantly permitted them to deduce where *Königsberg* could be expected to be found in it. And so she was, barely visible, on 30 October by cruiser *Chatham* of King-Hall's squadron. Other cruisers soon arrived, and a months-long blockade began.

Locating *Königsberg* was one thing; dealing with her was another, for she simply moved upriver beyond sight of the cruisers and also out of range, for the British ships drew too much water

(2 to 4ft more than the German vessel) to enable them to follow her. As the weeks went by the Germans erected a series of entrenchments, armed with machine guns and small-calibre cannon, and observation posts along the river banks. Meanwhile, a British collier was sunk to block one of the delta's outlets, but other main channels were still open to her.

The full story of the *Königsberg* siege is long and complicated, beyond the scope of this study. Suffice to say it was quickly realised that what was required to extirpate her were shallow-draught vessels able to penetrate the delta, plus aircraft to locate her. An initial request for these was refused; the only suitable ships were busily engaged off the Belgian coast and no aircraft could be spared.

Admiral King-Hall, however, discovered there were two Curtiss flying boats at Durban, owned by a South African mining engineer who had hired a British civilian aviator, H Dennis Cutler, to fly them. King-Hall arranged to hire one of them, co-opted Cutler into the RNAS with a temporary commission, and dispatched both to Niororo Island, 18 miles northeast of the delta, aboard the auxiliary cruiser *Kinfauns Castle*. (The second Curtiss was cannabalised later to provide parts, including even the hull, damaged on the first.)

Cutler's first flight on 19 November nearly ended in disaster when he lost his bearings, had to come down at sea, and was not discovered for six hours. The flying boat's radiator was damaged, but replaced by one from a Ford automobile, and on 22 November Cutler spotted *Königsberg* up the river. The cruiser now could be kept under surveillance, but there were still no means of attacking her. Even the surveillance ended when on 10 December the Curtiss was lost to a combination of engine failure and ground fire and Cutler was captured.

An aerial hiatus followed until arrival at Niororo on 21 February 1915 of two Sopwith 807s and a party of RNAS personnel dispatched by the Admiralty in response to another request by King-Hall. It had been intended to use these seaplanes to bomb *Königsberg*, but the hot and humid climate wreaked havoc on their fabric, fittings, floats and engines: '. . . the first attempt to get off the water was made with a load of two 50lb and four 16lb bombs, full petrol, and an observer. This proved hopeless. By a process of elimination. . . one of the seaplanes at last got away with only the pilot, without bombs, and with but one hour's supply of petrol. Even then the seaplane would not go above 1,500ft, and all hopes of the immediate destruction of the *Königsberg* by bombing vanished' and 'before the first week had passed one of [the Sopwiths] had been wrecked beyond repair.'[14]

In March the Admiralty finally assigned to King-Hall the shallow-draught vessels for which he had been pleading. They were the river monitors *Severn* and *Mersey,* two of three ships completed in early 1914 for Brazil but which had remained in the builder's possession when that nation was unable to pay for them. Taken over by the Royal Navy at the start of the war and renamed, they had served off the Belgian coast and then laid up for refits in which the armament of *Severn* and *Mersey* was altered and rearranged. In March they were at Malta, where they had been sent in hopes of operating them on the Danube if the Dardanelles expedition succeeded.[15]

Towed out from Malta, they arrived off the Rufiji on 3 June, basing at Mafia Island, which had been captured from the Germans in January, was closer to the delta, and became the main British naval and air centre. The monitors' average 6ft draught would permit them to enter the delta and their armament of two 6in guns each would be adequate to cope with *Königsberg,* although her 4.1in guns outranged the British 6in.

Meanwhile, another contingent of aircraft had arrived in late April — three Short Folders. These were old, very weary machines, having seen hard service in the North Sea (two of them had taken part in the Cuxhaven Raid).

They were only marginally superior to the Sopwiths, but could be flown with a two-man crew, and soon had *Königsberg* under observation again. Although one was damaged by German fire on the first flight, on 25 April, its observer took photos of the cruiser that were to be of considerable value later in the operation. One Short was lost to ground fire on 5 May.

A more substantial aerial reinforcement arrived shortly in the form of four landplanes — two Caudron G IIIs and two Henry Farman F 27s (the latter with steel airframes that could better resist the climate), along with wireless sets that would allow them to spot for the monitors. A field was cleared for them on Mafia and a hangar erected.

Three weeks were required to make the monitors serviceable again after their long and harrowing passage from Malta, and then time was needed for ships and aeroplanes to practice the virtually untried technique of aerial fire spotting. During this period one of the Caudrons and one of the Farmans were wrecked in crashes. On July 2 one of the remaining two tried unsuccessfully to bomb *Königsberg.*

The attack on the cruiser finally began on 6 July, preceded by another unsuccessful bombing run intended as a diversion as the monitors entered the delta. The day's results were mixed; *Königsberg* took three hits, but gave as good as she received, her highly-accurate fire, directed by observation points ashore, causing the monitors to shift position several times and inflicting damage and casualties on both.

In a port-mortem after they had withdrawn to lick their wounds, it was determined that of more than 600 shells fired the aerial observer had been to spot the fall of only seventy-eight. This was primarily because the monitors fired simultaneously, making it difficult for the observer to ascertain whose shots were hitting where. After a few days to sort this matter out and repair the monitors, the attack was renewed on 11 July, this time successfully. Guided by the Farman, *Severn* hit *Königsberg* with her eighth salvo and thereafter, but fire from the cruiser downed the aircraft (its occupants were uninjured). The Caudron took over and by 1450hrs *Königsberg* was a flaming hulk. The victory was marred by a bad landing that wrecked the Caudron, and it was not until early August, with arrival of new G IIIs, that aerial reconnaissance could confirm the success conclusively. The British did not wait for this to celebrate. Amid glad cries, the remaining Folders were ceremoniously burned on 13 July, and two days later a gala dinner was held, featuring 'soup a la Rufiji' and 'dessert de Keonigsberg' [*sic*].

The victory had one marring aftermath — *Königsberg*'s 4.1in guns were removed and, mounted on improvised carriages, provided the heavy artillery for the German field forces that tied down more than 200,000 Allied troops in interior Africa for the entire rest of the war.

Königsberg's demise was followed by a series of coastal amphibious operations, assisted by *Manica* (now equipped to operate a seaplane as well as her balloon) and aircraft embarked on auxiliary cruisers, which by the end of 1916 had put virtually the entire coast of German East Africa under British control. RNAS units subsequently served inland, assisting Allied forces in their vain pursuit of the elusive German army commanded by Lieutenant-Colonel (later Lieutenant-General) Paul von Lettow-Vorbeck.

In one of the most unusual episodes of the war in Africa, one of four Short seaplanes turned over to the Belgians succeeded in inflicting bomb damage on the German armed steamer *Graf Goetzen* on Lake Tanganyika on 10 June 1916.[16]

* * *

It is the modern view that once *Königsberg* was bottled up she ceased to be a factor in the naval war and could simply be ignored, but that does not seem to have the opinion at the time. Despite the rigour of the blockade, there remained a lingering fear that she might slip out to disrupt the trade routes again. Her destruction ended this forboding, enabled merchantmen to ply the Indian Ocean freely, and reduced the need for troopship escort. Moreover, it released a number of ships to be employed more profitably elsewhere. The 7½-month siege had tied down, at one time or another and for various periods, two battleships, ten cruisers and at least six additional ships, not to mention colliers and other auxiliaries. Thus, the *Königsberg* operation can be considered a strategic as well as a tactical triumph for naval aviation. Despite the many setbacks and long delays, it was only by aircraft that the cruiser could be accurately located, kept under sustained surveillance, and finally eradicated.[17] By coincidence the next German cruiser to be named *Königsberg* also fell victim to aviation, sunk by Fleet Air Arm dive bombers in 1940.

Notes

1. Jones, *The War in the Air*, Vol 5, p160.
2. Some sources list only two additional aircraft. Some of the Nieuports had been built for Turkey and were confiscated at the outbreak of the war. Nieuport floatplanes were fairly widely used by the French navy during the early war years but were later superseded by various models of flying boats.
3. Jones, *The War in the Air*, Vol 5, p160.
4. For details of these vessels, see Layman, *Before the Aircraft Carrier*.
5. Weldon describes his experiences with *Anne* in *'Hard Lying': Eastern Mediterreanean 1914–1919* (London: Herbert Jenkins, 1925).
6. Jones, *The War in the Air*, Vol 5, p163. For the story of the Turkish repulse, see Corbett, Vol 2, and Sir George MacMunn and Cyril Falls, *Military Operations, Egypt & Palestine*, Vol 1, *From the Outbreak of War With Germany to June 1917* (London: HMSO, 1928).
7. MacMunn and Falls, Vol 1, p49.
8. Ibid, fn.
9. Ibid, p29. An extensive description of the seaplanes' work from the carriers and earlier from the cruisers is given, virtually flight by flight, in Dick [R C] Cronin, *Royal Navy Shipboard Aircraft Developments 1912–1931* (Tonbridge, Kent: Air-Britain, 1990).
10. Jones, *The War in the Air*, Vol 5, p161.
11. Stephen Nelsen, 'French Naval Aircraft', *Cross & Cockade*, Vol 7 No 3, 1966.
12. Jones, *The War in the Air*, Vol 5, p162.
13. Keith Middlemas, *Command the Far Seas: A Naval Campaign of the First World War* (London: Hutchinson, 1962), p15.
14. Jones, *The War in the Air*, Vol 3, p6.
15. For details and histories of these vessels, see Buxton, *Big Gun Monitors*.

16. I A Grant, W H Bidgood and C de Saint Hubert, 'Belgian Air Operations Over Lake Tanganyika', *Naval Notebook*, No 3, 1979. Only sixteen copies of this publication exist.
17. Sources on the Rufiji operation abound. I have relied mainly on *The War in the Air*, Vol 3; *Naval Operations*, Vols 1 and 3, and the highly detailed account in Cronin, *Royal Navy Shipboard Aircraft Developments*, which reproduces the menu of the British victory dinner. Also useful were Middlemas, *Command the Far Seas*, Cato, *The Navy Everywhere*, Arthur Pollen, *The Navy in Battle* (Toronto: McClelland, Goodchild & Stewart, nd), and Edward L Leiser, 'Loss of the *Konigsberg*', *Cross & Cockade*, Vol 13 No 4, 1972. Pollen includes a long first-person narrative by an unidentified officer aboard *Severn* and also an extended discussion of the problems involved in indirect fire control — this, however, should be read with some caution, for Pollen had an axe to grind as the deviser of a fire-control system that lost to a rival method in competition for adoption by the Royal Navy, although most modern critics believe his system was superior; see Jon Tetsuro Sumida, 'British Capital Ship Design and Fire Control in the Dreadnought Era: Sir John Fisher, Arthur Hungerford Pollen, and the Battle Cruiser', *Journal of Modern History*, Vol 51 No 2, 1979. Leiser's article is based in part on the memoirs of Harold E M Watkins, who as an RNAS flight lieutenant was the pilot of the Caudron on 6 and 11 July. He rose postwar to the rank of RAF wing commander; the last survivor of the Rufiji aerial campaign, he died in 1971 at the age of 91. A more recent account of the *Königsberg* saga, aimed at the general reader but well-researched and accurate, is given in Dick Houston, 'The Admiralty's orders were clear: "Sink or destroy the *Königsberg*" ', *Smithsonian*, Vol 20 No 6, September 1989.

CHAPTER 14

The Dardanelles and Gallipoli: Reconnaissance and Strategic Failure

———— · ————

Probably more forests have been felled and more oceans of ink spilled in works devoted to the operations that can be lumped together as the Dardanelles/Gallipoli campaign than for any other purely military aspect of the First World War save the Western Front. The campaign's genesis, planning, execution, ramifications and aftermath have been, and continue to be, ceaselessly discussed, described, analysed, argued over and evaluated. Although a failure, it has been hailed as perhaps the most brilliant strategic initiative of the war; because it failed it has been condemned as perhaps the worst. It remains one of history's most tantalising 'what ifs'.

So vast and complex a subject is far beyond the scope of this book and the competence of its author to describe; the discussion will centre on the influence of aviation on the venture.[1]

*   *   *

Originally, the operation was to be strictly naval. A Franco-British fleet would steam through the Dardanelles, the narrow strait that separates European Turkey and its Gallipoli Peninsula from the Anatolian mainland, cross the Sea of Marmora and reach Constantinople, the capital, heart, nerve centre and major metropolis of the Ottoman Empire. What this fleet was supposed to do once it got there is disputed, but the assumption was that its presence would cause Turkey to quit the war, thus restoring the flow of Ukrainian grain to the West, open an all-weather supply line to Russia, free Russian forces fighting Turkey for use elsewhere and induce the Balkan states to (at best) join the Entente or (at least) remain neutral. In essence, a very simple strategy — but again, 'the simplest thing is difficult'.

Concealed under the mass of verbiage surrounding the naval plan, but breaking surface enough times to become apparent, is the fact that *the existence of aviation* was a major factor, perhaps a crucial one, underlying the decision that the operation was strategically viable.

To apprehend this, one must understand the prevailing opinion in regard to ships engaging land fortifications — in which the Dardanelles abounded, especially on the European side. It was considered axiomatic that ships were at a great disadvantage when confronting land artillery able to deliver high-angle plunging fire against decks, which were more lightly armoured than the sides, to which vessels could reply with only relatively low-trajectory fire.

In early 1915, however, aviation promised a means of overcoming the naval disadvantage. Wireless-equipped aircraft could guide indirect fire by warships standing outside the range and/or sight of land artillery and observe the results, signalling required changes of range and direction. Here it seemed was the solution to the problem of cracking the Dardanelles, offering a way of neutralizing the forts on the seaward sides of the Gallipoli Peninsula and Asiatic Turkey. The idea appealed to the air-minded Churchill, as well as to other naval officials.

That the potential offered by aviation exerted a strong influence on the decision to proceed with the operation cannot be doubted. Of the reasons for that decision, the British air history declares, 'One of the chief was the new air weapon. The effectiveness of naval bombardment . . . was enormously increased by this new power of observation.'[2] This assessment virtually repeated the earlier prediction by Maurice Hankey, the influential secretary of the War Council, that 'the value of naval bombardment . . . would be enormously increased' by the use of aircraft. A more recent historian agrees on the influence of aviation: 'It is clear that the enhanced capabilities which air observation was expected to give to naval guns played an important part in the decision to go ahead with the naval bombardment.'[3]

The value of aerial reconnaissance and spotting was clear to Vice Admiral Sir Sackville H Carden, who had been commanding a naval squadron positioned off the Dardanelles to intercept *Goeben* and *Breslau* should they reappear, and who was the choice to head the naval expedition should it be approved. Asked by the

Admiralty to estimate the type and number of ships he would require for the venture, he included in his reply of 11 January 1915 'four seaplanes, and the *Foudre*', and declared 'frequent reconnaissance by seaplanes indispensable'.[4]

Use of *Foudre* and her seaplanes also was recommended by Vice Admiral Sir Henry Jackson in January in an assessment asked for by the Admiralty War Staff, to which he was a consultant.[5] He added that 'Seaplanes with incendiary and other bombs should be in readiness to assist by every means in their power in the work of destruction and reconnaissance.'[6]

That *Foudre* should be suggested and requested was logical. Although the British cruisers had proved that seaplanes could work from warships, *Foudre* was the sole vessel afloat in the entire Mediterranean with the facilities to maintain and repair aircraft. Even more significantly, the French Nieuports were the *only* Allied seaplanes of any type available in January. As late as early March, the Admiralty cabled Port Said to send six of them to the Dardanelles[7] — an order impossible to obey, for two had been lost, three were aboard *Anne*, which was with a battleship/cruiser force operating in the Gulf of Smyrna, and two were aboard *Raven II* off the Palestine coast, leaving no more than one at Port Said.

Why this directive was issued is puzzling, for Churchill had a more potent aerial ace up his sleeve, and he had already played it — the seaplane carrier *Ark Royal*. *Ark Royal* was not mentioned in a previous chapter discussing the evolution of the British aviation vessel, for she did not figure in the line of descent. She was *sui generis*, the first British aviation vessel, authorised under the pre-war 1914–15 naval estimates as the result of experience gained by the cruiser *Hermes'* operation of seaplanes during 1913 manoeuvres.

Ark Royal has almost always been called a mercantile conversion, but that is true only in the most tenuous sense. Her builders' original plans do indeed show a typical 'tramp steamer' of the period, with superstructure and machinery amidships and cargo holds fore and aft.[8] But when purchased in May 1914 she was in a very early stage of construction, and upon completion the only vestiges of her mercantile origin were the keel and basic frame. A radical redesign placed superstructure and machinery right aft, leaving a long, unobstructed, sheerless upper deck. This apparently was intended to permit take-off by seaplanes on trollies or, it has been suggested, landplanes on their wheels. To further rid this deck of obstacles, the anchor cables were worked from the next deck below.

The design pioneered a basic feature of future carriers, an internal below-deck hangar. Access to it was gained by a large sliding hatch; seaplanes were handled by steam cranes on each beam. It can truly be said that *Ark Royal* was the first ship designed and built as an aviation vessel, and the last such for some time, all the other wartime examples down to *Argus* being converted or modified merchantmen or warships. As such, and because of her features, highly unusual for the time, she can be considered the primogenitor of the aircraft carrier in the same sense as USS *Monitor* was the primogenitor of the dreadnought.[9]

Ark Royal was completed in early December 1914 and was working up as plans for the Dardanelles were taking shape. Churchill was quick to enlist her in the operation. In a 13 January 1915 memo to Fisher he wrote: 'The director of the Air Department [Sueter] should be instructed to hold *Ark Royal* with eight seaplanes and aeroplanes in readiness for service "in Egypt". We cannot rely on French seaplanes for our spotting. The Army have developed a system of wireless telephone from aeroplanes spotting for artillery, which is most effective. Full details of this should be at once obtained, and some of the machines fitted accordingly. Meanwhile the French should be asked not to fly over the Pola [code name for the Dardanelles] area, as it will only lead to the mounting of Anti-Aircraft guns and complicate spotting later.'[10] (To close the books on *Foudre*, it may be mentioned that she and some of her seaplanes did take part in the operation, from 15 March to 23 May, but the Nieuports, lacking wireless communication, were useless for spotting — as Churchill had foreseen.)

Ark Royal sailed for the Aegean on 1 February with six seaplanes — two Wight Type A 1 Improved Navyplanes, large pusher-engine machines; three Sopwith 807s, and the Short Admiralty No 136, one of the models intermediate between the Folder and the Type 184 and which the ship's captain, RNAS Wing Commander/RN Commander Robert H Clark-Hall, termed the 'most valuable and only rough-weather seaplane on board'.[11] There were also four Sopwith Tabloids, single-seat landplanes. Among the complement of RNAS aviators — including several destined for high rank and influence in the future Royal Air Force — was Hugh Williamson, mentioned earlier in these pages.

The ship arrived on 17 February at the Greek island of Tenedos. This island and nearby Lemnos, which was the main base of the Franco-British fleet, had become available thanks to the pro-Allied Greek Prime Minister Eletherois Venizelos.

Tenedos, Lemnos and other Aegean islands, formerly Turkish, had come under Greek occupation as a result of the First Balkan War, but Turkey refused to abandon *de jure* sovereignty over them. Venizelos' ploy had been to remove their Greek garrisons, which, because of Turkey's continuing claim, made them nominally 'enemy' territory and so open to Allied occupation. Thus did the isles of Greece where burning Sappho loved and sung become naval and air bases.

By now Carden's fleet was growing to a strength of sixteen pre-dreadnought battleships (twelve British, four French), stiffened by the battlecruiser *Inflexible* and the brand-new dreadnought *Queen Elizabeth*, whose 15in guns were the largest naval ordnance afloat, plus a host of supporting vessels including mine-sweeping trawlers.

The first flights were attempted immediately upon *Ark Royal*'s arrival and were an ominous harbinger of the future — engine trouble kept two seaplanes on the water and a third could not 'unstick' in a calm sea.

The bombardment of the outer Gallipoli forts began on 19 February and continued in fits and starts for the next month. It became clear immediately that Churchill and others had been hopelessly over-optimistic in their belief that aerial spotting would solve all the problems. Valid as the technique was in principle, it was in practice plagued by a host of technical and tactical difficulties that had been unforseen or unsuspected — or if suspected, ignored. It apparently had been assumed that the seaplanes could fly whenever and wherever required, but this, of course, was far from the case. They had to depend on a benign sea — neither too rough nor too calm — to get airborne, and the sea was often uncooperative. Time and again take-offs were thwarted by sea conditions. Further, a successful take-off did not guarantee a safe return, for floats and their struts had a nasty habit of collapsing when they hit the water, often necessitating lengthy repair.

Another major problem was engine failure, which occurred with frustrating frequency. As I have written elsewhere, Clark-Hall's 'description of the various failures reads like a catalogue of every conceivable trouble to which an internal combustion engine can be subject'.[12] The problem is exemplified by Short No 136, the most reliable aircraft — it made twenty-six flights between 17 February and 31 May, during which it sustained sixteen engine failures.

Once the seaplanes were aloft, the low horsepower of their engines relative to weight of airframes and payload often prevented them from reaching altitudes from which spotting was effective. As Arthur Marder put it, in a greatly oversimplified but crudely accurate assessment, 'they were unable on account of the weight of their floats to fly high enough to do their job properly'.[13]

Unreliability of air-to-surface communication was another handicapping factor. The wireless sets, manufactured by the Sterling Telephone Company to the design of an RNAS officer, were barely out of the experimental stage and plagued by bugs nobody yet understood. Moreover, there were originally only two sets, so if a seaplane carrying one became unserviceable the bulky apparatus had to be transferred to another.

Undoubtedly, however, the greatest obstacle to success was total inexperience in techniques and methods for aerial spotting for naval gunfire. This was entirely novel; as far as can be ascertained, only once before the war had there been such a test in the Royal Navy — a brief experiment in 1907 by the battleship *Revenge*, utilising a man-lifting kite, and British warships had not practised or carried out large-scale firing at shore targets since the bombardment of Alexandria in 1882.

Thus aerial observers and warship gunnery officers at the Dardanelles had to devise an *ad hoc* system of signalling and coding on the spot under combat conditions, with no experience or precedents to guide them, complicated by the fact that the wireless sets could transmit but not receive.

Despite all these handicaps, some progress was made. Several of the older forts, with high parapets and unconcealed guns, were silenced by air-guided bombardment. But more modern works survived, and the naval guns were unable to deal with the mobile howitzers (many of Austro-Hungarian manufacture) with which the peninsula was being reinforced.

By mid-March, Admiral Carden, encouraged by preliminary success in minesweeping and aerial reports of damage inflicted on the outer defensive works, decided it was time to advance up the strait and engage the forts at its slimmest point, called The Narrows. He scheduled the operation for 17 March. But just at this juncture, the admiral, suffering a breakdown in health, abruptly resigned his command, citing medical advice. He was succeeded by his second in command, Vice Admiral John W de Robeck. This delayed the operation by one day.

The Allied debacle of 18 March has been so often and thoroughly described that no exposition is needed here. In summary, the British battleships *Irresistable* and *Ocean* and the French *Bouvet* were sunk by mines, which also heavily damaged *Inflexible*, and the French *Gaulois* and *Suffren* were severely damaged by gunfire. The minesweeping trawlers were forced to retreat under a hail of howitzer fire. *Ark Royal*'s seaplanes were supposed to supply a running reconnaissance of the bombardment, but the first could not get into the air until an hour after it started.

The main cause of the slaughter was a line of mines parallel to the Asiatic shore put down by the little Turkish minelayer *Nousret* on 8 March and which had gone undetected. The *Ark Royal* fliers had previously been able to spot mines, but failed to see these — possibly, it has been suggested, because their colour blended with that of the strait's bottom.

Although a few firebrands, such as Roger Keyes, pressed for a renewed effort, the defeat put paid to the purely naval venture. The fleet had been caught in a vicious dilemma: guns that could not be silenced until mines were swept, mines that could not be swept until guns were silenced.

* * *

The view quickly arose and persisted that the failure was the fault of aviation, specifically because the aircraft were seaplanes. This was one of the main conclusions of the so-called Mitchell Report, one of the numerous autopsies of the operation.[14] All hands became united in the belief that things would have gone swimmingly if only land-based aircraft had been available. As the Mitchell Report put it, 'The lack of aeroplane observation was throughout the operations found to be the heaviest handicap.'

It is imperative to understand that in this and other criticisms and analyses, *aeroplane* in British parlance of the period (and for a long time afterward) meant strictly a heavier-than-air machine with wheel undercarriage — the craft this book, for want of a better term, calls a landplane.

Even Churchill joined the chorus, writing later that 'Had aeroplane observation been possible, there is little doubt that great damage would have been done to the forts' and complaining of 'inadequate arrangements for observation from the air'[15] — strange words from one who had borne heavy responsibility for making those arrangements.

British seaplane carrier *Ark Royal* (left foreground) at Kephalo Bay, Imbros. In the background are (from left) the French battleship *Henri IV*, the British battleship *Exmouth* and the British cruisers *Bacchante* and *Edgar*. (J M Bruce/G S Leslie collection)

A French Voisin of No 3 Wing, RNAS, at Imbros in August 1915. This unit, equipped with a mixed bag of French and British aircraft and supplemented by *Ark Royal*'s seaplanes, bore the brunt of aerial operations during the early phases of the Gallipoli campaign. (Brian P Flanagan collection via August G Blume)

Zeppelin *L 53*, one of the first 'height climbers,' emerging from her shed. The last German airship to be lost in the war, perished aboard was her commander, *Kapitänleutant der Reserve* Eduard Prölss, who as commander of *L 13* on 19 August 1916 has been held responsible for a misleading report that averted what might have been the decisive naval battle of the war, as recounted in Chapter 17. (Courtesy of Dr Douglas H Robinson)

The Nordholz airship base in 1916, after expansion. In the foreground is one of the anti-aircraft guns installed as a result of the so-called Cuxhaven Raid of 25 December 1914. At left are the single airship sheds named *Nora* and *Norbart*. The large structure in the distance is the double shed *Norman*. The airship aloft at the far right is a training craft, probably *L 16*. (Courtesy of Dr U-H Opperman)

Short 184 No 8359, the aircraft flown at Jutland, astern of its carrier, *Engadine*. Its pilot at Jutland, Flight Lieutenant Frederick J Rutland, is at the extreme left. (Fleet Air Arm Museum)

Fregattenkapitän Peter Strasser, the indefatigable commander of the Naval Airship Division from 1913 until his fiery death aboard *L 70* on 5 August 1918. (Courtesy of Dr U-H Opperman)

The extremely air-minded Admiral Sir David Beatty, commander of the Grand Fleet, 1916–18, aboard his flagship, *Queen Elizabeth*, during the surrender of the German fleet, 21 November 1918. (Author's collection)

A Sopwith T 1 Cuckoo dropping a torpedo during a practice run. Had the war continued it is possible that aircraft of this type would have attacked the German fleet in harbour. (J M Bruce/G S Leslie collection)

A Sopwith Baby piloted by Flight Sublieutenant Robert W Peel in flight over Mudros harbour, Aegean island of Lemnos, in late 1917 or early 1918. It was in this aircraft that Peel attempted to attack the German battlecruiser *Goeben* and was saved from being shot down by the first serving naval officer ever to fly a heavier-than-air maritime combat mission. (Courtesy of Robert W Peel)

Actually, there were a few 'aeroplanes' available throughout the operation — *Ark Royal's* Tabloids. But they were unusable; as Clark-Hall pointed out in a reply to an Admiralty query as to why he had not flown them from the carrier's deck, such take-offs were probably feasible but in the absence of any landing place ashore every flight would perforce result in loss of the machine. (Also, although not mentioned by Clark-Hall, it was doubtful that these little single-seaters could have accommodated the bulky and heavy wireless sets, so they would have been useless for spotting.) Interestingly, in his 13 January memo to Fisher, Churchill had stated the desirability of 'a landing-place for aeroplanes on Tenedos', but nothing had been done.

Marder, too, initially blamed the aerial failure on the deficiencies of the seaplanes in two derogatory (and the only) references to them in his account of the Dardanelles operation in *From the Dreadnought to Scapa Flow*, one of which was quoted above. Several years later he had second thoughts, after discovering Hugh Williamson's unpublished memoirs and subsequent correspondence with Williamson. In a paper published in the 1970s,[16] Marder contended that the failure of the seaplanes was due less to their unreliability than to their inefficient and inappropriate employment by Carden and his staff — a view in which he was supported by Williamson.

The latter complained that many of the reconnaissance flights were useless wastes of time, and from this Marder argued that much air time could have been spent better in spotting missions. This may be true to a certain extent, but as the British naval history points out 'efficient air reconnaissance was essential'[17] to locate concealed guns and determine damage to forts — exactly as Carden had noted in his original assessment of what would be required.

Marder and Williamson deplore the lack of practice in aerial spotting before the operation began — a valid criticism but one that ignores some realities. Marder seems to believe there was time to have detached a ship or two to rehearse the technique against some uninhabited Aegean island. But was there time? The bombardment began only two days after *Ark Royal* had arrived and immediately demonstrated that her seaplanes could not fly at will. Carden realised that time was of the essence if the enemy defences were to be overcome before they were reinforced — as of course they would be once the bombardment began.

Marder conceded that the seaplanes had 'disadvantages', but he failed to appreciate their frequency and severity. He believed the 'disadvantages' were offset by absence of enemy aerial opposition and anti-aircraft guns and the supposed ability of the sea-planes to attain altitudes beyond reach of small-arms fire.

Of course there was no aerial opposition — that would have required fighter aircraft, which had not been created anywhere by early 1915, and the few Turko-German aircraft available were totally incapable of aerial combat. There were initially no specialised anti-aircraft guns (although German batteries were supplied later) but twelve were improvised by rigging howitzers on high-angle mounts. And the seaplanes, seldom able to reach more than 3,000ft, were within range of ground fire. Admittedly, this threat was minimal, although at least five of them were hit by small-arms fire, one pilot was wounded and two aircraft so badly damaged that they eventually had to be written off.

In short, there are no grounds for believing that the seaplanes should have performed more adequately because they faced slight enemy opposition. They were imperilled far more by technical problems than by Turkish guns.

In *Dreadnought to Scapa Flow*, Marder condemned the seaplanes as 'inferior' and 'early types'. Of course they were 'early types' — the first British seaplane had flown only four years previously. As to inferiority, one must ask: Inferior to what? These craft were 'state of the art' in early 1915. No superior types existed.

One would expect that Royal Navy officers, intimately acquainted with the sea in all its states and under all its conditions, would have understood the problems facing seaplanes. But despite that knowledge, or perhaps because of it, they failed to comprehend the difficulties. In fairness, however, it must be realised that no one as yet understood all of the hydrodynamic and aerodynamic factors affecting flight from water.

Unquestionably, landplanes would have had one tremendous advantage — based on solid ground, they could have flown on many days when seaplanes could not. But there is no reason to suppose they would have been a panacea. Even had they been present from the start, their engines and wireless would have been no more reliable than those of the seaplanes and their fliers no more experienced in spotting.

* * *

Ultimately, the debate over wheels versus floats is irrelevant. The failure of aviation at the Dardanelles, responsible so largely for the failure of the naval effort, can be blamed on the fact that *too much faith had been placed in it.* To many minds, powered heavier-than-air flight was still a new and marvellous phenomenon, endowed by its very novelty with wonderous powers. This resulted in naval aviation becoming one of the main props supporting the entire Allied strategic venture, and with naïve trust it was asked and expected to perform a function which at this stage of its technological development and tactical inexperience it was incapable of performing adequately. And since 'naval aviation' at the Dardanelles was expressed in the seaplane, this type of machine became the scapegoat. Naturally, disillusionment set in but, perhaps surprisingly, not to the degree that might have been expected. On the contrary, continued reliance was to be placed in the air arm as the Dardanelles phase of the campaign turned into the Gallipoli phase.

* * *

There had been many in government and military circles who had voiced doubt that a purely naval attempt to force the Dardanelles could succeed, holding that it would be necessary for a land force to seize the Gallipoli peninsula before the fleet could proceed. Consequently, after much bickering over its composition, an Allied expeditionary force was being assembled well before 18 March, to be commanded by the British General Sir Ian Hamilton. On 12 March, the very day of his appointment, his designated chief of staff, Major-General W P Braithwaite, had an interview with Kitchener in which he requested a contingent of up-to-date RFC aircraft with experienced pilots and observers. Kitchener curtly and rather angrily refused. Various explanations have been advanced for the refusal, but whatever the reasons may have been the result was that the burden of the Aegean air war remained borne by the RNAS.

However, the long-desired 'aeroplanes' were soon on the way in the form of RNAS No 3 Squadron (later designated No 3 Wing). Its nucleus was what had been called the Eastchurch Squadron, which from the early days of the war had operated in Belgium and northern France under the command of the colourful Wing-Commander Charles R Samson. One of the first four British naval aviators, Samson had been the first anywhere to fly an aeroplane from a moving ship and while on the continent had pioneered the use of armoured cars in British military service.[18]

In its new guise the squadron was a mixed bag of eighteen landplanes (of five different British and French types), of which Samson was later to state that only five were capable of useful service. So much for the supposed superiority of landplanes, although Samson declared that Admiral de Robeck, in his ignorance, 'was quite delighted to have aeroplanes at his disposal, as the seaplanes which were available had a very poor performance'.[19]

The squadron arrived on 23 March at Tenedos, where thanks to the efforts of Clark-Hall an airfield had finally been prepared. The balloon ship *Manica*, as related earlier, arrived on 9 April. Meanwhile, *Ark Royal* had begun to receive replacement and reinforcement aircraft, including Schneiders and improved Short types — eventually, although not for some time, so many that she was unable to accommodate all of them and Clark-Hall had to enlist a collier as a depot ship.

All these aerial assets were employed in preparation for the troop landings scheduled for 25 April. The bulk of the work was borne by No 3 Squadron, whose aircraft, as the air history sums it up, were 'over the peninsula at every opportunity . . . [They] plotted the enemy positions; they controlled parts of the ships' fire against enemy batteries . . . they procured some crude but useful photographs of the landing beaches and the ground in their immediate neighborhood, and they wrote descriptions of the beaches as they appeared from the air; they corrected inaccurate maps; and they dropped bombs on batteries and camps.'[20] According to Samson, sixty such flights, eighteen of them photographic missions, were made before 25 April.

All aerial elements took part in the landings on the 25th, Samson's craft supporting those at Cape Helles on the peninsula's tip and *Ark Royal* and *Manica* those by the Australian-New Zealand Army Corps (ANZAC) farther north. *Manica's* balloon initially proved more valuable than the seaplanes. Turkish battery commanders quickly learned to cease fire when seaplanes were overhead, thus concealing their locations from the aerial observers, but they dared not keep silent for long and so were detectable by the balloon, which was a semi-permanent fixture in the sky. It remained aloft for more than seven hours on the 25th and made seven ascents the next day. On three occasions it directed fire from battleship *Triumph* against the Turkish battleship *Turgud Reis* in the strait, preventing her from shelling the ANZAC transports.

Manica later teamed with *Queen Elizabeth* to become what Keyes described as 'a very unpopular combination with the enemy'.[21] On the 27th the balloonists directed that ship's fire against a Turkish merchant vessel in the strait which was sunk by the third salvo at a range of seven miles.[22]

As for the work of the landplanes on the 25th and succeeding days, the air history sums it up: 'Once the troops were established [ashore] . . . the aeroplanes were in constant demand. They spotted for shore artillery with Very lights, as the batteries, in the beginning, were unable to take in wireless messages. The effectiveness of their fire control was apparent before the week following the landings, when there was a marked decrease in the Turkish fire. . . . The aeroplanes also bombed guns, camps, and troops, took photographs of the important inland positions, and reconnitered the whole peninsula . . .'[23]

That paragraph may stand as a summation of the work of No 3 Squadron (No 3 Wing as of June) for the rest of the long Gallipoli bloodbath. It was reinforced in May by a French *escadrille* and in August, as a result of an RNAS reorganisation, transferred to the island of Mudros, where it was joined by No 2 Wing, equipped largely with French landplanes, and later by a few of the SS airships.

The landplanes took over most of the functions of *Ark Royal*'s seaplanes, and that vessel was assigned to naval forces carrying out diversionary operations in the Aegean and eastern Mediterranean, although returning from time to time to help at the peninsula. Her work there ended in late May as the result of the appearance in the Aegean of the German submarine *U 21*, which sank the British battleships *Triumph* on the 25th of that month and *Majestic* two days later.

In the absence of any form of anti-submarine weaponry, this little submarine had a strategic impact out of all proportion to her size, causing the hasty withdrawal of most of the Allied capital ships, including *Queen Elizabeth*. This left naval fire support of the troops ashore up to cruisers and destroyers until the arrival of the first of the big-gun monitors. Vulnerable because of her slow speed (no more than 11kts at best), *Ark Royal* joined the exodus. After various wanderings she finally settled at Mudros, where she served as an aircraft depot ship for most of the rest of the war. In June, *Ark Royal* was replaced as fleet aviation vessel by the much faster *Ben-my-Chree*, bringing with her the first of the Short 184s, which, as related earlier, made the first aerial torpedo attacks.[24]

Meanwhile, Admiral de Robeck was so impressed by the work of *Manica* that he requested more balloons, and *Hector* was dispatched to supplement her; toward the end of the campaign *Manica* was replaced by *Canning*.

* * *

Within weeks of the landing, the Gallipoli fighting had bogged down into the stalemate so typical of most of the entire war — in essence, offence incapable of penetrating into and beyond well-sited, well-protected trench systems studded with machine guns and backed by artillery.

As a consequence, aircraft took on the roles there that they performed equally elsewhere, with reconnaissance and fire control the most important functions. As the stasis persisted, photographic reconnaissance proved highly useful. As higher-performance aircraft and more reliable wireless sets were provided, and greater experience gained, spotting improved enormously, and by mid-summer remarkable accuracy was being achieved. On several occasions preparations for Turkish attacks or counter-attacks were broken up by aerial-guided artillery fire. An efficient corps of observers was recruited — 'chiefly light-weight midshipmen who, following a request from . . . Samson, had been selected . . . from scores of volunteers from the fleet'.[25]

Air-spotted indirect fire at ships in the strait from vessels on the seaward side of the peninsula added to Turkish difficulties in supplying and reinforcing the Gallipoli defences, as on 30 August, when air-guided shells from a monitor disrupted an unloading operation and may have sunk a small steamer.

The interdiction of the Turkish sea lanes by submarines, assisted somewhat by aircraft, as mentioned earlier, caused a much greater reliance on the long land routes, and these were subjected to considerable aerial bombing. *Ark Royal*'s seaplanes had flown bombing missions, but, as at Suez, the bombs were too few and too lightweight, and the attacks too piecemeal, to have constituted more than a minor annoyance. However, the higher-performance landplanes, which could carry heavier bombloads and could fly more frequently, became a real menace. Air attacks on land supply convoys became so harassing that eventually they 'forced the enemy to split up his columns into sections . . . marching at intervals of a mile apart. . . . But even this did not suffice, and movements by day soon came to be made only when

absolutely necessary'.[26] This became a matter of serious concern
to the Turko-German command. As the air history comments,
'Had it been possible to close [the land route], especially at night,
by aircraft attack and ships' fire, the Turks . . . must quickly have
exhausted their stocks [of ammunition] and could have hardly
withstood [Allied] attacks.'[27]

When Bulgaria joined the war on the side of the Central Powers
in October, thus opening a direct route for German supplies to
Turkey, a rail bridge over the Maritza River and a rail junction at
the nearby town of Fereji became objects of aerial attacks, but
only slight damage could be inflicted on such difficult targets and
traffic was scarcely disrupted.

All these attempts at interdiction of supply lines failed because
the Allied aircraft were too few in number and could not function
at night, and aerial bombing was still too inaccurate. Another
factor may have been the potpourri of aircraft types, many of
which were either unfit for service or difficult, because of varying
degrees of performance, to operate in conjunction. Throughout
1915 and 1916 the Allies persisted in sending to the 'sideshows'
machines that were already obsolete.

Although the Allies had for almost the entire length of the
Dardanelles/Gallipoli campaign what was in effect aerial supremacy, they did not entirely occupy the sky. Turko-German
aerial strength gradually grew, and there were many cross-raids on
opposing airfields. Damage and casualties, however, were slight
on the Allied side and very probably so for their opponents. It was
not until the very final weeks, in January 1916, that aerial combat
became a factor, with the arrival of machine gun-armed Fokker
monoplanes that took a toll of several French and British aircraft.
Before this, Allied air losses had been due to operational accidents or ground fire.

* * *

By late 1915 the campaign was entering its anticlimatic conclusion. It had dragged on for more than seven months, enormous
casualties had been sustained, many ships had been lost, a second
landing had achieved no results, and the Allies were barely closer
to Constantinople than they had been in April. It had been a story
of muddle, poor planning, incompetent leadership, lost opportunities and just plain bad luck — a story far beyond the scope of
this book and which may be studied in innumerable sources.

Suffice to say that by the end of the year it was decided to abandon the venture, and the withdrawal from the peninsula was completed during December 1915 and January 1916 — so successfully
that although enormous amounts of material were left behind
there were scarcely any casualties. The air history credits this to
the work of the air arm: 'By constant patrol, the two [RNAS]
aeroplane wings prevented any hostile aircraft from flying over
the . . . beaches during [preparations for the withdrawal.'[28] Actually, one German aerial observer *did* discover the preparations,
but his report was discounted by the Turko-German high
command.[29]

* * *

In its role in the Dardanelles/Gallipoli venture, aviation for the
first time exerted influence not merely on battle or theatre
strategy but on *grand strategy*, for, as we have seen, belief in its
efficacy was a major factor in the decision to authorise the naval
operation. Had not such trust existed, it seems quite possible that
the Dardanelles phase of the campaign would not have been
undertaken, in which case it is unlikely there would have been a
Gallipoli phase. When that phase did develop, aviation exerted
the same strategic influence, although in narrower terms, as it did
on the Western Front and elsewhere.

The failure of the Allies to seize the peninsula, about which so
much has been written, is counter-balanced by the Turkish
failure, about which so little has been written, to drive the in-
vaders off it. There can hardly be any doubt that much of the
Turkish failure was caused by Allied mastery of the skies, which
deprived the Turks from achieving strategic or, often, even tactical surprise. Aerial reconnaissance was especially important on
the hilly peninsula, where the Turks almost always occupied the
high ground and thus could have concentrated assault forces on
reverse slopes, making them undetectable had it not been for
observation from the air. That observation could not only find
such concentrations and thus forewarn of an attack, but also
bring down on the Turkish troops the fire of naval guns possessing greater range and far heavier weight of shell than army
artillery.

The Allies achieved air supremacy/superiority simply because
until the final weeks they faced feeble aerial opposition. Had it
been possible for the Fokker fighters to have arrived earlier and in

greater numbers the situation would have been far different, for there were no Allied aircraft that could have countered them. The end then might have come not as a near-bloodless operation but as a Dunkirk-like disaster.

One historian of the campaign has gone so far as to claim that 'if Turkey had possessed considerable air superiority she could have broken up the [naval] attack with comparative ease',[30] but that is an anachronistic attribution of more offensive power to aircraft than they had in 1915.

Although the Allies failed to make any real headway despite their aerial advantage, the role of aviation in helping to nullify Turkish action produced the same indecisiveness at Gallipoli as it did in France and thus was a factor prolonging the campaign. It is possible to speculate that the campaign could not have been sustained as long as it was had that factor been absent.

It can be argued that much of the aerial activity during the Gallipoli land fighting had no connection with 'naval' aviation — that this work could have been carried out equally well by aviators in RFC rather than RNAS uniform. This is undoubtedly true, but the fact remains that because of Kitchener's refusal to let the RFC participate it was only the existence of British naval air units which permitted the work to be done at all. Moreover, the RNAS fliers had the advantage of the experience in spotting gained during the naval phase. It may be concluded that naval aviation was not only importantly responsible for the genesis of the Dardanelles/ Gallipoli venture but equally responsible for its continuation.

* * *

The war never returned to Gallipoli, but conflict continued on, over and under the Aegean for nearly three years.

In late January 1916 the Royal Navy established a formation unique to that date in its history, the East Indies and Egypt Seaplane Squadron, composed originally of the carriers *Ben-my-Chree, Empress* (dispatched from home waters) and our old friends *Anne* and *Raven II*, as well as the air unit at Port Said, which was the squadron's base. The squadron was 'placed at the disposal of the GOC, Egypt, as and when required'.[31] It was, in short, a 'carrier task force' operating under the dictates of a strategic high command — the first in the British navy and the only such specifically organised naval force anywhere during the war save for the Russian Black Sea hydrocruiser division.

The squadron was first commanded by Squadron Commander Cecil J L'Estrange Malone, who had been in charge of the carriers during the Cuxhaven Raid, but in May he was succeeded by Samson, the erstwhile leader of No 3 Squadron/Wing, with his flag in *Ben-my-Chree*.

For many months after its formation the squadron operated intensively and widely in a great arc around the Aegean and eastern Mediterranean coasts from Salonika to Port Said and even northern Africa, where *Ben-my-Chree* took part briefly in suppression of the Senussi uprising. As one of its participants described its scope: 'The name of the squadron implies a wide area of activity, but the actual area over which it worked was even wider. Its seaplane carriers were frequently in the Red Sea, and one of them cruised for some months in the Indian Ocean [during the hunt for *Wolf*]. . . . Egypt in this connection must be held to include the whole seacoast of Palestine and Syria, together with that of much of the southern provinces of Asia Minor. There were few important points in this long and irregular seaboard which did not at one time or another come within the vision of the squadron ships or the seaplanes which they carried.'[32]

The aircraft spotted fire for a large and varied number of British and French warships, reconnoitred far inland and bombed port installations, fortifications, ships in harbour, troop encampments, supply depots and convoys, warehouses, factories . . . and on and on.[33] An example of how extensive the squadron's activities were is given by the writer quoted above in describing an operation of 25–29 August 1916 in which 'the ships had altogether covered 2,626 miles, and in which almost every accessible district of territory on the enemy lines of communications had been visited'.[34]

The strategic work of the squadron is illustrated by the important attention paid to attacks on the Turkish rail system. Railway stations, lines, junctions, bridges and trains were repeatedly the targets of seaplane bombs. Only moderate success was achieved, for bridges are notoriously difficult to hit (as was proved as late as the Vietnam War) and railbed is not easily destroyed, but the results were enough to disrupt Turkish logistics to at least some extent. These attacks, although far from decisive, demonstrated — as did the Russian aerial blows at Turkey's Black Sea supply lines — how the far-ranging mobility of shipboard aviation enabled it to exert strategic effect on areas beyond the reach of land-based aircraft.

In Red Sea operations, the EI&E carriers on several occasions supported the insurgent Arab irregular forces raised and led by T E Lawrence ('Lawrence of Arabia'). A *Ben-my-Chree* aerial observer, describing the work of her seaplanes in the operation leading to the surrender of the Red Sea port of Jedda to the Arabs, later stated that 'one may fairly claim the capture of that city, by no means an unimportant event in the War, was a decisive event secured almost wholly by aircraft'.[35] The air history opines that 'Although this may perhaps be going too far there seems little doubt that the resistance of the Turkish defenders . . . snapped when the seaplanes got to work.'[36]

Anne and *Raven II* were paid off as RN vessels in August 1917 and assigned to mercantile service, the former replaced by *City of Oxford*, converted to a seaplane carrier from her role as balloon ship. *Ben-my-Chree* was sunk at Castelorizo Island off the Turkish coast on 9 January 1917 by artillery firing from the nearby mainland — the only aviation vessel of any nationality to be lost to enemy action during the war.[37]

British shipboard aviation strength grew in the Mediterranean during late 1917 and early 1918 as more carriers were assigned, including the original North Sea trio and three of the 'mixed carriers'. At the end of the war these vessels were operating nearly the entire length and breadth of that sea. But by then the Royal Naval Air Service had ceased to exist.

Notes

1. So vast is the literature on the subject that I have limited my following citations to works bearing on only the aeronaval aspects. Titles of a few related works may be found in the bibliography. For the general reader, Alan Moorehead's *Gallipoli* (New York: Harper & Brothers, 1965) remains an excellent one-volume account.
2. Jones, *The War in the Air*, Vol 2, p65.
3. W A B Douglas, 'The RNAS in Combined Operations, 1914–1918' in A M J Hyatt, ed, *Dreadnought to Polaris* (Annapolis: Naval Institute Press, 1973), p23.
4. Quoted in Churchill, *World Crisis*, Vol 1 (Carnes & Noble edition), p535. All following citations to this volume are from this edition.
5. Ibid, p547.
6. Ibid, p549.
7. MacNunn and Falls, *Military Operations, Egypt & Palestine*, Vol 1, p60.
8. I was fortunate enough to obtain a set of these plans from the ship's builder, the Blyth Dry Docks and Shipbuilding Company (formerly Blyth Shipbuilding and Dry Docks Company) shortly before it went out of business.
9. For design and construction of *Ark Royal*, see R D Layman, 'HMS Ark Royal–Pegasus 1914–1950', *Warship International*, Vol 13 No 2, 1976. *Ark Royal* was renamed *Pegasus* in 1934.
10. Reproduced in Churchill, *World Crisis*, Vol 1, p545.
11. Reports from HMS *Ark Royal*, Dardanelles Operations, February–May 1915, Series VII, August 1915. A copy of this document was supplied by the late Air Vice Marshal Sir Geoffrey Bromet, one of *Ark Royal*'s original air complement. I do not have its PRO file number.
12. Layman, 'HMS *Ark Royal–Pegasus*'.
13. Marder, *Dreadnought to Scapa Flow*, Vol 2, p215.

14. The official title is *Report of Committee Appointed to Investigate Attacks Delivered on and [sic] the Enemy Defenses of the Dardanelles Straits*, CB 1550, PRO. Its shortened title is derived from the name of the committee chairman, Commodore F H Mitchell.
15. Churchill, *World Crisis*, Vol 1, pp624–625.
16. Arthur J Marder, 'The Dardanelles Revisited: Further Thoughts on the Naval Prelude' in *From the Dardanelles to Oran: Studies of the Royal Navy in War and Peace 1915–1940* (London: Oxford University Press, 1974). An earlier version of this essay appeared in *Dreadnought to Polaris*, op cit.
17. Corbett, *Naval Operations*, Vol 2, p195.
18. See David Fletcher, *War Cars: British Armoured Cars in the First World War* (London: HMSO, 1987).
19. Charles Rumney Samson, *Fights and Flights* (London: Ernest Benn, 1930), p218.
20. Jones, *The War in the Air*, Vol 2, p37.
21. Roger Keyes, *Naval Memoirs*, Vol 1, p317.
22. British and German sources identify this vessel as a former British merchantman named *Scutari*. Warneck, op cit, lists a vessel sunk by *Queen Elizabeth* on 27 April but does not give a name. Langensiepen and Güleryüz, *Ottoman Steam Navy*, state that a 2,900grt vessel named *Üsküdar* was sunk by a shell from *Queen Elizabeth* but do not give a date.
23. Jones, *The War in the Air*, Vol 2, pp44–45.
24. For this ship's activity at the Dardanelles, see Ian M Burns, 'Over the Wine-Dark Sea', Part 2, 'Operations of HMS *Ben-my-Chree*, June 1915–January 1916,' *Over the Front*, Vol 9 No 2, 1994.
25. Jones, *The War in the Air*, Vol 2, p29.
26. Ibid, p71.
27. Ibid, pp70–71.
28. Ibid, p74.
29. Brian P Flanagan, 'The History of the Ottoman Air Force in the Great War: The Reports of Major Erich Serno' Part 1, 'Born in Battle', *Cross & Cockade*, Vol 11 No 2, 1970.
30. W D Puleston, *The Dardanelles Expedition: A Condensed Study*, (Annapolis: US Naval Institute, 2nd ed 1927), p164.
31. Jones, *The War in the Air*, Vol 5, p380, fn.
32. C E Hughes, *Above and Beyond Palestine: An Account of the Work of the East Indies and Egypt Seaplane Squadron 1916–1918* (London: Ernest Benn, 1930), p18.
33. A full account of the squadron's activities would require far more pages than this volume could accommodate. The work is described in Hughes, op cit, and Jones, Vol 5. An even more detailed account in given in Cronin, *Royal Navy Shipboard Aircraft Developments*. For a condensed version, see R D Layman, J[oseph] Caruana, L[eonard] Gray and P[eter] K Simpson, K[enneth] Macpherson, ed., 'Turncoat Carriers', *Warship International*, Vol 5 No 4, 1968.
34. Hughes, *Above and Beyond Palestine*, p84.
35. Wedgewood Benn, *In the Side Shows* (London, New York and Toronto: Hodder and Stoughton, 1919), pp98–99.
36. Jones, *The War in the Air*, Vol 5, p220.

CHAPTER 15

North Sea Aeronaval War I:
The Influence of the Airship

The reason for the German navy's hasty and enthusiastic embrace of the rigid airship has been described in Chapter 10. To recapitulate: the High Seas Fleet was, owing to Tirpitz' construction policy, sadly deficient in the scouting cruisers that it suddenly required for the unexpected conditions in which it found itself because of the British decision not to conduct an inshore offensive, which might have led to a decisive battle, but instead to rely on distant blockade.[1] The airship, specifically the Zeppelin, offered a relatively immediate, inexpensive and possibly even superior substitute.

The airships were too few to be of much consequence during the war months of 1914, but from early 1915 their numbers and activity grew greatly. This was in part because of the strategic bombing campaign envisioned for them, as described in Chapter 7, but probably more importantly because of the representations of Admiral Hugo von Pohl, who in February 1915 succeeded Admiral Friedrich von Ingenohl as commander of the High Seas Fleet.[2] Von Pohl continued his predecessor's policy of refusing to risk loss of capital ships — a *Diktat* of Kaiser Wilhelm — and rarely ventured his main body outside home waters.

All operations 'were preceded and accompanied by elaborate airship scouting, and it was actually von Pohl, who could not feel safe at sea without a ring of airships in the sky, who expanded the Naval Airship Division beyond the wildest dreams of its pre-war supporters'.[3] Airships accompanied the fleet for the first time on 29 March, and again on 17 and 22 April and 29–30 May. On 4 June, von Pohl wrote a recommendation to the naval authorities 'which largely determined the Navy's policy on lighter-than-air craft for the rest of the war'.[4] He first declared that 'With the shortage of suitable light cruisers, extensive airship reconnaissance with operations of the High Seas Fleet is a prerequisite', and then continued to extol airships as a means of combatting submarines, protecting minesweeping operations by detecting the advance of enemy forces against them, and spotting enemy mines. 'Considering the extraordinarily great significance of the airships for naval warfare', he wrote, 'I consider it urgently necessary to give priority to buiding more airship sheds by every possible means.' To provide for fleet needs and to insure against contingencies, von Pohl estimated that eighteen ships would be required. That figure was accepted, and construction was authorised for six more hangars, each to shelter two craft.

Although von Pohl was cognizant of the value of aerial reconnaissance, he was, from lack of prior experience, ignorant of its proper employment: 'The airships were taking the place of cruisers and they were assigned a role and position similar to that taken by the latter vessels in a normal fleet movement',[5] sometimes apparently tethered so closely to the surface units as to be with visual signalling distance. 'It is clear that neither von Pohl nor anyone else understood the possibility of using airships for long-distance strategic scouting — covering the remote areas of the North Sea to find where the British Grand Fleet in fact was located. Instead, von Pohl held them in a tight defensive girdle around the fleet.'[6]

* * *

British concern over what was perceived as the Zeppelin menace had, as noted earlier, mounted steadily before the war. The *Mayfly* disaster temporarily soured the Royal Navy on the rigid airship, but its continued development in Germany forced a reawakening of interest. In June 1912, Sueter and Mervyn O'Gorman, superintendent of the Royal Aircraft Factory, were sent on an aeronautical fact-finding mission to the Continent at the behest of the Technical Subcommittee of the Committee of Imperial Defence. They returned with a disquieting report on German progress, on which the subcommittee based its own report to its parent group. This 'dealt at length and in vivid language upon the immense advantage that the long-range airship would confer in a North Sea war, pointed out that Germany had already produced such craft, claimed that they could carry devastating loads of explosives, and . . . chastised critics of the *Mayfly* failure by stressing that the Germans had suffered even greater disaster and discouragement without losing heart. The report declared that "every one of the strategical and tactical advantages which the Committee of Imperial Defence anticipated when recommending construction of a rigid airship for the Navy, has been, or is in a fair way of being, realised by the German airships".'[7]

Agitation for construction of rigids was re-ignited, and among its leaders were Churchill (although he would later claim he had never held airships in great regard) and Jellicoe, then Second Sea Lord and being groomed to become the navy's sea-going chief, who had reached an appreciation of them in part, at least, because of his own Zeppelin flight (see Chapter 4).

A construction programme finally got under way, the painful story of which is beyond the scope of this book[8] — suffice to say that the expertise in airship design and manufacture gained by the Germans during nearly two decades could not be acquired quickly. Consequently, the first British rigids did not enter service until fairly late in the war (the early ones considerably inferior to their German counterparts) and played virtually no role in the conflict at sea.[9]

* * *

As increasing numbers of Zeppelins took to the skies, escorting the High Seas Fleet and beginning to bomb Britain, they posed a two-fold problem and peril. As a result of a request by Kitchener to Churchill on the eve of the First Battle of the Marne, the Royal Navy and its air service took responsibility for the entire air defence of the British isles — a burden they carried until early 1916, when defence over land was shifted to the army and the RFC. At the same time, and throughout the war, it was necessary to do something to counter the perceived German advantage in long-range aerial reconnaissance at sea. The obvious solution to both problems was simply to attack the Zeppelins anywhere and in any way possible. This resulted in Churchill's previously described campaign to hit them at their bases, which after 1914 became a totally sea-going effort following the German advances in Belgium that put the sheds beyond range of land-based aircraft.

The motives for attacking the airships, whether to prevent them from bombing or to prevent them from scouting, merged. The aim was to destroy them whatever their missions might be. A third motive for attacks on their bases was the hope that dangling a small force of aircraft-carrying ships in German waters might lure the High Seas Fleet out to where the Grand Fleet could pounce on it or elements of it. This was one of the aims of the Cuxhaven Raid in 1914. The Germans, however, only once rose to the bait, as will be recounted.

This type of anti-airship work, pioneered by the Cuxhaven Raid, was carried on energetically by the Harwich Force for many months afterward. Between 20 March and 6 June 1915 seven attempts were made to strike Zeppelin bases or their associated facilities, but all failed. Ships had to turn back because of bad weather, seas were too rough for take-off, aircraft propellers splintered, floats broke up in choppy water, seaplanes capsized in ship wakes, engines failed on the water or in the air, aviators failed to find their targets or got lost in fog; several machines were lost.[10]

A final attempt 'to continue the offensive against the Zeppelins which were habitually dogging the normal North Sea patrols sent out from Harwich'[11] was made on 4 July 'with the double objective of bringing the Zeppelins to action and of reconnoitring the Ems river',[12] where it was believed a group of transports was being collected. Of the five observation seaplanes, only two were able to take off and only one to return; four airships were sighted but the floats of all three Sopwith Schneiders embarked for Zeppelin attack broke up on the water. This final fiasco was disillusioning: 'Much had been risked to give the seaplanes their chance. Their repeated failures created a distrust of the Naval Air Service among many responsible naval commanders. Not until January of 1916 were any further combined operations against the German coast attempted.'[13] The distrust was justified. Here again was a case in which it was not based on any prejudice against aviation — else why would have eight aeronaval operations been authorised? — but on technological unreliability of aircraft.

The operations resuming in 1916 were made by the Harwich Force escorting HMS *Vindex*, the first of the 'mixed' carriers and from which the first landplane take-off had been made on 3 November 1915. The first two attempts, in late January and aimed at the Hage airship base, were foiled — first by fog, then by U-boat attack. For the next operation, on 25 March and directed against a Zeppelin base believed to be at Hoyer on the Schleswig coast, Tyrwhitt's Harwich Force and *Vindex* were given distant support by the Battle Cruiser Fleet. *Vindex* got off five seaplanes; only two returned, but one had discovered that the airship sheds were not at Hoyer but farther inland at Tondern (today Danish Tonder).

For the first time, this pinprick stirred the High Seas Fleet out of harbour. It was now commanded by the aggressive Admiral Reinhard Scheer, who in January had succeeded the cancer-stricken and dying von Pohl. Wireless-detected information of the German move brought the Battle Fleet out of Scapa Flow, and for a time it appeared an air operation had finally set the stage for a major battle. In a confusing series of actions, ships of the Harwich Force were bombed (unsuccessfully) by German seaplanes, sank two trawlers and a destroyer, and collided with each other. The expected battle, however, did not occur, because as the weather became increasingly rough, Scheer turned his main body homeward.

Discovery of the Tondern base prompted Tyrwhitt to propose an aerial strike against it, again with the aim of luring the German fleet out. Attempted on 4 May, it was probably the greatest failure of all. Of eleven Sopwith Babies embarked in *Vindex* and *Engadine*, 'four of them broke their propellers, three suffered engine failure, and one capsized in the wash of the destroyers. Of the three pilots who got off, one fouled the wireless aerial of the destroyer *Goshawk* and disappeared in the sea with the wreckage of his seaplane; the second had to return with engine trouble after a brief flight; the third alone reached Tondern',[14] where its two bombs missed their target.

The operation did, however, result in the destruction of one Zeppelin. *L 7*, which had left Tondern to search for the British force, was brought down by gunfire from the light cruisers *Galatea* and *Phaeton* and polished off by the deck gun of submarine *E 31*, which then rescued the seven survivors of the airship's crew.

Undaunted as always in his faith in the aeronaval combination, the indefatigable Tyrwhitt set about planning yet another blow at Tondern, but it was forestalled by developments, to be described later, that led to the Battle of Jutland. Tondern remained inviolate until 19 July 1918, when seven bomb-carrying Sopwith Camels flying from the deck of HMS *Furious* destroyed Zeppelins *L 54* and *L 60* there in the most outstandingly successful carrier operation of the war.[15] Fear of a similar attack caused Tondern to be abandoned as an active base for the rest of the conflict.

* * *

In addition to the early attempts at offensive blows against the Zeppelins, more strictly defensive seagoing measures were taken after the airship raids on Britain began. At the suggestion of Lord Fisher in April 1915, a special squadron of cruisers armed with anti-aircraft guns was formed to intercept airships at sea. The six vessels, each given one 6pdr and one 2pdr AA gun, were based on the Humber River. First designated the Anti-Airship Light Cruiser Squadron and later the 6th Light Cruiser Squadron, its operations were never successful and were eventually abandoned.

At the same time as Fisher's suggestion, Churchill proposed using submarines for the same purpose. This idea was put into practice in September 1915, when submarines *E 4* and *E 6* were each armed with four 6pdr AA guns and dispatched into the North Sea. *E 6* was able to engage Zeppelin *L 9*, but its gunfire failed to score any hits and the airship summoned up a seaplane that forced the submarine to break off the action.

In early 1916, Rear Admiral George A Ballard, who under the title Admiral of Patrols commanded coast defence flotillas, proposed patrols by aircraft-carrying ships to catch the Zeppelins at sea. The suggestion was accepted, and a number of vessels embarked Sopwith Schneiders and/or Babies to be flown off at dusk to intercept airships as they headed for Britain and at dawn as they returned. Eventually this effort involved five trawlers, two (possibly three) paddlewheel river ferries, two old torpedo gunboats, various of the Harwich cruisers and the carrier *Vindex*.[16]

There was even an attempt to enlist a submarine; in April 1916 *E 22* was fitted to carry two Schneiders to be floated off as the boat trimmed down by the stern. The technique worked after three tries, but the idea was abandoned because the special ramp installed for carriage of the aircraft hindered the submarine's underwater handling, and of course it could not submerge with the seaplanes aboard.[17]

In the end, the standing patrols proved futile. Airship sightings were infrequent. The sole aerial interception occurred on 2 August 1916 when a Bristol Scout flying from the platform on *Vindex* unsuccessfully attacked *L 17* with explosive darts and then was lost due to engine failure.

The diversion of ships, personnel and aircraft to this unproductive effort, and the amounts of fuel it consumed, while relatively small as an aspect of the overall naval war, constituted one more drain on British resources imposed by the German strategic bombing campaign.

The influence of the Zeppelin was reflected in the Admiralty design of the *Ascot* or 'Racecourse' class of paddle minesweepers that entered service in 1916. They were intended to carry two Sopwiths, with derricks to handle them, for anti-airship work. Tests on two of these vessels, however, found handling too difficult, apparently because of excessive ship roll, and as far as known none of the sweepers employed aircraft operationally. The derricks nevertheless were retained, and an officer on one of the vessels reported they became 'very useful for hoisting the beef and spuds, or, more important, "duty free" rum and tobacco'.[18] Thus did the Zeppelin, in a bizarrely indirect manner, benignly affect some British sailors.

*   *   *

Equally as strong a motive as preventing airship attack on Britain was the desire to blind them as aerial eyes over the North Sea. In that role the Zeppelins exerted a great, albeit inhibitory, influence on the strategies of both the German and British fleets.

The importance von Pohl had accorded to airship reconnaissance was carried to an even higher degree by Scheer, and under his regime there was virtually no major operation of the High Seas Fleet that was not predicated upon the availability or non-availability of airships. Scheer called them 'indispensable', declaring 'their wide field of vision, their high speed, and their great reliability when compared with the possibilities of scouting by warships, enabled the airships to lend us the greatest assistance'. Then, however, he added an important qualification: 'But only in fine weather. So the Fleet had to make its activities dependent on those of the airships, or do without them.'[19] But despite their weather-influenced limitations, the airships became an important instrument in the German fleet's strategy, as described in Chapter 10, to wear down the Grand Fleet by traps and ambushes.

Jellicoe, doubtless aware that he was, as Churchill would later characterise him, 'the only man on either side who could lose the war in an afternoon', was already fearful of such German 'guerrilla' tactics. With immense moral courage, he wrote to the Admiralty on 30 October 1914 to declare that he would turn his fleet away from anything that might be construed as an attempt to lure it over a line of submarines or mines, even though such an action 'may bring odium upon me'.[20] With equal moral courage, the Board of Admiralty endorsed his policy.[21]

Thus the strategies of the rival navies jelled early in the war — the commanders of the German fleet conscious of their battleline inferiority, the commander of the British fleet inhibited by fear of the new underwater weapons. Consequently, neither side was willing to accept battle except under conditions as favourable to itself and as unfavourable to its enemy as could possibly be obtained — attitudes hardly unusual in the history of warfare but perhaps in this case carried to extremes.

For both sides, then, adequate and sustained reconnaissance became essential, to enable them to obtain favourable positions or extricate them from unfavourable ones, to achieve surprise or avoid being surprised.

And so the airship joined the submarine and the mine as factors inhibiting Jellicoe. His correspondence is replete with mention of his aerial inferiority, and he was later to write that 'The German Zeppelins, as their numbers increased, were of great assistance to the enemy for scouting, each one being, in *favourable weather* [his emphasis], equal to at least two light cruisers for such a purpose.'[22] So hyper-sensitive did the admiral become about airships that one feels he began to resemble Coleridge's walker on a lonesome road who knows that a frightful fiend doth close behind him tread — or in this case over him.

Jellicoe's apprehension, however, was widely shared by many others, including Beatty, Sueter, Fisher, Churchill (who said the Admiralty War Staff thought one Zeppelin was equal to *six* cruisers for scouting), Maurice Hankey, Rear Admiral Sir Charles L Vaughan-Lee (who succeeded Sueter as director of the Air Department), and Vaughan-Lee's successor, Commodore (later Rear Admiral and Air Vice Marshal Sir) Godfrey M Paine, a veteran aviator who became Fifth Sea Lord (for Air Services) when that office was created in January 1917.[23]

Boiled down to their essence, their shared opinions can be summed up in the air history's description of Jellicoe's perceived predicament: 'The naval Zeppelins, housed in the distant sheds on the coast of North Germany, gave the Admiral of the High Seas Fleet a great advantage over Sir John Jellicoe. The Commander of the Grand Fleet had to face the possibility that every movement which he made by sea in the daylight hours could be promptly reported to his invisible enemy. He might be compelled to fight an action, without air support, against an enemy whose airships were cruising over him in undisputed supremacy.'[24]

It was the desire to rid themselves of this daytime aerial incubus that caused Jellicoe and Beatty to agitate so strongly for ships and aircraft to exorcise it. Until these were provided, there was a strong sense of impotency. 'If we saw them [airships] sailing overhead', Marder quotes Admiral William M James as declaring, 'we could do nothing but swear at them.'[25]

But that is not entirely true; from the Cuxhaven Raid to the aftermath of Jutland, British warships fired at Zeppelins with everything from rifles to 13.5in main battery guns. By the end of the war specialised anti-aircraft guns had become ubiquitous in the Royal Navy (and every other navy as well), mounted on vessels ranging from trawlers to super-dreadnoughts. Their record, however, was dismal. The problems of accurate anti-aircraft fire, difficult enough to solve on land, were magnified enormously when that fire had to be directed from a moving — and quite likely rolling, pitching or heeling — ship.[26]

Even such a large and relatively slow-moving target as an airship was far from easy to hit, and although some Zeppelins were damaged by British warship gunfire, only two were destroyed — *L 7* as noted above, and the German army's *LZ 85*, downed at Salonika. Aerial attack was equally difficult, due mainly to lack of effective weapons. Attempts to arm aircraft with small-calibre cannon, including the American recoilless Davis gun, never really worked out, and the first operational anti-airship weapon was the Ranken dart, named for its inventor, naval engineer officer Francis Ranken. This small missile was fitted with vanes which, after it struck an airship's envelope, would expand to grip it in place while an explosive warhead automatically detonated. The darts were carried in canisters of twenty-four and released three at a time.

They had, of course, to be dropped from above their target. This placed the heavier-than-air machine, and especially the seaplane, at a disadvantage, for the airship had a generally higher ceiling and by venting ballast could achieve a faster rate of climb. In the fifteen or so minutes it took a Sopwith Baby to reach 5,000ft, the airship it was after could be far off and away at a higher altitude, and even out of sight. No Zeppelin ever fell victim to a Ranken dart, and the attack on *L 7* apparently was the only time it was actually used against an airship.

A second weapon, adopted at the instigation of Admiral Vaughan-Lee, was a rocket developed by a French naval lieutenant, Y P G Le Prieur. Strongly resembling the sky rockets once seen at American Fourth of July celebrations, these were mounted on the interwing struts of biplanes and fired electrically from the cockpit. They were used with some success by 'balloon busters' on the Western Front, although they were wildly inaccurate at much beyond 400yds. A number of naval Pups were armed with Le Prieur rockets (four on each set of struts), but as far as can be ascertained none was ever actually fired at an airship.

It was the introduction of explosive and incendiary machine-gun ammunition that finally gave the aeroplane a deadly anti-airship weapon, and several Zeppelins were destroyed by naval landplanes and flying boats employing these bullets. These successes, however, were duplicated only twice by shipboard aircraft. The first was on 21 August 1917, when a Pup flying from a platform on the light cruiser *Yarmouth* destroyed Zeppelin *L 23*. The second did not occur until 11 August 1918, when a Camel taking off from a high-speed lighter towed by a destroyer downed *L 53*— the final Zeppelin casualty of the war.[27]

* * *

The British official air history argues that the navy's preoccupation with the Zeppelin, especially because of early naval responsibility for defence of home skies, plus the need to devote aerial resources to combat the U-boats, retarded development of a sea-going air arm: 'Had the provision of suitable aircraft to ensure scouting work for the fleet been the sole, or even the main, concern of the Admiralty Air Department, there is small doubt that ships' aircraft would have been more rapidly developed than they were. . . . The building up of an aeroplane organisation inside the Naval Air Service absorbed personnel and equipment which might otherwise have been available for the development of air co-operation with the fleet.'[28]

There is much justification for this view, especially as it applies to thinking and developments from early 1915 through mid- to late-1917. The pleas of Jellicoe, Beatty and others for aviation ships and aircraft stress the need to combat the Zeppelin more than the desire to give the Grand Fleet an aerial reconnaissance arm, although that desire is often mentioned. This is reflected in the fact that most of the aircraft designed or proposed for shipboard use were fighter types. The air history attributes the emphasis on 'offensive rather than reconnaissance aircraft' to the influence of the Zeppelin bombing campaign, but it is clear that an equally important factor was the desire to guard the fleet against aerial scouting.

In addition, Jellicoe, as noted earlier, was worried that the Zeppelins might spot fire for German ships during a fleet engagement. His fear was groundless, for the Germans never contemplated the idea, but Jellicoe, of course, could not have known this at the time.

For their own aerial scouting, the British admirals seemed wedded to the notion that the large rigid airship was the only suitable craft — a belief based probably in part on a carryover of pre-war apprehension about the Zeppelin, followed by its actual appearance over the North Sea, and seemingly confirmed by the unreliability of the seaplane. That unreliability was demonstrated during early attempts to operate seaplanes from *Campania*, which were so unsuccessful that serious consideration was given to abandoning her as an aviation vessel — a fate she escaped only by virtue of the deck take-offs in late 1915. These re-established her value as a 'fleet carrier', but she was absent on the two occasions in 1916 (described in the next chapters) when she might have played an important role.

In the absence of British rigid airships, attention was turned to using non-rigids for fleet reconnaissance. But although these 'blimps' could stay aloft for long periods, the limited amount of fuel they could carry restricted their range, and extended flight caused crew fatigue. These difficulties might be overcome if an airship could be towed by a surface vessel and replenished at sea. Successful experiments with towing were carried out in May 1916 by the cruiser *Carysfort* and airship *C 1* (the first of a new class of anti-submarine craft), followed in September by tests of refuelling *C 1* and changing its crew from the cruiser *Canterbury*. It was found the airship could be towed with ease at up to 26kts, and at 12kts crews could be changed either on deck or by using a boatswain's chair, and 60 gallons of petrol hosed up in eight minutes.[29] Despite this success, the technique, for reasons unknown, was never used operationally — and, in fact, only rarely did the non-rigids operate with the fleet.

The desire to extend the range and endurance of aircraft led to construction of lighters on which to tow flying boats into the North Sea. Delivered fairly late in the war, these craft were employed to allow aerial patrol and reconnaissance off the German coast but never worked with the main fleet.[30]

One must not overemphasise the role of the airship in restricting North Sea naval action. The submarine and the mine were far more inhibiting. Nevertheless, the existence of aerial reconnaissance as represented in the Zeppelin played a considerable part. Scheer, as noted above, tied his fleet operations to the availability of Zeppelins, and by doing so also tied them to the dictates of weather — as he admitted in the preceding quotation. The Zeppelins were fragile giants that could not function during the frequent North Sea storms. Even on the ground in their sheds they were at the mercy of the wind; velocities as slight as 12mph made it impossible to haul them out without the danger that they would be blown against the interior sides of the hangars during the process.[31]

Just how fair-weather a craft the airship was is indicated by statistics gathered by Robinson, showing that during the 1,559 days of the North Sea war scouting flights were made on only 399 days.[32] Even when airships were aloft, their vision was often restricted by fog or low clouds, in which the North Sea abounded. But despite these handicaps, Scheer's faith in the Zeppelin remained unshaken.

On the other hand, although Jellicoe and Beatty were likewise aware of the limitations that weather placed on their aerial opponents, their apprehension remained unshaken. We know in hindsight that their fears were largely groundless — that British wireless intelligence, secured by the cryptographers of the famous Room 40[33] and by a system of wireless direction-finding stations established in early 1915,[34] supplied them with far more, and far more accurate, information than was ever supplied by airships to von Pohl or Scheer. Such information, obtained though work top secret during and for some time after the war, was sometimes mishandled — transmitted to the British commanders too late or in misleading terms — but on the whole gave the Grand Fleet a tremendous edge. Room 40's forewarning of intended German moves on several occasions enabled the Grand Fleet to put to sea before a single anchor had been raised in the High Seas Fleet. In contrast, one searches in vain for a single instance in which information obtained by airship was of major value, or even any value at all, to the German admirals.

* * *

German faith in the airship and British concern over it resulted in the influence of aviation on the North Sea struggle, as expressed in aerial reconnaissance, resting on a paradox — it was exerted not by what it actually accomplished but on what German mentality *believed* it could accomplish and what British mentality *feared* it could accomplish. These differing perceptions combined to help prevent what might have been an all-out fleet action that would, in one way or another, have profoundly affected the character, duration and perhaps the outcome of the entire war.

Aerial reconnaissance helped forestall such a battle by reducing, as it did on land, the possibility of strategic surprise. Here was another paradox, for by the very act of employing such reconnaissance in attempt to achieve strategic surprise, the German fleet reduced the possibility of achieving it, since the knowledge of the existence of German aerial reconnaissance induced the British to act with greater wariness to avoid the traps that it might have enabled the Germans to set. On the other hand, it could have prevented — although there never arose a situation in which it did — the High Seas Fleet from falling into a British trap.

Thus aerial reconnaissance reduced the chances of a fleet action occurring by chance. It is highly unlikely to the point of virtual certainty that, had the rigid airship never been invented, the German fleet would have been handled more boldly or the British fleet less cautiously, but its absence would surely have increased the possibility of a fleet action developing from a happenstance collision of the two. In a following chapter we shall examine an exact instance in which a major action would have almost inevitably occured had it not been for aerial reconnaissance.

Some historians have criticised the airship bombing campaign as an unwise diversion of the craft from the oceanic reconnaissance role. Marder goes so far as to assert the German navy 'sadly mismanaged' the Zeppelins as a scouting force. Another writer declares 'The German ships were used in general very unwisely, inflicting relatively unimportant damage . . . in bombing raids at a terrible cost in destruction of their own machines and men',[35] and suggests airships could have assisted U-boats in the Atlantic by locating mercantile targets for them (as German long-range aircraft did in the Second World War).

There are some grounds for the charge of 'mismanagement'. Von Pohl's too-close disposition of airships has been mentioned. Even Scheer, who put them on a much longer leash, failed to exploit their capabilities to the full — never, for instance, sending them to reconnoitre or bomb the British naval bases at Scapa Flow or Rosyth, which their range would have permitted.

Whether the bombing campaign was justified has been discussed in Chapter 7. As to whether the airships would have been better employed solely for scouting, it must be pointed out that their greatest importance in that role existed only when the German fleet was aggressively active at sea out of home waters. Essentially, that was the case only for a period of six months or so in 1916. It is to that period that our discussion now turns.

Notes

1. Of the sixteen modern light cruisers (those of sufficient speed to serve as scouts) possessed by Germany at the start of the war, only six were assigned to the High Seas Fleet. The others were dispersed overseas or stationed in the Baltic.
2. Von Ingenohl was relieved of command as a result of the Battle of Dogger Bank, in which the armoured cruiser *Blücher* was lost and the battlecruiser *Seydlitz* badly damaged.
3. Robinson, *The Zeppelin in Combat*, p82.
4. Ibid, p92.
5. Cuneo, *The Air Weapon*, p306.
6. Robinson, *The Zeppelin in Combat*, pp84–85.
7. Layman, *To Ascend From a Floating Base*, pp181–182.
8. For the full story, see Higham, *The British Rigid Airship*.
9. As far as I can ascertain, only once did a British rigid actually engage in what might be called combat, when on 29 September 1918 airship *R 29* assisted in the destruction of submarine *UB 115*.
10. All these failed operations are described in Jones, *The War in the Air*, Vol 2.
11. Jones, *The War in the Air*, Vol 2, p385.
12. Ibid, p360.
13. Ibid, p361.
14. Ibid, pp402–403.
15. For this operation, see Jones, *The War in the Air*, Vol 6, pp306–307; Robinson, *The Zeppelin in Combat*, pp319–321; Rimell, *Zeppelin!*, pp200–205; R D Layman, '*Furious* and the Tondern Raid', *Warship International*, Vol 10 No 4, 1973, and Dick [R C] Cronin, 'Tondern: Prelude, Climax and Aftermath,' *Cross & Cockade International*, Vol 25 No 2, 1994.
16. For details of these ships and their activities (except those of the Harwich cruisers and *Vindex*), see Cronin, *Royal Navy Shipboard Aircraft Developments*.
17. The technique of floating the seaplanes off was the same used by German submarine *U 12* in early 1915. The wooden ramp was still aboard *E 22* when she was sunk by *UB 18* on 22 April 1916 and pieces of it kept one of the only two survivors of the boat afloat until he was picked up by the German submarine. See A S Evans, *Beneath the Waves: A History of HM Submarine Losses* (London: William Kimber, 1986).
18. R Moore, ' "Racecourse Class" Paddle Minesweepers', *Model Maker & Model Boats*, Vol 16 No 188, August 1966.
19. Scheer, *Germany's High Sea Fleet*, p211.
20. Most of this letter is quoted in Marder, *Dreadnought to Scapa Flow*, Vol 2, p76. Jellicoe was obsessed with the idea that the Germans would lay mines in front of his fleet, something they never contemplated. However, his fear of the underwater threat was justified — during the first seven months of the war submarines or mines took a toll of two British battleships, six cruisers, two torpedo gunboats and at least one submarine.
21. Jellicoe did indeed suffer 'odium' in later years. Many historians writing during the 1920s and 1930s criticised him for supposed timidity. More recent commentators, however, generally agree that his Admiralty-endorsed policy of containing the German fleet without risking loss of battleline superiority was sensible and effective. For an excellent analysis, see Trevor Wilson, *The Myriad Faces of War: Britain and the Great War, 1914–1918* (Cambridge: Polity Press, 1988).
22. Admiral Viscount Jellicoe of Scapa (Sir John Jellicoe), *The Grand Fleet 1914–1916: Its Creation, Development and Work* (New York: George H Doran, 1919), p32.
23. For these opinions, see the documents listed in Roskill, *Documents*, as Nos 211, 331, 460, 469 and 533.
24. Jones, *The War in the Air*, Vol 2, pp356–357.
25. Marder, *Dreadnought to Scapa Flow*, Vol 2, p46.
26. For a brief survey of the problems and development of shipboard anti-aircraft weapons, see Layman, *To Ascend From a Floating Base*, pp248–251.
27. This episode is described in S[tephen] W Roskill, 'The Destruction of Zeppelin *L 53*,' *US Naval Institute Proceedings*, Vol 86 No 8, August 1960.
28. Jones, *The War in the Air*, Vol 2, p338.
29. These experiments are described in Jones, *The War in the Air*, Vol 2, pp389–391, and Higham, *The British Rigid Airship*, pp119–120. Higham is critical of Beatty's handling of the airships.
30. For a full description of these craft, see Michael H Goodall, 'Lighters', *Cross & Cockade (Great Britain) Journal*, Vol 12 No 2, 1981. It was from one of these lighters, adopted for high-speed towing, that the Camel which downed *L 53* took off.
31. Mooring masts, which permitted airships tethered to them to ride freely in the wind, were not yet in use. There was one revolving shed — but only one, for as Scheer commented, 'it involves a great deal of time and uncommonly large expense to build them' as well as requiring huge amounts of material (Scheer, *Germany's High Sea Fleet*, p207).
32. Robinson, *The Zeppelin in Combat*, p347.

33. The story of how through serendipitous means the British were able to obtain copies of the German naval codes, and how these allowed the strange assemblage of Room 40 intellectuals to track and predict German fleet and ship movement, is far beyond the scope of this book. A detailed history is Patrick Beesly, *Room 40: British Naval Intelligence 1914–1918* (New York: Harcourt Brace Jovanovich, 1982). See also Christopher Andrew, *Secret Service: The Making of the British Intelligence Community* (London: William Heinemann, 1985). One of the first pieces of British luck came when the Russian navy recovered code books from the German cruiser *Magdeburg* after she ran aground in the Baltic on 26 August 1914 and sent one to the Admiralty. There are several conflicting versions as to exactly how these books were discovered and retrieved; perhaps the most accurate is David Kahn, 'The Wreck of the *Magdeburg*', *The Quarterly Journal of Military History*, Vol 2 No 2, 1990.

34. The workings of these stations are described by Sir Arthur Hezlet, *Electronics and Sea Power* (New York: Stein and Day, 1975).

35. Abbott, *The British Airship at War*, p118.

CHAPTER 16

Jutland

———————— · ————————

The High Seas Fleet's most active period began shortly after Scheer's appointment to its command. It stemmed from a meeting of naval authorities, including Scheer, in Berlin on 1 February 1916, at which the overall naval situation was discussed. Two important decisions resulted: to resume unrestricted submarine warfare and to allow more aggressive action by the fleet. Confirmation and approval of these decisions was given by Kaiser Wilhelm when he visited the fleet at Wilhelmshaven on 23 February. 'This [the Kaiser's] announcement was of great value to me', Scheer would write, 'as thereby . . . I was invested with authority which gave me liberty of action to an extent I myself had defined.'[1]

As a later writer put it: 'The fleet offensive could take the following forms: mining operations, airship attacks, destroyer and cruiser raids, bombardments of the English coast, and advances with the entire Fleet.'[2]

The unrestricted U-boat campaign was cancelled in early May, again as a result of American protests, but this was somewhat of a blessing for Scheer, as it freed the submarines to act in co-ordination with the fleet. The unfettering of the fleet from the Kaiser's previous strictures coincided with the British attempts to lure it into action by means of the seaplane raids described in the previous chapter, and as a result there were several skirmishes involving surface, sub-surface and aerial elements. The early sorties of the High Seas Fleet were to some extent more or less limbering-up exercises; the first major operation, on 25 April, was a bombardment by Scouting Group I (the battlecruisers) of Lowestoft and Yarmouth, after which it skirmished with vessels of the Harwich Force. Three Zeppelins scouted for the fleet on this occasion and seven flew bombing missions inland, but the scouts were unable to provide information and the bombing was scattered and ineffective.

Thanks to wireless intelligence and direction-finding, the British were forewarned of the German fleet's projected movement and probable location; both Beatty's Battle Cruiser Fleet and Jellicoe's Battle Fleet were at sea, and only a timely German retreat averted what could have been a major battle. Air waves had proved more useful than airships in the information-gathering role, although neither side was aware of it.

The 25 April operation was in a way a dress rehearsal for an even bolder operation which Scheer, unaware of his close call on that occasion and unshaken in his confidence in aerial reconnaissance, began planning for the next month — an operation that would result, due to the influence of aviation, in the greatest naval clash of the war: the Battle of Jutland.[3]

* * *

Scheer's scheme was once again based on an effort to defeat an inferior enemy force, in this case Beatty's battlecruisers, and to lure them out he planned a bombardment of Sunderland, far closer to Beatty's base at Rosyth than Lowestoft and Yarmouth. The plan is succinctly described by one historian of Jutland: 'Submarines were to lay mines off the British bases and to report the exit of British forces from them. Airships were to observe the English coast and scout on the flanks of the High Seas Fleet. The scouting forces [Hipper's battlecruisers] would bombard Sunderland early in the morning. The main body would be in a supporting position in the centre of the North Sea. . . . When the British forces emerged . . . submarines and airships would report their movements. The High Seas Fleet would then surprise and annihilate inferior detachments.'[4]

Scheer deemed aerial reconnaissance crucial to the plan, so much so that he predicated the entire operation upon the availability of airships and their ability to function at long range. In regard to the latter aspect, 'it is apparent', as Robinson states, 'that Scheer had made a clean break with von Pohl's doctrine of confining the airships to close tactical missions. At last they were to be flung boldly out into the distant reaches of the North Sea for the strategic reconnaissance for which they were so pre-eminently suited . . .'[5]

The operation was initially scheduled for 19 May, and fifteen submarines sailed on the 15th to take stations. However, delays were necessary, first to the 23rd and then to the 29th, in order to complete repair of the battlecruiser *Seydlitz*, which had struck a mine during the April operation, and to correct a spate of condenser defects that ships of Battle Squadron III had sustained during the same sortie.

Time was now growing short, for the U-boats would have reached the limit of their endurance by 1 June. Just at this juncture, the weather turned against Scheer. Strong adverse winds set in, against which the Zeppelins could make only slow progress, or none at all, and immobilising some of them in their sheds.

Consequently, as Scheer later wrote, he decided on the 30th to switch to an alternate plan while the submarines were still on station — 'an advance in the direction of the Skagerrak, [where the object would be 'a campaign against cruisers and merchantmen'] as the vicinity of the [Danish] Jutland coast offered a certain cover against surprise. An extensive aerial reconnaissance was an imperative necessity for an advance on Sunderland in the north-west, as it would lead us into waters where we could not allow ourselves to be forced into giving battle. As, however, the course now to be adopted, the distance from the enemy points of support was considerably greater, aerial reconnaissance was desirable, though not absolutely necessary.'[6]

Optimstically, the airship force commander, Strasser, ordered five Zeppelins to lift off on the morning of the 31st, but the adverse winds persisted. 'Thus, it should be emphasised, the Naval Airship Division, by its inability to cover the High Seas Fleet in the western part of the North Sea, determined in a negative way the place as well as the time of the Battle of Jutland.'[7]

Scheer sailed on the early morning of the 31st, unaware that Room 40's omnipresent electronic ears had alerted his enemy that he was to be on the move, and that Jellicoe and Beatty had put to sea several hours earlier. By early afternoon the winds had abated sufficiently that four airships could take off, but they had barely crossed the German coast when the battle began and later were unable to observe anything through mist and low clouds that reduced visibility to as low as half a mile. One had to turn back when it lost a propeller and the others returned at various times during the night and early morning.

Even as they were retiring, a second wave of five ships had lifted off around midnight, to take position should the battle be renewed on the morning of 1 June. The actions of only two of these, *L 24* and *L 11*, warrant description. Both, during the dark hours, saw flashes from gunfire and heard explosions as Scheer's ships, retreating homeward, tangled with the destroyer flotillas at the rear of the now diverging British fleet. As first light broke around 0300hrs, they began to transmit observation reports. Later knowledge showed that those of *L 24* were utterly false and misleading. At least five times it reported spotting ships that existed only in the imagination of its observers. The most misleading was a report at 0300hrs that it had located and bombed a large number of enemy vessels, including submarines, in a bay off northern Denmark. This led Scheer to the mistaken conclusion that the British fleet had settled there at nightfall. Postwar research established that no warships of either side were in that locality, and whatever *L 24*'s crewmen thought they had seen and bombed remains a mystery.

L 11 performed more creditable work, four times observing units of the enemy fleet and in signals transmitted at 0310hrs, 0340hrs, 0400hrs and 0410hrs reported reasonably accurately, in spite of decreasing visibility, their type, number and courses (although once confusing battlecruisers with battleships, a relatively trivial error). Unfortunately, however, the airship's navigation was faulty, and its reports placed the British ships 25 to 30 miles from their actual positions.

During its brushes with the British vessels, *L 11* came under intense fire, even the main battery guns of the capital ships taking potshots at it. The airship was not hit, but shells burst close enough to buffet it, causing its commander to break off contact. Shortly after its 0410hrs report visibility became so poor that no more observations could be made.

Subsequently, Scheer was satisfied he was in no further danger from the British fleet and at 0608hrs signaled Strasser that aerial reconnaissance was no longer needed.[8]

* * *

Despite Scheer's disclaimer that aerial reconnaissance was 'not absolutely necessary' for his advance to the Skagerrak, it is obvious that he was more than willing and eager to employ it when events unfolded as they did — especially eager on the morning of 1 June, when he was uncertain if the British fleet had been able to interpose itself across his line of retreat. The presence of the British was a surprise to Scheer — he had not expected to encounter the entire Grand Fleet so relatively close to his home waters, and when he did encounter it his main concern was to retire in the face of enemy numerical superiority. The fact that Scheer was surprised, that as far as he was concerned the battle developed by accident, reinforces the argument stated above that the absence of aerial reconnaissance would have resulted in more chances of a clash occurring by happenstance. Had weather permitted airships to scout ahead of the High Seas Fleet on 31 May it is doubtful, assuming they would have located the Grand Fleet, that there would have been a Battle of Jutland. It can be concluded that although the influence of aviation on Jutland was negative, that influence was unquestionably exerted.

* * *

There was also a British aerial presence at Jutland, in the form of the seaplane carrier *Engadine*, which after work with the Harwich Force had been serving for several months as the aviation vessel for Beatty's Battle Cruiser Fleet with a standard complement of two Short 184s for reconnaissance and two Sopwith Babies for anti-airship work. For tactical purposes she was attached to the four-ship 3rd Light Cruiser Squadron, taking her place with it in the so-called A–K scouting line.

As Beatty's units steamed toward a rendezvous with Jellicoe's on the afternoon of 31 May, the carrier forged 4 miles ahead of that line, making her the foremost ship of the force. This move has puzzled some writers, who have questioned why such a weak vessel was in the scouting line at all instead of being tucked away safely to the rear of the battlecruisers.

Actually, her positioning made a great deal of sense. Carriers such as *Engadine* required up to half-an-hour to prepare a seaplane for flight and then had to stop to hoist it onto what had to be relatively calm water and stop again to recover it. At the rear of the fleet *Engadine* would have been steaming through water roiled by the wakes of dozens of ships, and such turbulence could capsize an aircraft or cause its floats to break up — as happened during the seaplane raids of 1915 and early 1916. The carrier then would have had to wait for the turbulence to subside or haul off to find a smoother spot, which would not have only delayed flight and recovery but left the vessel well behind the advancing fleet, probably out of visual sight, and even at her best speed of 22kts *Engadine* would have been hard-pressed to catch up with it.

In her advanced position, *Engadine* would have been able to heave-to and launch her aircraft in unruffled waters. As things developed, however, this advantage was lost, for shortly before the first contact was made with German vessels Beatty changed course northward for the rendezvous with Jellicoe. This left *Engadine* as the rearmost vessel, which so worried the commander of the 3rd LCS that he ordered her to put on speed and close the battlecruisers. But then Beatty, after cruiser skirmishing had broken out, signalled another change of course, to the south-south-east — a manoeuvre intended to cut off what appeared to be the German main body (which was in fact only an outer screen) from its line of retreat. But *Engadine*, obedient to her last order, continued northward at 22kts and soon met the battlecruisers on an opposite course. Beatty thereupon signalled the carrier visually from his flagship, *Lion*, to make an aerial search to the north-north-east. This has been criticised as the wrong direction in which to seek the enemy main body, but it would seem logical at the time since that was the direction where the first contact with German vessels had been made.

Engadine, after hauling clear of the battlecruisers, launched a Short in the time of 27 minutes — a considerable achievement at sea, for this had never been accomplished in less than 20 minutes in the calm waters of a harbour.[9] Twenty minutes later the seaplane, although visibility was poor, sighted the cruisers and destroyers of Hipper's Scouting Group II. Its observer's three messages radioed to *Engadine* identified the vessels correctly by type and course, including the significant fact of their radical change of course to the south-east, during which they fired ineffectively at the aircraft. The carrier, however, was unable to pass this information along despite repeated efforts by searchlight and perhaps by wireless.[10] Fortunately, the turn had also been observed by a cruiser that was able to make contact with Beatty.

Soon after the last message from the Short its fuel line ruptured and it had to alight, being picked up by *Engadine* at 1604hrs. In the absence of further orders, no more flights were attempted — they would probably have been impossible anyhow under worsening sea conditions and visibility. *Engadine* fell in with the armoured cruiser *Warrior*, severely damaged by German gunfire, took her under tow and embarked the survivors of her crew before she sank the next morning.[11]

The conduct of *Engadine* at Jutland has been subjected to a good deal of misguided criticism. Marder, for instance, states that the carrier had not 'fulfilled her reconnaissance role'[12] because she launched only one of her four aircraft. He did not understand that scouting was one of two roles assigned to her, the second being attack on airships. That is why she carried the Sopwiths, which, lacking wireless, were useless for reconnaissance. Certainly, both of the wireless-equipped Shorts could have been flown, but simple common sense dictated that one should be reserved for whatever future missions might be required.

The Grand Fleet's 1916 doctrine of restricting aerial reconnaissance until contact had been made with an enemy force has also been criticised. But again, there were quite logical reasons for this policy. As I have noted elsewhere: 'Until the advent of the flight-deck carrier, an aircraft operating beyond range of land had perforce to be a seaplane unless every flight were to be a one-shot sacrifice mission. And the seaplane was totally dependent on sea conditions . . . for take-off and recovery. A 1916 admiral simply could not be certain that he could order aerial reconnaissance whenever he desired, and if his aircraft did get aloft he could never be sure if they would be able to return.'[13]

One of Beatty's biographers, referring specifically to *Engadine*, put it this way: '. . . the range of her seaplanes was very limited, and once they had flown off the water it was problematical if they would ever return. It was not possible to maintain an air reconnaissance patrol for any length of time, so it was the usual practice to conserve the seaplanes until there was some indication that the enemy was in the immediate vicinity.'[14]

Rare is a history of Jutland failing to remark that it was the first major naval battle in which a heavier-than-air craft took part, but to the best of my knowledge none has noted that it was also the *only* and *last* such occasion, for no sea action ever again saw such a mass of dreadnoughts engaged.[15]

* * *

There could, and should, have been an even greater British aerial presence at Jutland had not a still somewhat baffling series of mixups resulted in the absence of HMS *Campania*, Jellicoe's aviation vessel.

Campania had received two visual signals on the afternoon of 30 May telling her to prepare to sail, but somehow missed the final one that ordered the fleet to sea, apparently because of decreasing visibility. It was not until nearly midnight that her captain discovered the fleet had gone. He weighed anchor immediately and set out in pursuit. By strenuous effort her aging engines were driven to 20.5kts, at which rate she would have caught up with the Battle Fleet some hours before Jellicoe arrayed it against Scheer's main body. Jellicoe, however, believed that *Campania* was good for no more than 19kts[16] and also feared that the unescorted vessel would be vulnerable to submarine attack, so at 0437hrs on the 31st ordered her back to Scapa (wireless silence now having been abandoned).

The question inevitably arises: What might have happened had *Campania* been present? Her ten or so seaplanes were a mix of Sopwiths and Shorts, and the latter would have permitted a multiple aerial search. They could have been flown off her platform on their trollies while she was under way, although she would have had to turn into whatever the prevalent wind would have been. She could also have recovered them more easily; unlike *Engadine*, she was equipped to pluck them from the water while under way, although only at very low speed (no more than 6kts).

But how Jellicoe might have employed these aircraft must forever remain a mystery — as also what they might have discovered in the poor visibility that plagued the Zeppelins and *Engadine*'s Short. However, it can be speculated that the outcome of Jutland could have been quite different had Jellicoe been aware of what speed *Campania* could achieve.

Notes

1. Scheer, *Germany's High Sea Fleet*, p110.
2. Holloway H Frost, *The Battle of Jutland* (Annapolis: US Naval Institute, 1936), p30.
3. The literature on Jutland is so extensive that my citations are limited to those bearing on only the aerial aspects.
4. Frost, *The Battle of Jutland*, p95.
5. Robinson, *The Zeppelin in Combat*, p147.
6. Scheer, *Germany's High Sea Fleet*, p136.
7. Robinson, *The Zeppelin in Combat*, p147.
8. Detailed accounts of the Zeppelin activity can be found in Robinson, Cuneo and Frost, all op cit, and N J M Campbell, *Jutland: An Analysis of the Fighting* (London: Conway Maritime Press, 1986). Frost is highly critical of the airships, repeatedly denigrating them. Cuneo is more charitable.
9. The pilot was Flight Lieutenant Frederick J Rutland, who inevitably was called 'Rutland of Jutland'. He was later a pioneer of platform and deck flying. After the war he became an aeronautical adviser to the Mitsubishi industrial firm in Japan. In the late 1930s he settled in the United States, going into business as an investment broker but acting as a sort of low-grade espionage agent, supplying the Japanese navy with information on US naval aviation developments. He returned to Britain shortly after the Pearl Harbour attack, apparently voluntarily, but was imprisoned until 1943 under the 1939 Defence Regulations although no formal charge was ever lodged against him. Much mystery still surrounds this episode. He died by suicide in 1949.
10. British communications were extremely muddled at Jutland — over and over again signals were unreceived, delayed, misplaced or ignored — and *Engadine* was apparently a victim of this confusion, which may have been abetted by the notorious incompetence of Beatty's flag lieutenant, Lieutenant Commander Ralph Seymour. See Layman 'Engadine at Jutland', which also gives a full account of the flight.
11. Layman, 'Engadine at Jutland'.

12. Marder, *Dreadnought to Scapa Flow*, Vol 3, p56.
13. Layman, 'Engadine at Jutland'.
14. W S Chalmers, *The Life and Letters of David, Earl Beatty, Admiral of the Fleet* (London: Hodder and Stoughton, 1951), p225.
15. Battleship vs battleship clashes of the Second World War never involved more than a handful of vessels. To the best of my knowledge, the only occasion in which opposing battleships both employed their shipboard seaplanes was the Italo-British encounter of 9 July 1940.
16. It was not until ten years later that Jellicoe learned *Campania*'s actual speed.

CHAPTER 17

North Sea Aeronaval War II: The Greatest Battle Never Fought

_____ · _____

As the High Seas Fleet licked its wounds after Jutland, Scheer believed he had been well served by the airships. He was not alone; writing some years later, a former Zeppelin commander was convinced that 'the enemy . . . rapidly retreated to the west as soon as our airships had got in touch with them'.[1] On the other side of the North Sea, Jellicoe's sense of aerial inferiority was reinforced. Neither he nor anyone else in his fleet could know that _L 11_ was the only Zeppelin that had been seen; its repeated appearances seemed to indicate that the airships were as ubiquitous as feared. A memo prepared for the Admiralty in 1917 by a group of airship advocates stated: 'It is no small achievement for [the] Zeppelins to have saved the High Seas Fleet at the Battle of Jutland', and this was widely quoted for some time. It would take years of research to establish that, for all practical purposes, the work of the Zeppelins at Jutland was worthless.

* * *

Scheer was determined to try his Sunderland plan in its original form, and as soon as possible, if only to keep his fleet's fighting edge honed. His preparatory orders stressed that aerial reconnaissance was 'essential', and so once more he had to depend on propitious weather, which turned out to be in mid-August.

The plan was virtually identical to the earlier scheme — a bombardment of Sunderland to lure out Beatty — only this time an even greater number of submarines (twenty-four of them) would be stationed to ambush and reconnoitre. Eight airships would be employed: four to patrol a line extending roughly from Norway to Scotland to watch for Jellicoe, three to take station, respectively, off the Firth of Forth, the Tyne and the Humber, and one, _L 13_, to stand guard in the area the Germans called the Hoofden (the waters off the Dutch coast where the English Channel blends into the North Sea), there to warn against any enemy approach from the south.

The High Seas Fleet sailed in the evening of 18 August, and the airships lifted off during the early hours of the 19th. But German wireless chatter had once again enabled the Grand Fleet to steal a march; alerted by Room 40, Jellicoe had sailed on the afternoon of the 18th, followed in the evening by Beatty and Tyrwhitt's Harwich Force. The British Battle Fleet thus passed south of the northern aerial scouting line before its craft even arrived on station.[2]

Some of the other airships were able to sight various British ships at various times steering on various courses, but here we encounter a discrepancy concerning visibility. Apparently, due to a phenomenon not infrequent in the North Sea, visibility was better from the surface than from the air. Jellicoe declares flat out 'the weather was clear'[3] and Scheer states 'the visibility in the locality of the Fleet justified the assumption that our airships commanded a clear view over the whole sea areas'.[4] But reports from the Zeppelins, as given in many sources, are full of references to low clouds (down to 650ft), rain squalls, mist and thunderstorms.

Nevertheless, during nearly 10 hours of flight, three airships, *L 11*, *L 13* and *L 31*, were able to report eleven sightings of enemy vessels.[5] The first two reports were from *L 13*, which spotted the Harwich Force, accurately identifying it as composed of cruisers and destroyers and stating it was proceeding in a general southerly direction. Scheer therefore dismissed this force as inconsequential and blithely continued to head for Sunderland. Actually, however, Tyrwhitt's course as reported by *L 13* was temporary while he manoeuvred to take up a patrol position.

I do not intend to attempt to describe in detail the ensuing movements of the rival fleets or their times; these may be studied in many sources. What follows is a condensation.

Jellicoe and Beatty had joined forces and were steaming south, on a course that would have led them to encounter Hipper and Scheer fairly quickly, when the submarine *U 52* sank the light cruiser *Nottingham* of Beatty's screen. It was not immediately evident, however, whether the cruiser was the victim of a torpedo or a mine. Jellicoe, with his persistant fear of a mine trap, therefore reversed course to the north until the facts could be sorted out.

This move was seen and reported to Scheer by submarine *U 53* and somewhat later by *L 31*.

Two hours later, after Jellicoe was assured that *Nottingham* had not struck a mine, he turned south again. But Scheer's subsurface and aerial scouts had now lost contact with the Grand Fleet, and the reversal of the British course was *not* reported to him.

Shortly after noon the British and German fleets, converging at right angles, were within about 40 miles of each other — an hour or so of steaming would have brought them into contact. The British wireless directional stations had located the High Seas Fleet, and this information was passed to Jellicoe by the Admiralty. He increased fleet speed and gave preparatory battle orders. Scheer, of course, was totally unaware that instead of springing a trap he was sailing into one — from the information he had received it seemed that enemy forces to the north and south were steaming away from him.

Just at this juncture, when a battle appeared inevitable, Scheer received a startling message from *L 13* — that it had spotted about thirty enemy vessels, including battlecruisers, battleships and sixteen destroyers, heading north. The report added that the airship was under heavy fire. From the size and composition of this force, Scheer concluded that it would be Beatty's fleet or old battleships from the Channel Fleet.

Here, at last, appeared the long-awaited opportunity — the chance to inflict decisive losses on an inferior British force. Scheer immediately changed course south, taking his fleet directly away from Jellicoe's.

But *L 13* had committed what one writer, with considerable justification, has called 'the worst airship blunder of the entire war'.[6] What its crewmen saw were the ships of the Harwich Force. Tyrwhitt, informed by a British submarine that the Germans were at sea, had abandoned his patrol and headed north with the aim of making a torpedo attack. After a fruitless search, he too turned south temporarily.

Scheer asked *L 13* for more details on the types of ships it had seen, but clouds, and possibly the AA fire, had caused the airship to lose contact; no further information was forthcoming.

Scheer's chase after a phantom fleet was unavailing; after a submarine report of enemy heavy units to the northward, and deciding that it was now too late to bombard Sunderland, he shaped course for home. The rest of the day was anti-climatic, although both sides scored submarine successes, the British

losing another light cruiser, HMS *Falmouth,* and the German battleship *Westfalen* being damaged.

* * *

Why *L 13* misidentified the Harwich ships after twice having reported them accurately earlier remains unexplained. Latter-day
historians, blessed with hindsight, have heaped blame on the airship commander, *Kapitänleutant der Reserve* Eduard Prölss, on the
basis that as a reserve officer with presumably little sea time (in
civilian life he was chief of the Magdeburg municipal fire department), he was too inexperienced in warship identification.[7]
Perhaps, but it is equally possible that the error was simply due to
the difficulties of peering through clouds while under shellfire.

Whatever the reason, the mistake marked a major turning
point in the naval war. The immediate consequence was the pre-
vention of what would quite possibly have been a decisive fleet
engagement; a long summer afternoon stretched ahead and apparently surface visibility — unlike that at Jutland — was excellent. Thousands of pages of speculation have been published on
what the outcome and results of such a battle might have been.
But let us indulge in a bit more.

The first thing to be considered is the composition and disposition of the two fleets. Scheer was at a huge disadvantage, with
eighteen battleships against twenty-nine and two battlecruisers
against six, and farther from home waters than he had been at
Jutland. There had not been time enough for the British to correct the matériel defects discovered at Jutland — flaws in protection and munitions — but tactical reforms had been undertaken.
As always, the Battle Cruiser Fleet was stationed well ahead of the
main body (30 miles on this day) but the two forces now were
linked by a line of cruisers permitting visual passage of signals.
Hipper was not quite as far ahead of Scheer (20 miles) but had no
visual link, so that signals had to be sent by wireless — making
them subject to interception by Room 40 and the direction-
finding stations.

Hipper's Scouting Group I was now reduced to two battlecruisers — one had been lost at Jutland and two were still
under repair from the battering they took there. To compensate,
Scheer assigned Hipper three battleships, but this destroyed SG
I's value as a fast scouting/striking arm by limiting its speed to no
more than 21kts. True, one of the battleships was the new *Bayern,*

the first German capital ship with 15in guns, but she could have faced the equally armed 5th Battle Squadron of the five *Queen Elizabeth* class, which had been detached from Beatty and were now directly under Jellicoe. Their guns outranged *Bayern*'s by about 1,000 yards and fired a heavier shell, and they had a speed advantage. More importantly, there were forty British 15in guns against eight German.

Altogether, the odds were high that Jellicoe would have inflicted substantial losses on the High Seas Fleet had he been willing to take advantage of his advantages. Although it is most improbable he could have achieved a Tsushima-like annihilation, a substantial victory could have eliminated the German battle fleet as a real threat.

The consequences can only be conjectured, but one might have been the forestalling of the German submarine campaign. British light forces, free from the threat of enemy heavy units while protected by their own, could have cleared the Heligoland Bight of its defensive mines and destroyed the U-boats off their ports. Endurance and range of minesweepers and destroyers employed in these duties could have been extended by seizing one or more of the Frisian islands (or even Heligoland itself) as bases — an option that had been considered in 1914. Possibly there would have been a penetration into the Baltic, as had been advocated by Lord Fisher.

To suppose a decisive German victory on 19 August is to enter the realm of fantasy, but if disbelief can be suspended the potential consequences are staggering to contemplate. An immediate result would have been the end of the British blockade. The High Seas Fleet could have broken out of the North Sea. The battlecruisers might have raided Atlantic trade routes — an idea that had been presented to and endorsed by Hipper in late 1914.[8] It is conceivable that consideration might have been given to the even more radical (and controversial) proposal advanced in 1915 by *Korvettenkapitän* Wolfgang Wegener, a High Seas Fleet staff officer, that the Faeroe, Azores and Cape Verde islands be seized as fleet bases.[9]

With the breaking of the blockade, direct trade with the United States could have resumed in German hulls. Thus there would have been no need for the submarine campaign, which became such a major factor in the American decision to enter the war. There would have been no German industrial sabotage in the United States nor the anti-US intrigues revealed in the Zimmerman Telegram.[10] The end of the blockade would have permitted resumption of food importation, thus ending the food riots that by the end of 1916 had erupted in more than thirty German cities, preventing a portion of the more than 760,000 civilian deaths attributed to blockade-related causes by the end of the war,[11] and maintaining home-front morale.

Such fanciful speculation aside, it can be stated with certainty that the results of a major battle, whatever they might have been, would have had a profound positive influence on the nature, duration and perhaps the outcome of the war. As it turned out, the events of 19 August actually did exert an influence, but in a totally negative fashion by marking the end of efforts to fight such a battle.

The German submarine activity that day worried Jellicoe deeply. His fear that he could be led into a submarine trap seemed confirmed. The U-boats had fired sixteen torpedoes, including those that hit the two cruisers, and most or all of their wakes had been seen by British vessels. The losses convinced Jellicoe that even light cruisers required anti-submarine escort by destroyers, a type of which the Grand Fleet was always short of the 100 he believed it needed. In the absence of that number, he determined that the fleet should never again venture as far south as it had on the 19th except in an emergency or if Scheer could be caught at a clear-cut disadvantage. His submission of that policy to the Admiralty was intensely discussed during the next several weeks, and finally approved. It was adhered to by Beatty when he took command of the fleet after Jellicoe's elevation to First Sea Lord.

The Zeppelins had also disturbed Jellicoe; once again they seemed omnipresent. 'From 8:24am [British time] onwards', he wrote, 'Zeppelins were frequently in sight from both the Battle Fleet, and the Battlecruiser Fleet, and were fired at, but they kept at too long a range for our fire to be effective. . . . Commodore Tyrwhitt, who was at sea with the Harwich Force . . . stated later that his force was shadowed by airships during the whole period of daylight on the 19th. . . . It was evident that a very large force of airships was out. A total of at least ten was identified by our directional wireless stations and they appeared to stretch right across the North Sea.'[12]

Scheer was satisfied with the work of his submarines, both for reconnaissance (their reports had in fact been more accurate than those of the airships) and in attack (one was mistakenly believed to have torpedoed a battlecruiser). He was somewhat less happy about the Zeppelins, wanting them in future to abandon standing patrol and take a more positive role in determining where the enemy fleet was rather than where it wasn't, but still deemed them indispensible to his operations. He was, of course, at this time blissfully unaware that *L 13*'s inaccurate report had saved him from potential disaster.

Believing his Sunderland expedition had come close to success, Scheer determined to repeat it. Bad weather thwarted an attempt in September, and then the *Admiralstab* had began to have doubts that a North Sea offensive was wise or useful, and before a new operation could be arranged came the high-level decision to re-sume the submarine war on commerce, albeit under prize rules.[13] It was ordered that this would take precedence over U-boat co-operation with the High Seas Fleet, and thus Scheer lost the use of the craft he considered imperative for his operations. 'The work of the fleet', he wrote, 'was from that time onward chiefly directed to the support of the [submarine] campaign.'[14] Al-though it is not true, as has often been stated, that the High Seas Fleet never ventured out again, the emphasis on the submarine campaign, especially after unrestricted operations resumed in early 1917, did result in long periods of idleness and the transfer of many of the fleet's best and brightest personnel to the U-boats — factors contributing to the mutinies of 1918.

* * *

The far-reaching impact that the naval policy decisions made after 19 August 1916 had on grand strategy, and thus the course of the war, the fate of nations and the shape of future history, has been well-recognised and emphasised by historians: 'The naval war in the North Sea, as far as the battle-fleets were concerned, came to a virtual standstill in the autumn of 1916. Seen in this light, the operation of 19 August could be rated as one of the most decisive in the history of the entire war.'[15]

And 'August 19 . . . marks a definite turning point in the war at sea.'[16]

And 'August 19 . . . was at once a finale and a prologue. The first part of the great drama was over. The curtain rang down on the excursions of the German Fleet, just as they were beginning to offer a promise of success. It was to rise again, not on serried fleets seeking one another . . . but on submarines toiling . . . in relentless search for prey, while behind them a host of relentless pursuers followed hard.'[17]

And 'A deadlock had . . . been reached, and it seemed that for the future the two great battle fleets could but lie inactive, watching one another across a sort of "No-Man's Sea", where attack and defence were concerned only with transport and commerce.'[18]

Would this situation have developed had it not been for *L 13*'s inaccurate report? All we can be sure of is that *something* would have happened had Scheer continued on his collision course with the Grand Fleet, but that nothing *did* happen was the direct result of that report. In this respect, that message represents probably the greatest single influence exerted by aviation not only on the course of the naval war but on the entire 1914–18 conflict.

Marder, in a phrase that has been widely quoted, characterised the events of 19 August as a game of 'blind man's buff'. Scheer was not entirely sightless, but even in the country of the blind the one-eyed man cannot be king if he does not know what he is seeing.

Notes

1. Heinrich Hollender, 'Lighter-Than-Air Craft', in Neumann, *The German Air Force in the Great War*, p111.
2. A remarkably similar episode occurred 26 years later, when, before the Battle of Midway, American aircraft carriers advanced beyond the position of a patrol line of Japanese submarines before the enemy boats reached station. The Americans in 1942, like the British in 1916, had been alerted through decoding of intercepted wireless communications.
3. Jellicoe, *The Grand Fleet*, p439.
4. Scheer, *Germany's High Sea Fleet*, p182.
5. A complete tabulation of these reports is given in Cuneo, *The Air Weapon*, p333.
6. Frost, *The Battle of Jutland*, p521.
7. I am inclined to think this criticism unjustified. Quite a number of airship commanders came from the reserve (including Max Dietrich, an uncle of the future famous actress Marlene Dietrich) and they seem in general to have been no less competent than regular officers. If Prölss were indeed the villain of 19 August, he suffered a horrible retribution, for he was commanding *L 53* when it was flamed down in August 1918 by the lighter-launched Camel as noted in an earlier chapter.
8. The suggestion came from *Kapitän* Max Hahn of the battlecruiser *Von der Tann*. See Philbin, *Admiral von Hipper*, pp91–94.
9. This proposal was only part of a far-ranging critique of German naval policy and strategy. See Wolfgang Wegener (Holger H Herwig, trans), *The Naval Strategy of the World War* (Annapolis: Naval Institute Press, 1989).
10. The war had been a boon to American industry and agriculture because of the Allied need for US products, but there can hardly be a doubt that US manufacturers and farmers would have been just as happy to sell to Germany had the British blockade not prevented it.
11. These figures are approximations taken from Martin Gilbert, *First World War Atlas* (New York: Macmillan, 1970), p77.
12. Jellicoe, *The Grand Fleet*, p436.
13. *ie*, merchant ships were not to be sunk indiscriminately, but stopped and searched, and if then sunk provision made for the safety of their crews.
14. Scheer, *Germany's High Sea Fleet*, p199.
15. Paul M Kennedy, *The Rise and Fall of British Naval Mastery* (London and Atlantic Highlands, NJ: Ashfield Press, reprint ed 1988), p249.
16. British Naval Staff Monograph, *Home Waters. From June 1916 to November 1916*, quoted in Marder, *Dreadnought to Scapa Flow*, Vol 3, p235.
17. Ibid, quoted in Marder, p254.
18. Newbolt, *Naval Operations*, Vol 4, p49.

CHAPTER 18

'Taranto' 1918 and Jan Smuts' Revenge

———— · ————

The British aerial presence on 19 August was even more minimal than at Jutland, when at least one aircraft got aloft. *Campania* was again absent, this time laid up for repair of engine room defects. Her balloon, however, had been transferred to the battleship *Hercules* for a test of towing endurance at sea. It was flown for 28 hours, although unmanned. Even had it lofted observers, it was so far in the rear of the Battle Fleet that their field of vision would have been no greater than that of the advance screen. This prompted Beatty to comment 'the balloon should be flown from a ship in the advance cruiser line to increase the range of vision ahead of the Fleet. Had the balloon been well forward during the operations, I am of opinion that the enemy might possibly have been sighted.'[1] *Engadine* again accompanied the battlecruisers, but the sea was too rough for her floatplanes. The one attempt to get a Sopwith up to attack a Zeppelin failed when a wave smashed its propeller.[2]

The seeming ubiquity of the Zeppelins on the 19th brought renewed calls for ships capable of carrying aircraft. Only in the air, it appeared, could these monsters be countered; fairly intense gunfire directed at them had been unsuccessful.

Actually, unbeknowst to the British, the airships were ceasing to be a factor at sea, due mainly to the general inactivity of the High Seas Fleet after October 1916. Never again would they be used in the strategic reconnaissance role.

Their measure as strategic bombers was beginning to be taken in 1916. By the end of the year four had been shot down by aeroplanes using the new incendiary ammunition. Their only safety, it seemed, lay in altitude, and a new generation of Zeppelins was produced — the 'height climbers,' able to reach what was then the unprecedented altitude of 16,000 to 20,000ft, well above the ceiling of British aeroplanes. However, bombing and observation from these heights were even more inaccurate than before, and losses continued to mount during 1917–18 when the ships descended to altitudes suitable for these functions. By the end of the war the Naval Airship Division was virtually moribund. The death of its *Führer*, Peter Strasser, when *L 70* was shot down on 5 August 1918 — the penultimate airship loss of the war — deprived it of much of its driving force.

Had the war continued, the airships almost certainly would have been succeeded by the huge Dornier and Staaken seaplanes, which had range and endurance greater than even the largest British flying boats and would have been far less vulnerable than the hydrogen-filled Zeppelins. These aircraft, however, were still in the prototype stage when the war ended.

Although aerial activity continued briskly off the Belgian coast during the last years of the war, the sort of British shipboard offensives mounted by the seaplanes during 1915–16 more or less ceased until mid-1918. Then, in July, *Furious* staged the raid on Tondern described earlier. Toward the end of 1918 some attempts were made by aircraft towed on lighters, but the only success of consequence was the destruction of *L 53*. The grandiose American plans for seaborne aerial attacks on the U-boat bases came to nothing.

Meanwhile, however, the Royal Navy was equipping its ships with landplanes, seaplanes and balloons at a rapid pace and planning — and even commissioning — aviation vessels, while at the same time devoting many of its aerial assets to the anti-submarine effort.

*　　*　　*

The stasis in the North Sea that began following August 1916 continued after November, when Jellicoe became First Sea Lord and Beatty succeeded him as Grand Fleet commander. Beatty adhered to his predecessor's strategy of distant containment; he refused to venture into the sea's southerly waters until the fleet's deficit in destroyers had been remedied. He was willing to accept battle, under favourable conditions, only in its northern reaches, but that was where Scheer would not venture without submarines.

Those craft inaugurated the greatest crisis of the naval war in early 1917 with adoption of the unrestricted campaign against merchant shipping. Convoy and other measures began to ameliorate the situation, but these were long-term solutions. A more immediate remedy required direct action, the most obvious of which would be to choke the U-boats off at their northern German ports by mining, close patrol or even blockships. Such action, however, would be impossible unless or until the High Seas Fleet were neutralised. Since it was apparent that this was not going to be achieved by battle, other means were needed, and in a sort of *Zeitgeist* several minds turned almost simultaneously to use of the air.

Sueter had long been advocating aerial torpedo attack on the German and Austro-Hungarian fleets. He was given the chance to try the technique in the Adriatic, using the Short Admiralty Type 320 seaplane, an improved version of the Type 184 able to carry an 18in torpedo (the 184 could barely stagger into the air under the weight of a 14in weapon). The attempted attack on Pola failed, however, when gale-force winds prevented the aircraft, which were being towed, from taking off. It was another example of the unreliability of seaplanes, especially heavily-loaded torpedo craft, for use on the high seas.[3]

The Sopwith T 1 Cuckoo, the first landplane designed (largely at Sueter's instigation) as a torpedo carrier and which could also loft an 18in missile,[4] offered a better alternative, and it was the craft that suggested itself as ideas for an aerial blow at the German fleet circulated in the Admiralty in 1917. These finally coalesced into a plan involving the carriers *Argus, Furious* and *Campania*, plus the 'large light cruisers' *Glorious* and *Courageous*, which were to have half their main batteries replaced by aircraft platforms as on *Furious*. The aircraft were to be Cuckoos, of which 100 would be ordered along with 200 torpedoes for them.

This was obviously a long-term scheme, for *Argus* was not expected to be completed until the spring of 1918 (in the event, the design changes previously described delayed her completion until September 1918) and the conversion of *Glorious* and *Courageous* would be a fairly lengthy process. The first Cuckoos were ordered (on 16 August), but unexpected delays occurred. The aircraft was designed to take a Hispano-Suiza engine, but that was in too great demand for SE 5a fighters, so the Sunbeam Arab was substituted. This necessitated structural modifications, the Arab proved to have teething problems, and the Sopwith subcontractors were inexperienced in aircraft construction. Ultimately, orders for the Cuckoo totalled 300 or more,[5] but only ninety had been completed by the Armistice.

Unexplained in the Admiralty scheme is what the fate of the Cuckoos was to be after the attack; of the carriers proposed for the operation, only *Argus* had a full flight deck to which they could have returned. Perhaps most of their pilots would have been expected to ditch and await rescue. Whatever the case, the plan eventually died a-borning.

While it was being mulled over, Beatty came up with an independent scheme for an aerial attack. Entitled 'Considerations of an Attack by Torpedo Planes on the High Sea Fleet' and submitted to the Admiralty on 11 September 1917, it was an elaboration of proposals presented to Beatty in August by Captain (later Admiral Sir) Herbert W Richmond, commanding officer of the battleship *Conqueror*,[6] and Flight Commander Frederick Rutland, who had flown *Engadine*'s seaplane at Jutland.

Over-optimistic and unrealistic in some respects, it was nevertheless a bold, ambitious, imaginative and prescient plan; the documents describing it[7] should be required reading for those who still maintain that the 'Battleship Admirals' of British naval officialdom were blind to the value of 'air power'.

Beatty began with the premise that to permit the inshore operations necessary to prevent passage of the submarines it was 'of the highest importance to immobilise the High Sea Fleet, or, if that be not completely effected, to drive it to the East [*ie*, into the Baltic] and block its return'.

He continued: 'It is suggested that the new type of Torpedo plane [which although not identified is obviously the Cuckoo] affords us a weapon with which this can be done, provided it is produced in large numbers and used in masses, and that the full benefit of surprise is obtained by means of complete secrecy of our intentions.'

The attack would be carried out by 120 torpedo planes taken to within an hour's flying time from Wilhelmshaven, the German fleet's main base, aboard eight carriers converted from speedy (16 to 20kts) merchant ships by fitting them with 'decks for flying-off and flying-on, and the installation of lifts etc'. (This description may hint that full flight decks were envisaged.) Each carrier would embark fifteen torpedo planes plus two fighters for escort.[8]

This force would assemble at Scapa Flow and proceed south to the vicinity of the Humber, where it would be joined by escorting cruisers and destroyers. For protection against torpedoes and mines, the carriers would be fitted with blisters (bulges as fitted on monitors) and paravanes.

The aircraft would strike at dawn in three successive waves of forty machines, each wave divided into eight flights of five machines. Targets, in order of priority, would be battlecruisers and battleships (including pre-dreadnoughts), dock gates and floating docks, light cruisers and, finally, destroyers and submarines. Each five-unit formation attacking capital ships would have one specific target. After the attack the aircraft would rendezvous with the carriers at some specified point off the Dutch coast.

The torpedo planes would not be the only strike force. They were to be joined at dawn by Curtiss H 12 'Large America' flying boats (number not specified) proceeding by night directly from the British coast. To guide them, a line of ships would be stationed to show lights from which the aircraft could take bearings. The flying boats would carry 230lb bombs for use against 'floating docks, engine houses, the mine store, and submarines in the basin'. There are indications that lock gates of the Kaiser Wilhelm (Kiel) Canal would also be targeted by them, to prevent the German ships from taking shelter in that waterway.[9]

This portion of the plan seems unrealistic. Beatty stated 'the radius of action of these craft [the H 12s] is understood to be about 600 miles.' It would appear that if he expected the flying boats to return directly to Britain, he was confusing radius with range. An H 12 did indeed have a *range* of around 600 statute miles but its *radius* was not much more than half that. The margin of fuel left for a return flight would be cut to a dangerous level if the aircraft encountered adverse winds during the outward flight or had to spend more than a bare minimum of time over their targets.[10] Perhaps, however, this danger was realised, for the plan contained a fallback provision: 'Flying boats which should be unable to complete the return journey, to proceed along the Dutch Coast and refuel, arrangements being made to refuel from destroyers at specified places. . . . Boats unable to reach so far, to intern themselves in Holland.'

The Admiralty reply to Beatty, on 23 September,[11] was not encouraging. The plan, it stated, would involve 'a great sacrifice of valuable carrying capacity' and the time required for conversion of the ships into carriers 'would inevitably be so long as to preclude their employment during the Summer of 1918'. An alternative would be construction of special vessels, 'which could not possibly be completed in less than 18 months'. Finally, it was doubtful that the proposed number of torpedo planes would be available until late in 1918.

Beatty returned to the matter on 7 October in a letter more or less pooh-poohing some of the Admiralty objections and urging haste in provision of torpedo planes. This time the rejection was emphatic. 'Lord Commissioners of the Admiralty . . . regret they are unable to agree to the proposal to withdraw eight merchant ships of speed from 16–20kts . . . from the service on which they are at present engaged.'[12] It was pointed out that the Cuckoo, although a single-seater, was a quite sizeable aircraft even with wings folded, and therefore a ship able to carry fifteen of them would have to be large as well as speedy. There were few such vessels available, and in view of the shipping crisis caused by the U-boat campaign they were vitally needed in merchant service. Moreover, the conversion work would require much dockyard time and labour that was needed for new construction and for repair of damaged ships.

These were valid, practical arguments. The rejection was not based on disdain for aviation or belief the idea was unfeasible, but on the realities of the time. Indeed, the concept was embraced in principle, for the reply went on to state: 'It is generally accepted by Their Lordships that, under existing circumstances, the air presents the greatest facilities for conducting an offensive against the enemy's vessels and bases, and the possibilities of developing such an offensive in the future are being fully considered.'[13]

Ultimately, the issue was academic because of the delays in the Cuckoo production programme, which had fallen far behind schedule. By July 1918 no more than a dozen T 1s were in hand, and no pilots had yet been trained on them. The first Cuckoos and their fliers did not go aboard *Argus* until 19 October 1918; they and the ship were still working up when the war ended. It is possible that had the conflict continued into 1919 an aerial torpedo attack would have been made on the German fleet, although far below the scale proposed by Beatty. Or perhaps not; it must be remembered that the original purpose was to neutralise the High Seas Fleet so as to permit close anti-submarine operations, and by mid-1918 the U-boats had been well mastered by other means.

Assuming that the resources for such an attack had been available in the numbers projected by Beatty, and that surprise had been achieved, it might have been fairly successful. Although one of the Admiralty objections had been that the 18in torpedo — which while weighing 1,000lbs had an explosive charge of only about 170lbs — would have been ineffective against the stoutly-

protected German capital ships, 120 of these missiles, or a sizeable percentage of that number, would have been sufficient to
produce considerable havoc. There undoubtedly would have
been a large sacrifice of British aircraft, and perhaps lives.
German aerial opposition would have been slight, for aside from a
few local defence flights at some of the airship bases most of the
German naval fighting aircraft were at the Belgian ports, the
Frisian islands or in Flanders. But the inevitable operational
accidents — caused by navigational error, engine failure, fuel
exhaustion — would have taken a toll.

What the results of such an attack would have been can, of
course, only be conjectured. But even a moderate success might
well have resulted in 'Wilhelmshaven' rather than 'Taranto' becoming the symbolic synonym for an aerial blow at a harbour-
bound fleet.

* * *

If the reader has by now discerned that this book has focused
largely on the British navy's air arm, it is because the Royal Navy
was the world's foremost leader and pioneer in virtually every
facet of naval aviation — strategically, tactically, technologically
and administratively. In operational doctrine it was rivalled (and
actually in a few respects excelled) only by the Russian navy in the
Black Sea,[14] but the Russian activity was restricted to a limited
geographical area whereas British naval aviation exerted influence from Scapa Flow to Aden.

British leadership, however, was destined soon to perish, with
the creation of the Royal Air Force as a separate, independent
third service. The desirability or need for the air as a separate
entity had become an issue of divisive dispute even before the war
(the RFC had originally been established as such) that grew more
politically bitter after the outbreak of the conflict. To settle the
matter, committee after committee, board after board, was
established, deliberated, bickered, argued, debated, recrimi-
nated, recommended and dissolved (often in rancour), only to be
succeeded by one that repeated the process.

This Byzantine story is — thank God! — well beyond the pur-
view of this book.[15] Suffice it to say matters came to a head with
reaction to the German daylight aeroplane raids in mid-1917.
This resulted in the commissioning of one final study group
whose nominal chairman was Prime Minister David Lloyd George

but whose actual head was Lieutenant General Jan Christian Smuts, Britain's Boer War foe, now South African defence minister, who had been co-opted into the War Cabinet. As an 'outsider' to British internal politics, he was credited with impartiality on the issue.

His committee's final report — the Smuts Report, as it came to be known[16] — concluded strongly that the air should be separated. Much debate followed, but eventually it was so ordained. 'Essential is the understanding', one writer has stressed, 'that formation of the Royal Air Force resulted from a political, not a military, decision.'[17] On 1 April 1918 the RNAS and the RFC officially ceased to exist and the RAF was born.

There was, naturally, considerable resistance in naval circles to the loss of the air arm. But, astonishingly, Beatty readily acquiesced — not only acquiesced, but embraced the change. With what seems incredible naiveté, he apparently believed that all it took to become a naval aviator was the ability to fly an aircraft, that 'the knowledge required to be of value to the fleet should not be difficult to acquire'.[18] As Marder remarks, 'His seemingly supine attitude . . . is beyond rational explanation.'[19] He would later, after becoming First Sea Lord, bitterly regret his blithe acceptance of the destruction of the RNAS.

The transformation had little real effect on naval aviation during the remainder of the war. RNAS squadrons were redesignated by advancing their numbers by 200 (thus No 8 Squadron RNAS became 208 Squadron RAF); aviators donned new uniforms[20] and were given army-style ranks that remained in effect until air force ranks were established in 1920. The effect was least felt in the shipboard units, where they became 'air force contingents' whose functions remained the same. Harmony prevailed.

This was not the case, however, for the land-based units, many of those which had been performing maritime functions being diverted to other duties. Roger Keyes, commanding the Dover Patrol, complained bitterly in a 28 May 1918 letter to the Admiralty that his air organisation at Dunkirk 'has been entirely disintegrated', with six of its eight fighter squadrons withdrawn, while of the former six naval bombing squadrons only one remained and that not under his command.[21]

The most pernicious effects, however, were not felt until after the war, and the worst of these was the departure from the navy of its ablest and most experienced airmen — those who had been with the RNAS from its foundation and had skillfully and courageously built it into the world's finest naval air arm. Given a choice between staying with the senior service or joining the new junior one, they almost to a man took the latter course.

Many of them felt, rightly or wrongly, that they had been treated unfairly by the Admiralty, denied advancement and their efforts unappreciated. Many undoubtedly saw the writing on the wall; even had the RNAS continued to exist, it was obvious that it would shrink drastically after the war. Its tremendous growth during the conflict had been the result of direct entry, which in some respects was a necessary evil. It had been realised early on that the number of personnel needed could not possibly be supplied from the ranks of those already serving. Volunteers, to train exclusively for air duty, would be required. And they came — eager young men with no knowledge of the navy or how it functioned, who could scarcely tell a dory from a destroyer, whose exuberance would sometimes slide into irresponsibility and pose disciplinary problems, especially in the early days of wildfire RNAS expansion (one reason for the RNAS reorganisation of 1915).[22]

These would vanish with the rose after the war, leaving the cadre of professional air officers facing the prospect of being stranded for years in their current ranks or, worse still, the dread possibility of half-pay. The new service offered greater chances for promotion, with concomitant increases in pay and prestige — and indeed, many of those who opted for it did achieve high rank. There was also the challenge of helping to develop new technology and a new organisation and — a strong psychological motive not to be underestimated — the sheer enjoyment of flying.

It is thus difficult to criticise these men for the choice they made, but the fact remains that in their departure from their parent service they deprived it of a solid core of experts who might well have integrated aviation into it as successfully and importantly as their counterparts did in the American navy.

There followed, as one of the few airmen who choose to remain with the RN called it, 'Nineteen Years of Friction',[23] while Air Ministry and Admiralty fought for status and funds. It was not until nearly the eve of the Second World War that the Royal Navy regained control of shipboard aircraft — and *only* shipboard aircraft. But the hour was late, and as a consequence 'when Britain went to war in 1939, her naval aircraft were obsolete and ridiculously few in number, her naval airmen were inexperienced and junior, her seaborne air doctrine was obscurantist and mistaken, and her admirals were determined to do without [aviation] if they could'.[24]

If Jan Smuts harboured any subconscious resentment over his defeat at British hands long before 1917, he unwittingly took his revenge that year by creating a document that would seriously cripple Britain's sea power.

Notes

1. Quoted in Jones, *The War in the Air*, Vol 2, p419.
2. The pilot was again Rutland, now promoted to flight commander as a result of his Jutland flight.
3. The aborted mission was undertaken on 3–4 September 1917. Sueter was in personal command aboard the Italian destroyer *Ippolito Nievo*, which with three other destroyers escorted six Short 320s towed by motor launches. See Sueter, *Airmen or Noahs*, pp42–43.
4. This was the aircraft that Sueter later berated the Admiralty for its failure to have ordered into production earlier. Later, two rivals to the Cuckoo were designed, the Blackburn Blackburd and the Short Shirl, capable of carrying a torpedo with a heavier explosive charge. Only prototypes were produced, and their performance was inferior to that of the T 1.
5. Bruce, *British Aeroplanes*, and other sources state the orders totalled 350, but only 300 are listed in Ray Sturtivart and Gordon Page, *Royal Navy Aircraft Serials and Units 1911–1919* (Tonbridge: Air-Britain, 1992).
6. Richmond, who earlier and later held various staff positions, has been called one of the RN's most brilliant officers, but he was an iconoclast in bad odour at the Admiralty — so much so that Beatty concealed his identification as a contributor to the plan, lest mention of his name should prove prejudicial.
7. Letters No 2243/H.F.022 in Adm 1/8486 and 2484/0022 in Air 1/6641, documents Nos 189 and 197 in Roskill, *Documents*. The first of these is not given in full in Roskill, but supplemental information can be found in John Bullen, 'The Royal Navy and air power: the projected torpedo-bomber attack on the High Seas Fleet at Wilhemshaven in 1918', *Imperial War Museum Review*, No 2 1987, which is an excellent exposition of the plan and why it failed to come to fruition. I am grateful to Professor Irwin H Roth for drawing this article to my attention.
8. There are some discrepancies in the number of aircraft projected. Beatty speaks repeatedly of 121 torpedo machines rather than the 120 that would be the total if each carrier stowed fifteen. There is also some doubt whether the number aboard each carrier would be seventeen *including* two fighters or seventeen *plus* two fighters. If the former, the total number of aircraft would be 136; if the latter, it would be 152.
9. On the first day of hostilities civilian aviator Claude Grahame-White reportedly proposed to Churchill that an air attack be made on the lock gates, the aircraft to be carried on destroyers and flown by private pilots. See Graham Wallace, *Claude Grahame-White: A Biography* (London: Putnam, 1967), p196.
10. The British Felixstowe flying boats, whose performance was comparable or superior to that of the H 12, were unable to span the North Sea and return when fully fuelled and carrying a full bombload. For the few (and unsuccessful) attempts to use them to bomb German bases they were towed out on lighters.
11. Admiralty letter M 00219 in Adm 1/8486, document No 194 in Roskill, *Documents*.
12. Admiralty letter M 013083 in Air 1/641, document No 197 in Roskill, *Documents*.
13. Ibid. On 1 October Jellicoe proposed a carrier attack on the submarine construction slips at Bremen, but it was deemed that the only two existing carriers, *Campania* and *Furious*, could not embark aircraft in sufficient number to make the effort worthwhile. See Marder, *Dreadnought to Scapa Flow*, Vol 4, p239fn.
14. At the risk of hubris, I pride myself as being, thanks to the generous assistance of the late Boris P Drashpil in the United States and the late Edgar Meos in what was then the Estonian SSR, perhaps the first to present some of this story in English. It is obvious now (in 1995) that some of my work was inadequate and flawed. With the opening of hitherto secret archives since the demise of the Soviet Union, more competent researchers than I are at work and I have no doubt that within a few years many fascinating facts will be presented.
15. This tangled tale runs *passim* through many of the volumes of *The War in the Air*; among many other sources are Stephen Roskill, *Navy Policy Between the Wars*, Vol 1 (New York: Walker and Company, 1968); Geoffrey Till, *Air Power and the Royal Navy 1914–1945: A Historical Survey* (London: Jane's Publishing Company, 1979) and Malcolm Cooper, *The Birth of Independent Air Power: British Air Policy in the First World War* (London: Allen & Unwin, 1986).
16. The official title is 'Air Organisation. Second Report of the Prime Minister's Committee on Air Organisation and Home Defence Against Air Raids. 17 August 1917'. It is reproduced in full in the appendix volume of *The War in the Air*.

17. Paul C Phillips, 'Decision and Dissension — Birth of the RAF', *Aerospace Historian*, Vol 18 No 1, 1971.
18. Beatty letter of 22 August 1917 to the First Sea Lord, Adm 116/1606, document No 182 in Roskill, *Documents.*
19. Marder, *Dreadnought to Scapa Flow*, Vol 4, p333fn.
20. Sometimes not even that; Robert Peel, mentioned in my preface, did not lay eyes on an RAF uniform until after the Armistice.
21. Keyes, *Naval Memoirs*, Vol 2, p40.
22. Of the approximately 55,000 RNAS officers, NCOs and ratings in March 1918, more than 51,000 came from direct entry, according to figures (which differ slightly from other sources) in B J Hurren, *Perchance: A Short History of British Naval Aviation* (London: Nicholson & Watson, 1949). Interestingly, quite a number of RNAS aviators were Canadian volunteers. See William Guy Carr, *Good Hunting: Being Volume Three of 'By Guess and By God'* (London: Hutchinson & Co, 1940).
23. The title of Chapter 14 in Bell Davies, *Sailor in the Air.*
24. N W Emmott, 'RAF, the Impossible Dream', *US Naval Institute Proceedings*, Vol 95 No 802, 1969.

CHAPTER 19

Conclusions

————————— . —————————

There has too often been a tendency to characterise naval aviation of 1914–18 as a sort of experiment, a mere testing of the potential of the power it would unleash in the Second World War and against which its achievements have been measured, always to its detriment.

This is a fallacy — its value during the earlier conflict was seen as positive, and it was employed for immediate, practical purposes. Had this not been the case, naval air arms would not have experienced the enormous expansions shown in Appendix 1.

The influence of aviation on the naval war of 1914–18 must be evaluated in terms of the four main general functions of aviation as stated in Chapter 1 — aerial combat, tactical offence, strategic offence and reconnaissance.

Let us evaluate:

Aerial combat, although sometimes waged intensely, was a minor factor; its necessity was seldom as urgent over the sea as it was over land and opportunities for it were fewer. It generated only to a slight degree the cycle of 'reciprocal force development' and 'symmetrical response' that it created on the land fronts.

Tactical offence, although never as major a factor as it was to become in the Second World War, was on some occasions and in some areas (the Dardanelles and the Anatolian coast, for instance) effective enough to be disruptive. Offensive action by aircraft, however, never vitally affected the naval war — aircraft never sank a major warship or decided the outcome of a naval engagement.[1] The one occasion in which aircraft alone actually defeated a surface force — the massacre of the British motor torpedo-boats in August 1918 — was a very minor skirmish in a very large war.

For shipboard aviation, tactical offence took on a characteristic that has come to be dominant: it was directed principally against coastal or inland targets — military installations, harbour facilities, factories, ships in port, communications centres, supply lines (bridges, rail lines and stations, road junctions), aircraft bases and the like. This type of offensive action has become virtually the *raison d'etre* of the aircraft carrier. It is how carriers have been employed (for all practical purposes solely) since the Second World War — in the Korean War, the Suez crisis, the Vietnam War, the Persian Gulf conflict and the many American overseas interventions and shows of force during the Cold War. Seen in this light, the carrier vs carrier battles of the Pacific war, which took place during the span of merely three years, are anomalies; they have never been repeated and it is difficult to imagine any future situation in which they would be. The function of the carrier, as pioneered in the First World War, has become the projection of sea power over land by means of the air.

The influence of strategic aerial offence, as practiced by the German and British navies in the Great War, is difficult to ascertain. It, too, was disruptive, but never to the point of decisiveness that its proponents predicted. It can be said that its real impact was political and would be felt in the future, for it helped lay the groundwork for the pernicious philosophy of air power, with its theory (which has long been a keystone of American foreign policy) that any problem can be solved and any conflict concluded by dropping explosives from the sky.

And so we come to reconnaissance, which at sea as on land was aviation's overwhelmingly most important and most influential function in the Great War. In previous chapters I have divided this function into the traditional 'tactical' and 'strategic' categories and under its general definition included aerial direction of gunfire for, although this is not exactly scouting, it is accomplished by the same means: observation from the air of things below.[2]

Some years ago an analyst of naval strategy split the function into 'fleet reconnaissance' and 'detached reconnaissance', with this explanation: 'In fleet work immediate information of the enemy's exact position is required, but the detached force seeks more the general nature of the enemy's activities and an estimate of what he is likely to do in the future.'[3]

It might also be possible to define these functions as 'active' and 'passive'. An example of 'tactical,' 'fleet' or 'active' aerial reconnaissance would be Beatty's dispatch of the seaplane on a specific vector at Jutland; an example of 'strategic', 'detached' or 'passive' would be Scheer's stationing of a line of airships for the Sunderland operation.

Tactical aerial reconnaissance at sea never affected matters to any important degree, unless the unfortunate work of *L 13* be considered an example. Actually, 'fleet' reconnaissance was never really undertaken except by the German navy. What it might have accomplished had *Campania* accompanied the Grand Fleet at Jutland and/or in August 1916 must forever remain unknown.

It was on the strategic level that naval aerial observation, like its counterpart on land, exerted true and significant influence. It was a major factor in frustrating the Turkish strategic goal of seizing the Suez Canal; although performed on the tactical level for the destruction of *Königsberg*, it accomplished the strategic aim of freeing Indian Ocean shipping from what was considered a potential threat. The mere fact of its existence was an important element in the strategic decision to attempt the Dardanelles operation. By contributing greatly to the defeat of the U-boats it helped to counter Germany's deadliest maritime strategy. And probably most importantly, it determined to a considerable degree the strategies of the rival fleets in the North Sea.

Paradoxically, much of this influence was exerted negatively, caused by what aircraft failed to do or were unable to do. Failure of seaplanes to achieve during the Dardanelles naval campaign what they were believed capable of influenced the strategic decision to undertake the Gallipoli land campaign. Inability of airships to function at the right time and in the right place caused Scheer to take the course that resulted in the Battle of Jutland, and the failure of one to identify warships accurately in August 1916 averted what almost certainly would have been a greater Jutland.

The paradoxical nature of aviation's influence on the North Sea war has been discussed in Chapter 15, but must be stressed again: it was exerted not by what aviation achieved but by what German admirals optimistically hoped it could achieve and what British admirals pessimistically feared it could achieve.

Both sides were deceived, and it has been strongly suggested that Scheer was more duped than Jellicoe. One historian, assessing the Sunderland operation, was moved to declare it proved 'that the airships upon which Scheer had placed such great reliance were not only useless but positively dangerous, due to their highly inaccurate reports',[4] a judgment echoed by another writer: '[The airships] were . . . anything but an unqualified success. They either failed to take the air or made reports that were so inaccurate as to be seriously misleading.'[5]

But these are hindsight views, and also ignore the irony that it was an inaccurate aerial report which spared Scheer from a possibly decisive defeat and perhaps his own death.

The errors made by the Zeppelins were due considerably to inexperience in aerial observation and lack of training in that skill. This was a problem common to all navies in the early years of aerial warfare; some time elapsed before it was realised that simply putting a naval officer in the sky could not ensure that he could identify with certainly what he saw below, that even with the best of visibility things on the surface could take on a different perspective from the air and that specialised training was necessary. The problem may have been exacerbated in the German navy by the need to train airship commanders and crews rapidly to man the expanding Zeppelin fleet. The usual instructional period was about six months, but sometimes even more hurried, and much of this time was necessarily devoted to technical matters.[6]

*   *   *

The previous chapters have, I trust, exploded the myth that navies of the First World War era were indifferent or inimical to aviation, proving to the contrary that they embraced it almost too eagerly, trusting that the reconnaissance revolution effected by the combination of aircraft and wireless provided a means of rapid acquisition and instantaneous transmission of information that previously could be gleaned only by long and patient surface search and communicated only relatively slowly.

This trust was ultimately justified, but during 1914–18 this supposedly wonderful new power of observation failed to meet all expectations because of aviation's state of technological adolescence. Despite disappointments, however, astonishing progress was made during those years. By the date of the armistice aviation had become thoroughly entrenched as an element of sea power — an element that would gain steadily in importance until within a relatively few years it would transform naval warfare as radically as had the gun and the steam engine.

It has been suggested that early aviation's problems and limitations would have been more readily recognised had naval commanders been more personally acquainted with aircraft. Certainly, there was much ignorance in these respects. Of all the air-minded high-echelon naval officers/administrators mentioned in this book only Churchill and Prince Heinrich had ever actually handled the controls of an aeroplane; few of the others had been aloft even once as passengers. But to insist that an admiral who saw the potential of aviation must himself have experienced flight and learn how an aircraft was piloted is rather like insisting that an admiral who saw the potential of the submarine must himself have cruised aboard one and learned how to adjust a torpedo's depth-setting mechanism.[7] Beatty did not need Jellicoe's experience of a Zeppelin flight to appreciate that craft's potential for reconnaissance; Bradley Fiske filed his torpedo plane patent application a month before he went into the air for the first (and apparently the only) time.

*   *   *

It is the paradoxical and frequently negative influence of 1914–18 naval aviation that has caused it to be so ignored, discounted or denigrated. In the study of history it is usually easier to determine why something happened than it is discover why something did not happen, and naval aviation prevented a number of things from happening.

It is in this respect that it vitally affected the nature and duration of the First World War, exercising an influence parallel to, as Charles Bright so congently argues, aviation in general exerted. In the absence of naval aviation the conflict would unquestionably have taken different turns in several places and at several times, with an outcome which through the haze of history can be only the subject of wild surmise.

Notes

1. The only occasion I can find of aircraft intervening in a battle between relatively major surface vessels occurred in mid-May of 1917 during a clash of Austro-Hungarian light cruisers with a mixed force of British cruisers and Italian and French destroyers in the Adriatic. Austro-Hungarian and Italian aircraft both attempted, unsuccessfully, to bomb enemy ships and the former reportedly directed cruiser gunfire — which if true would seem to be the only instance of its kind in the First World War. For a description of this action see Newbolt, *Naval Operations*, Vol 4, pp297–306.
2. Aircraft directing naval gunfire against shore targets, however, might be considered performing offensive action rather than observation — the dividing line here is thin.
3. John Creswell, *Naval Strategy: An Introductory Study* (Brooklyn: Chemical Publishing Co, 2nd ed revised 1942), p264.
4. Frost, *The Battle of Jutland*, p524. Cuneo (*The Air Weapon*) takes umbrage with Frost's severe criticism of the German airships, especially of their often inaccurate position reports, noting that Frost himself, in his book on Jutland, cites more than thirty instances in which British warships made equal or greater errors.
5. Creswell, *Navy Strategy*, pp263–264.
6. Judging from the airship reports, it seems that some identification of warship types was based on a vessel's number of funnels or type of masts. Considering the state of the art of naval architecture of

the period, this was hardly an accurate gauge. A vessel with three funnels could be a battleship, cruiser or destroyer; one with tripod masts could be either a battleship or a battlecruiser.

7. In the United States the supposed gap between sea and air was bridged by legislation mandating that no officer could command an aviation vessel or naval air station without first qualifying as an aviator or aerial observer. This rule could be open to abuse; some middle-aged and relatively high-ranking officers took air training (usually the observer's course) purely for the sake of career advancement, seldom if ever going aloft again. In the long run, however, the results were probably salutary. The policy stands in stark contrast to that of the Royal Navy during the interwar years, under which RAF fliers serving afloat were excluded from all but the most trivial shipboard duties.

Appendix 1: Growth of Naval Air Arms, 1914–1918

These figures, taken from official, semi-official and unofficial sources, cannot be guaranteed to be totally accurate to the final digit, but do illustrate the great expansion that naval aviation underwent. Discrepancies are indicated by two numbers separated by a slash. 'HTA' (heavier-than-air) includes landplanes and seaplanes. The figures for aircraft should be read with some caution, for they do not reflect only the numbers on active combat service but also include those used for training, obsolete but still on inventory, unserviceable or under repair, in reserve, and experimental or prototype machines. The numbers are far from representative of the totals of naval aircraft produced, which because of losses in combat, by accident or being discarded came to many hundreds more than those given for 1918.

Great Britain

Date	HTA Craft	Airships	Balloons	Personnel
4 August 1914[1]	93/95	6[2]	2 ?[3]	727[4]
1 April 1918[5]	2,949	111[6]	200 ?[7]	55,066[8]

1. Date of declaration of war against Germany.
2. Only two operational; total includes four transferred from army.
3. Possibly more; old spherical types transferred from army.
4. As of 15 August 1914.
5. Date of creation of RAF and disestablishment of RNAS.
6. As of 1 November 1918; total includes eight rigids. Of 266 non-rigids constructed or reconstructed, 100 were lost or discarded and twenty-three transferred to other nations. The Admiralty retained control of naval lighter-than-air craft after establishment of the RAF.
7. No official figure can be located. This estimate is based on the statement in Air 1/2103 that 180 vessels were equipped to operate balloons.
8. As of 15 March 1918, two weeks before disestablishment of the RNAS. This figure is taken from Roskill, *Documents*. Hurren, *Perchance*, gives the number as 55,165 later in March.

Germany

Date	HTA Craft	Airships	Balloons[1]	Personnel
1 August 1914[2]	24	1[3]	—	c200
11 November 1918	1,478	19[4]	—	16,122

1. Some spherical types were used for training and meteorology.
2. Date of declaration of war against Russia.
3. Plus one commercial airship under charter for crew training.
4. This figure is extremely deceptive. Altogether, the German navy acquired eighty-three airships during 1914–18, of which most were lost to enemy action, destroyed by accident or discarded. Of the nineteen survivors, seven were wrecked by their crews after the Armistice; the others were parcelled out among the Allied nations. The highest number of airship personnel was 5,965 as of 1 April 1917.

France

Date	HTA Craft	Airships	Balloons	Personnel
4 August 1914[1]	8[2]	—	—	208
11 November 1918	1,264	37[3]	198/200	11,059

1. Date of declaration of war against Germany.
2. Operational types only.
3. Including two transferred from Britain; four others transferred to the United States.

United States

Date	HTA Craft	Airships	Balloons	Personnel
6 April 1917[1]	54	1[2]	2	267
11 November 1918	2,107	20	117/215	39,871[3]

1. Date of declaration of war against Germany.
2. Non-operational.
3. Including Marine Corps personnel.

Austria-Hungary

Date	HTA Craft	Airships	Balloons	Personnel
28 July 1914[1]	22	—[2]	—[3]	—[4]
4 November 1918[5]	249/268	—	—	—[6]

1. Date of declaration of war against Serbia.
2. Three in prewar service transferred to army in 1914.
3. Nine in prewar service transferred to army in 1914.
4. Number at start of hostilities unknown; 224 at end of December 1914.
5. Date of armistice with Italy.
6. Exact number at end of hostilities uncertain; highest apparent total was 2,142 as of 1 July 1917.

Italy

Date	HTA Craft	Airships	Balloons	Personnel
23 May 1915[1]	15/30	3	2	385
4 November 1918[2]	638	36	16[3]	4,382

1. Date of declaration of war against Austria-Hungary.
2. Date of armistice with Austria-Hungary.
3. There were also 150 barrage balloons.

Russia

No reliable figures can be given, although it is known that as of 1 August 1914 the Russian navy possessed twenty-four HTA craft, all seaplanes — sixteen in the Black Sea and eight, including a float version of the four-engine Sikorsky *Ilya Mourmetz*, in the Baltic. By 30 June 1917 the Black Sea Fleet had been assigned more than 200 aircraft. The navy had turned all its lighter-than-air craft over to the army after the Russo-Japanese War.

Appendix 2: Ships Sunk, Permanently Disabled, Captured, Interned or Otherwise Incapacitated by Direct or Indirect Aerial Action

Surface Warships and Auxiliaries

British

Net vessel (trawler) *Rosies*: Bombed and sunk by Austro-Hungarian seaplanes.

Motor torpedo boat *CMB 39*: Severely damaged by German seaplane strafing; interned in Holland.

Motor torpedo boat *CMB 40*: Scuttled after German seaplane strafing.

Motor torpedo boat *CMB 41*: Severely damaged by German seaplane strafing; interned in Holland.

Motor torpedo boat *CMB 42*: Severely damaged by German seaplane strafing; interned in Holland.

Motor torpedo boat *CMB 42*: Scuttled after German seaplane strafing.

Motor torpedo boat *CMB 47*: Scuttled after German seaplane strafing.

German

Torpedo boat *A 13*: Bombed and sunk in harbour by British landplane(s); raised but damaged beyond repair.

Tug *Zuiderzee*: Bombed and sunk in harbour by British landplane(s); raised and repaired; scuttled in 1918.

Harbour craft *Hafenwache II*: Bombed and sunk in harbour by British landplane(s).

Austro-Hungarian

Auxiliary minesweeper *Elöre*: Bombed and sunk in harbour by Italian landplane(s); raised and repaired; ultimate fate unknown.

Russian

Destroyer *Okhotnik*: Sunk by mine laid by German seaplane.

Torpedo boat *Stroini*: Bombed by German seaplanes after ground-
ing; damage delayed refloating; subsequently destroyed by
storms.

Note: Bolshevik destroyer *Moskvityanin* bombed and sunk by British seaplane at Alexandrovsk on the Caspian, 21 May 1919.

Turkish

Destroyer *Yadighair-i-Milet*: Bombed and sunk by British Handley-
Page landplane; raised but damaged beyond repair. Largest
warship to be destroyed by aerial attack during 1914–18.

Merchant Vessels

British

Gena: Torpedoed and sunk by German seaplane.

Kankatee: Torpedoed and sunk by German seaplane.

Storm: Torpedoed, bombed and sunk by German seaplanes.

Wairuna (New Zealand): Captured by German raider *Wolf* and
seaplane; later sunk.

Matunga (Australian): Captured by German raider *Wolf* and seaplane; later sunk.

American

Winslow (schooner): Captured by German raider *Wolf* and seaplane; later burned.

Japanese

Hitachi Maru: Captured by German raider *Wolf* and seaplane; later
sunk.

Dutch

Gelderland: Captured by German seaplanes as contraband carrier.

Norwegian

Royal (schooner): Captured by German Zeppelin as contraband
carrier.

Turkish

Immingard: Bombed and sunk in harbour by Russian seaplane(s);
raised and repaired; lost later to Russian submarine; sinking by
aerial attack is disputed.

Mahmut Şevket Paşa (?): Torpedoed by British seaplane while aground; destruction by aerial attack is disputed.

Unidentified vessel: Torpedoed by British seaplane; sinking is unverified.

Unidentified vessel, possibly a lighter: Torpedoed by British seaplane; sinking is unverified.

Scutari (?) or *Usküsar* (?): Sunk by balloon-guided gunfire of British battleship *Queen Elizabeth.*

Submarines

British

B 10: Bombed and sunk in harbour by Austro-Hungarian seaplanes; raised but destroyed by accidental fire while under repair.

C 25: Constructive total loss after strafing and bombing by German seaplanes.

D 3: Bombed and sunk by mistake by French airship.

German

U 39: Interned in Spain after being damaged in bombing attack by French seaplanes.

UB 31: Sunk by surface vessels after being located by British airship.

UB 32: Bombed by British seaplane.

UB 59: Bombed in dry dock by British landplane(s); constructive total loss; blown up.

UB 83: Sunk by British destroyer after being located from balloon.

UB 103: Sunk by surface vessels after being located by British airship.

UB 115: Sunk by joint attack of surface vessels and British rigid airship.

UC 70: Sunk in harbour by aerial-guided gunfire of British monitor; raised and repaired; sunk by joint attack of British landplane and destroyer.

French

Foucault: Bombed by Austro-Hungarian seaplanes; scuttled.

Appendix 3: A Note on the Development of Aerial Direction of Naval Gunfire

The British navy pioneered techniques of guiding indirect fire by warships by means of aircraft, and put them into practice more frequently and successfully than any other navy during 1914–18.

The first attempts on the Belgian coast in 1914 by use of a balloon were hampered by a complicated and lengthy chain of communication, and do not appear to have been very effective. Experiments in February 1915 involving heavier-than-air craft and the old battleship *Revenge* proved that wireless communication was essential. Wireless sets had already been issued to *Ark Royal* for her work at the Dardanelles. The first method used there was quite *ad hoc*, devised on the spot, and necessarily very simple: the aerial observer would estimate the range to the target, then note the fall of shot and signal whether the shells were bursting 'over or short,' 'right or left'. Gradual adjustments were made in this manner until accuracy was achieved. The procedure was tedious at best, when it worked at all, but improved with experience.

Meanwhile, in January 1915 an RFC officer, D S Lewis, had devised what became known as the clock-code system. As described by him, it employed a celluloid disc, laid over a map, 'with circles inserted at 25, 100, 200, 300, 400 yards radius according to the scale of the map. Outside are painted the figures of a clock. The circles are lettered A to E. The disc is pinned with its centre on the target and its XII–VI diameter towards the battery firing. Shots are then signalled down according to their position on the map, C9, B2, etc'. (Quoted in Jones, *The War in the Air*, Vol 2, p86.) This system was first used at the Battle of Neuve Chapelle in March 1915 and in improved form became standard in the RFC for direction of artillery fire.

Experiments with *Revenge* and aircraft resumed in April 1915, stimulated by the success of *Manica*'s balloon at Gallipoli. They failed initially because of wireless technical problems, but when improved wireless sets were obtained considerable success was achieved. Subsequently, a school was established for training observers in the technique.

The clock-code system had come to the favourable attention of the navy, but whether it saw naval use is debatable. It was reportedly employed during the operations against *Königsberg*, but in view of what several officers involved there have written that is unlikely; the method seems to have been no more advanced than that employed initially at the Dardanelles.

Later in the Gallipoli campaign, *Ark Royal*'s seaplanes used a different technique: 'Panoramic and vertical photographs were first taken of the targets on which spotting observation by the seaplanes was required. With the panoramic view before him, the observer could pick up his target without waste of time. Over his vertical photograph he had a transparent scale showing the actual distances on the ground, and, by first flying over the ship and setting the scale to the line of fire he could, on the photograph, identify the fall of each shell and read, on the scale, the error in range and deflection.' (Jones, *The War in the Air*, Vol 2, p73.)

Select Bibliography

———————— • ————————

The works listed here are supplemental to those cited in chapter notes.

Alexandrov, Andrei, 'All-Russian 'Boats: Grigorovich Flying Boats 1913–1918', *Air Enthusiast*, No 57, 1995.

Angelucci, Enzo, *The Rand McNally Encyclopedia of Military Aircraft 1914–1980*, Chicago: Rand McNally, 1980.

Arthur, Reginald Wright, *Contact!: Careers of US Naval Aviators Assigned Numbers 1 to 2000*, Washington: Naval Aviation Register, 1967.

Barjot, Pierre, *Histoire de la guerre aéro-navale*, Paris: Flammarion, 1961.

Bartlett, C P O, 'Bomber Pilot: 1916–1918', *Cross & Cockade*, Vol 17 No 3, 1976.

Brassey, Thomas [Earl Brassey], and Leyland, John, eds, 'The Royal Naval Air Service in the War', *The Naval Annual 1919*, London: William Clowes and Sons, 1919.

Brembach, Hellmuth, *Adler über see: 50 jahre deutsche marineflieger*, Oldenburg: Gerhard Stalling, 1962.

Brown, David, 'The Genesis of Naval Aviation 1909–1918', paper for symposium *Les Marines de Guerre du Dreadnought au Nucleaire*, Paris, 23 November 1988.

Brown, D K, *The Surface Fleet of World War I*, Bath: David Brown, nd.

Bruce, J M, 'Sopwith 2F 1 Camel', *Air Pictorial*, Vol 26 No 8, August 1964.

—, *Britain's First Warplanes*, Poole, Dorset: Arms and Armour Press, 1987.

—, *The Sopwith Pup*, Leatherhead, Surrey: Profile Publications, 1965.

—, *The Short 184*, Leatherhead, Surrey: Profile Publications, 1966.

—, *The Sopwith 1½ Strutter*, Leatherhead, Surrey: Profile Publications, 1966.

—, 'Carrier Operations—the Pioneers', *Aircraft Illustrated Extra*, No 12, 'Naval Aviation, 1912–1945,' London: Ian Allan, nd.

Burdick, Charles B, *The Japanese Siege of Tsingtau*, Hamden, Conn: Archon Books, 1976.

Bureau of Naval Personnel, *Navy Wings*, Washington: Government Printing Office, 1955.

Caidin, Martin, *Golden Wings: A Pictorial History of the United States Navy and Marine Corps in the Air*, New York: Random House, 1960.

Campbell, Christy, ed, *Naval Aircraft*, London: Phoebus Publishing/BPC Publishing, 1977.

Cassar, George H, *The French and the Dardanelles: A Study of Failure in the Conduct of War*, London: George Allen & Unwin, 1971.

Chatterson, E Keble, *Seas of Adventure: The Story of the Naval Operations in the Mediterranean, Adriatic, and Aegean*, London: Hurst & Blackett, 1936.

Chinn, George M, *The Machine Gun*, Vol 1, *History, Evolution and Development of Manually Operated, Full Automatic, and Power Driven Aircraft Machine Guns*. Washington: Bureau of Ordnance, Department of the Navy, 1951.

Coletta, Paolo E, *Patrick N L Bellinger and US Naval Aviation*, Lamham, Md: University Press of America, 1987.

Couhat, Jean Labayle, *French Warships of World War I*, London: Ian Allan, 1974.

Cronin, Dick [R C], 'Camel Lighters', *Cross & Cockade International*, Vol 26 No 2, 1995.

D'Ami, Rinaldo, 'French Aviation Units in Italy', *Cross & Cockade*, Vol 19 No 3, 1978.

Dittmar, F J and Colledge, J J, *British Warships 1914–1918*, London: Ian Allan, 1972.

Dooly, William G Jr, *Great Weapons of World War I*, New York: Walker and Company, 1969.

Dousset, Francis, *Les navires de guerre francais de 1850 a nos jours*, Rennes: Editions de la Cité, 1975.

Edzards, Heinz, *Lutfschiffhafen Ahlhorn: ein breitrag zum jubiläumsjahr 1965*, Ahlhorn: Günher Kirchgeorg, 1965.

Emme, Eugene M, ed, *The Impact of Air Power: National Security and World Politics*, Princeton, NJ: D Van Nostrand Co, 1959.

Ewing, WIlliam, *From Gallipoli to Baghdad*, London: Hodder and Stoughton, nd, *c*1917.

Fraccaroli, Aldo, *Italian Warships of World War I*, London: Ian Allan, 1970.

Friedman, Norman, *Carrier Air Power*, London: Conway Maritime Press, 1981.

Gibbs-Smith, Charles H, *Aviation: An Historical Survey from Its Origins to the End of World War II*, London: HMSO, 1970.

Gillett, Ross, *Wings Across the Sea*, Sydney: Aerospace Publications, 1988.

Goldrick, James, *The King's Ships Were at Sea: The War in the North Sea August 1914–February 1915*, Annapolis: Naval Institute Press, 1984.

Gordon, T Crouther, *Early Flying in Orkney: Seaplanes in World War I*, Kirkwall: BBC Radio Orkney, 1985.

Gretton, Peter, *Winston Churchill and the Royal Navy*, New York: Coward McCann, 1967.

Grey, C[harles] G, *Sea-Flyers*, London: Faber and Faber, 1942.

—, *The History of Combat Airplanes*, Northfield, Ver: Norwich University, 1942.

Grosz, Peter M, 'German Naval Aircraft', *Cross & Cockade*, Vol 4 No 1, 1963.

Halpern, Paul G, 'Naval Contribution to Victory in 1918', Paper presented at Great War Society fifth annual seminar, Bethesda, Md, 29 September 1995.

Hartcup, Guy, *The War of Invention: Scientific Developments, 1914–1918*, London: Brassey's Defence Publishers, 1988.

Heinkel, Ernst (Jürgen Thorwald, ed), *Stormy Life: Memoirs of a Pioneer of the Air Age*, New York: E P Dutton, 1956.

Herwig, Holger H, and Heyman, Neil M, *Biographical Dictionary of World War I*, Westport, Conn: Greenwood Press, 1982.

Hezlet, Arthur, *Aircraft and Sea Power*, New York: Stein and Day, 1970.

Higgins, Trumbull, *Winston Churchill and the Dardanelles: A Dialogue in Ends and Means*, New York: Macmillan, 1963.

Hoyt, Edwin P Jr, *The Germans Who Never Lost: The Story of the Königsberg*, New York: Funk Wagnalls, 1968.

Hurd, Archibald, *Italian Sea Power in the Great War*, London: Constable and Co, 1918.

Jackson, Robert, *Strike From the Sea: A Survey of British Naval Air Operations, 1909–69*, London: Arthur Baker, 1970.

Joubert, Philip de la Ferté, *The Third Service: The Story Behind the Royal Air Force*, London: Thames and Hudson, 1955.

Kemp, P K, *Fleet Air Arm*, London: Herbert Jenkins, 1954.

Kennedy, Paul, *The Rise and Fall of the Great Powers: Economic Change and Military Conflict from 1500 to 2000*, New York: Random House, 1987.

Kerr, Mark, *Land, Sea, and Air: Reminiscences of Mark Kerr*, London: Longmans, Green, 1927.

Killen, John, *A History of Marine Aviation 1911–68*, London: Frederick Muller, 1969.

King, H F, *Armament of British Aircraft 1909–1939*, London: Putnam, 1971.

Klachko, Mary, with Trask, David F, *Admiral William Shepherd Benson, First Chief of Naval Operations*, Annapolis: Naval Institute Press, 1987.

Köppen, Paul, *Der krieg zur see: die überwasserstreikräfte und ihre technik*, Berlin: Mittler, 1930.

Layman, R D, 'The Quiet Revolution: Aviation in the Great War', in Layman, R D, and McLaughlin, Stephen, eds, *From Sarajevo to Sarajevo: The Great War and the Twentieth Century—Essays in Honor of Agnes Peterson*, Palo Alto, Calif: The Great War Society, 1994.

Le Fleming, H M, *Warships of World War I*, combined vol, London: Ian Alan, nd.

Longmore, Arthur, *From Sea to Sky 1910–1945*, London: Geoffrey Bles, 1946.

MacDonald, Scott, *Evolution of Aircraft Carriers*, Washington: Government Printing Office, 1964.

Macintyre, Donald, *Wings of Neptune: The Story of Naval Aviation*, New York: W W Norton, 1963.

—, *Aircraft Carrier: The Majestic Weapon*, New York: Ballantine Books, 1968.

Macksey, Kenneth, *The Technology of War*, London: Arms and Armour, 1986.

Martiny, Nikolaus von, *Bilddokumente aus österreich-ungarns seekrieg 1914–1918*, 2 vols, Graz: Akademische Druck-u Velagsanstait, 1975.

Mau, Hans-Joachim and Scurrell, Charles E, *Flugzeugträger—trägerflugzeuge*, Berlin: Transpress, 1991.

McNeill, William H, *The Pursuit of Power: Technology, Armed Force, and Society since AD 1000*, Chicago: University of Chicago Press, 1982.

Meos, Edgar, 'Aircraft of the Russian Navy During World War I', *Cross & Cockade*, Vol 4 No 1, 1963.

Miller, Harold Blaine, *Navy Wings*, New York: Dodd, Mead & Co, 1937.

Miller, Thomas G Jr, ed, 'Naval Aviation Overseas, 1917–1918', *Cross & Cockade*, Vol 4 No 1, 1963.

—, and Robinson, Douglas H, 'Nonrigid Airships in World War I', *Cross & Cockade*, Vol 5 No 2, 1964.

—, ed, 'The Hornets of Zeebrugge', *Cross & Cockade*, Vol 11 No 1, 1970.

Morrisette, Raymond F, 'The Rotary Aircraft Engine in World War I', *Relevance*, Vol 4 No 2, 1995, new series (Journal of The Great War Society).

Morrow, John H, Jr, *The Great War in the Air: Military Aviation from 1909 to 1921*, Washington: Smithsonian Institution Press, 1993.

Munson, Kenneth, *Aircraft of World War I*, London and Garden City, NY: Ian Allan and Doubleday, 1968.

Naish, G P B, *Flying in the Royal Navy 1914–64*, London: HMSO, 1964.

Nelsen, Stephen, 'Italian Naval Aircraft', *Cross & Cockade*, Vol 5 No 3, 1964.

—, 'Austrian Naval Aircraft', *Cross & Cockade*, Vol 7 No 2, 1965.

North, John, *Gallipoli: The Fading Vision*, London: Faber and Faber, 1966.

Parkes, Oscar, and Prendergast, Maurice, eds, *Jane's Fighting Ships 1919*, London and Edinburgh: Sampson Low, Marston, 1919.

Parks, James J, 'Award of the Naval Victory Trophy', *Cross & Cockade*, Vol 18 No 2, 1977.

Phelan, Joseph A, *Heroes & Aeroplanes of the Great War 1914–1918*, New York: Grosset & Dunlap, 1966.

Preston, Anthony, *Battle Ships of World War I*, New York: Galahad Books, 1972.

Rawlings, John D R, *Pictorial History of the Fleet Air Arm*, London: Ian Allan, 1973.

Rehder, Jacob (Sander, Helmut, ed), *Die verluste der kriegsflotten 1914–1918*, rev ed, Munich: J F Lehmanns, 1969.

Reynolds, Clark G, *Admiral John H Towers: The Struggle for Naval Air Supremacy*, Annapolis: Naval Institute Press, 1991.

Robinson, Douglas H, 'Hydrogen for German Airships in World War I', *Cross & Cockade*, Vol 7 No 4, 1966.

Roskill, Stephen, *Admiral of the Fleet Earl Beatty, the Last Naval Hero: An Intimate Biography*, New York: Atheneum, 1981.

Schieffelin, John H, 'Boat Pilot', *Cross & Cockade*, Vol 11 No 1, 1970.

Shock, James R, *US Navy Pressure Airships 1915–1962*, Edgewater, Fla: Atlantis Productions, 1993.

Silverstone, Paul, *US Warships of World War I*, Garden City, NY: Doubleday & Co, 1970.

Skiera, Joseph A, ed, *Aircraft Carriers in War and Peace*, New York: Franklin Watts, 1965.

Smith, Peter C, *The Story of the Torpedo Bomber*, London: Almark, 1974.

Sondhaus, Lawrence, *The Naval Policy of Austria-Hungary 1867–1918: Navalism, Industrial Development, and the Politics of Dualism*, West Lafayette, Ind: Purdue University Press, 1994.

Sprout, Harold, and Sprout, Margaret, *Toward a New Order of Sea Power: American Naval Policy and the World Scene, 1918–1922*, Princeton, NJ: Princeton University Press, 1940.

Stormer, Fritz (Kilduff, Peter, trans), 'Seaplanes in Combat: The Reminiscences of Dr Fritz Stormer', *Cross & Cockade*, Vol 20 No 2, 1979.

Swansborough, Gordon, and Bowers, Peter M, *United States Navy Aircraft since 1911*, 1st ed, New York: Funk and Wagnalls, 1968.

Taylor, John C, *German Warships of World War I*, Garden City, NY: Doubleday & Co, 1970.

Taylor, John W R, *Fleet Air Arm*, London: Ian Alan, nd.

Thetford, Owen, *British Naval Aircraft 1912–1958*, London: Putnam, 1958.

Topping, A D, 'The Etymology of "Blimp" ', *American Aviation Historical Society Journal*, Vol 8 No 4, 1963.

Trask, David F, *Captains & Cabinets: Anglo-American Naval Relations, 1917–1918*, Columbia, Mo: University of Missouri Press, 1972.

Trimble, William F, *Wings for the Navy: A History of the Naval Aircraft Factory, 1917–1956*, Annapolis: Naval Institute Press, 1990.

Turner, Charles C, *Aircraft of To-day: A Popular Account of the Conquest of the Air*, London: Seeley, Service & Co, 1918.

Turpin, Brian J, 'Coastal Patrol Airships 1915–1918', *Cross & Cockade (Great Britain)*, Vol 15 No 3, 1984.

Van Wyen, Adrian O and Pearson, Lee M, eds, *United States Naval Aviation 1910–60*, Washington: Government Printing Office, 1961.

Watson, Eric A, 'An In-Depth Look at the SS Zero Airship', *The 1418 Journal*, 1975–6 (Journal of the Australian Society of World War One Aero Historians).

Waugh, Colin, 'North Sea Flyer', *Cross & Cockade*, Vol 16 No 3, 1975.

Whistler, Richard T, 'Photographs from the Italian Front', *Cross & Cockade*, Vol 14 No 1, 1973.

Whitehouse, Arch, *Squadrons of the Sea*, Garden City, NY: Doubleday & Co, 1962.

Woodhouse, Henry [Casalegno, Mario Terenzio Enrico], *Textbook of Naval Aeronautics*, 2nd ed, New York: Century, 1918.

Wragg, David, *Wings Over the Sea: A History of Naval Aviation*, New York: Arco, 1979.

Young, Desmond, *Rutland of Jutland*, London: Cassell, 1963.

Zelinsky, Robert, 'Rotaries', *Cross & Cockade*, Vol 14, no 4, 1973.

Index

———— · ————